Library of
Davidson College

SPEECH PERCEPTION AND PRODUCTION
Studies in Selective Adaptation

SPEECH PERCEPTION AND PRODUCTION
Studies in Selective Adaptation

William E. Cooper
Harvard University

Ablex Publishing Corporation
Norwood, New Jersey 07648

Copyright © 1979 by Ablex Publishing Corporation.

All rights reserved. No part of this book may be reproduced
in any form, by photostat, microfilm, retrieval system, or any other means,
without the prior permission of the publisher.

Printed in the United States of America.

Library of Congress Cataloging in Publication Data

Cooper, William E, 1951–
  Speech perception and production.

  (Language and being)
  Bibliography: p.
  Includes indexes.
  1. Speech perception. 2. Speech. I. Title.
II. Series.
BF455.C68   153   79-17281
ISBN 0-89391-027-9

ABLEX Publishing Corporation
355 Chestnut Street
Norwood, New Jersey 07648

For Jeanne and The Houndstooth

LANGUAGE AND BEING

edited by
George Lakoff

and

John Robert Ross

A. L. BECKER and ARAM A. YENGOYAN • *The Imagination of Reality: Essays in Southeast Asian Coherence Systems,* 1979

WILLIAM E. COOPER • *Speech Perception and Production: Studies in Selective Adaptation,* 1979

In Preparation

CHARLOTTE LINDE • *Autobiographical Narratives*
LIVIA POLANYI • *The American Story*
JOHN ROBERT ROSS • *Infinite Syntax*
TERRY WINOGRAD and FERNANDO FLORES • *Understanding Cognition as Understanding*

PREAMBLE TO THE SERIES

Our purpose in these books is to bring together as wide a variety of thinkers on language as we can. We feel a certain urgency in this task, for we perceive the field of linguistics to be deeply divided already, with no end in sight to current factionalism. Indeed, the prospects are for more, not fewer, theoretical splits.

And our perception has been that as theories and controversies have multiplied, the issues between groups of researchers have grown to seem bigger than they are. We see the present isolationism leading to a limiting introversion.

We believe, however, that many people may be working together *without knowing it*, because of the theoretical walls between them. Our hope is that juxtaposing their thoughts in this series may make an implicit consensus more apparent.

And what could the features of such an unperceived consensus be? Here we do not feel ourselves on sure ground, but the following broad-brush styles of thinking may unite many workers.

1. A rejection of constraints on data, a widening of the field of view to include phenomena that have sometimes been held to be "outside" linguistics. Some may wish to reject entirely any inside/outside dichotomy with regard to the study of language, in particular any distinction between the structure of a language and its use.

2. An attempt to integrate any study of language into the wide set of disciplines which relate human beings to reality: not only the traditionally more or less tightly connected fields of psychology, cognitive science, philosophy, anthropology, sociology and poetics, but also areas like law, therapy, music, education, politics, religion, and probably many more.

3. A conviction that knowledge can emerge not only through the success of some formal mode of description. Each formal theory provides both a way of seeing and a set of blinders. The value of a formal theory may lie as much or more in its 'failures' as in its 'successes.' And the purpose of clarity will often be best served by a refusal to impose a criterion of formal description upon the presentation of research results.

4. A change from the widespread research strategy of seeking the truth by generalizing over a number of cases to a strategy of studying the single case in all its richness, to find a general truth in the principles of organization that the individual displays. This reverence for the unique may focus on a single text, or on an idiolect, or on a particular history of acquisition, etc.

5. A sense of the futility of polemics, of wrangling. A willingness to listen. In George Miller's words,

> In order to understand what another person is saying, you must assume it is true and try to imagine what it could be true of.

We are groping as we write these words, as we launch this series. We are searching for a richer, more deeply connected, ultimately more *human*, linguistics. We invite you to join with us in this search.

GEORGE LAKOFF   JOHN ROBERT ROSS

CONTENTS

preface xiii

chapter one
Introduction 1
    Speech Production *2*
    Speech Sounds *6*
    Speech Perception *10*
    A Model of Speech Perception *15*

I SPEECH PERCEPTION

chapter two
Place of Articulation 27

    study 1 *27*
    Introduction *27*
    Experiment 1 Identification *30*
    Experiment 2 Discrimination *34*
    Experiment 3 *39*
    General Discussion *44*

    postscript to study 1 *47*
    Reinterpretation *47*
    Related Studies *47*

study 2   50

Conclusions   *63*

postscript to study 2   64

chapter three
Voicing   67

study 3   67

postscript to study 3   77

study 4   78

postscript to study 4   83

chapter four
Stop Consonants and Glides   89

study 5   89
Experiment 1   *90*
Experiment 2   *96*
Experiment 3   *100*

postscript to study 5   107

II THE RELATION BETWEEN SPEECH PERCEPTION AND PRODUCTION

chapter five
Perceptuo–Motor Adaptation   115

study 6   115

study 7   125

study 8
Experiment 1   *128*
Measurements of Vowel Duration and Closure Gap   *131*
Experiment 2   *133*
Experiment 3   *136*
General Discussion   *138*
A Neural Model of the Perceptuo–Motor System   *139*

appendix A   143

postscript to study 8   145

study 9 *146*
Experiment 1 *148*
Experiment 2 *152*
Experiment 3 *155*
General Discussion *156*

postscript to study 9 *158*
New Perceptuo–Motor Studies *159*

chapter six
Motor-Perceptual Adaptation 161

study 10 *161*

postscript to study 10 *173*

chapter seven
New Directions 175

bibliography 187

author index 199

subject index 203

PREFACE

This study is an attempt to uncover processes that mediate the perception and production of speech in normal adults. The goal was pursued using variations of a single experimental method, *selective adaptation,* a method widely used in psychological research for many years but only recently applied to speech processing. Adherence to a single method restricted the range of approachable issues, and this monograph is not intended to provide a balanced view of the entire field of speech research. The emphasis here is rather on an in-depth treatment of a relatively narrow but important set of topics. By the end of the discussion, it should be clear that restricting the study in this manner has nonetheless provided a foundation for extension to a broader range of problems.

There were practical advantages to keeping within the framework of a single method, once it had yielded a first round of useful results. Among these was the relative ease of conducting a large series of experiments using similar test procedures. The single-method strategy also enabled us to obtain a good feel for the technique's limitations and flexibility.

These advantages were potentially offset by two important drawbacks, well-known to those who have applied a single method over a prolonged period. One problem was boredom, to be overcome only by a continued effort to extend the method's usefulness beyond its present borders; the other, ironically, was developing such an affinity for the method that its own idiosyncrasies became a main object of study. We tried to avoid both pitfalls.

The work reported here dates to the early 1970s, and it has already spurred (and been spurred by) similar efforts at a number of experimental laboratories in the United States, Canada, and Europe. These include laboratories at Brown

University, Carnegie-Mellon University, Cornell University, Haskins Laboratories, Kresge Hearing Research Laboratory of the South, Indiana University, Massachusetts Institute of Technology, Northeastern University, Queen's University of Belfast, State University of New York at Buffalo, University of Keele, University of Minnesota, University of Sussex, University of Texas, University of Waterloo, and University of Wisconsin, among others. The growing interest in this topic, evidenced both by the number of research groups and by their published reports, made it seem appropriate to take stock of the work at this stage of development, even though much still remains to be done.

Beginning in 1975, research in our own laboratory shifted to other topics in speech processing, but many other laboratories continued to focus their efforts on selective adaptation. The text incorporates into the discussion almost all the studies on this topic that have appeared in print as of Spring 1979.

In organizing this monograph, I have presented work of our laboratory in considerable detail and have drawn on related work of other laboratories in subsequent discussions. This organization permitted a coinciding logical and chronological sequence, and it should illustrate how one laboratory has gone about the business of conducting a long-term study. At the same time, convergences and divergences between studies conducted at different laboratories have played a major role in directing ongoing research, and the impact of these studies is evidenced throughout.

Specialists in speech perception will find reprinted portions of a number of familiar and readily accessible journal articles, and some of these readers might reasonably ask why such a book is being published at all. Chapters 1 and 7 are completely new, and a good deal of updating and critical discussion appears at the end of each chapter. This new material is, to be sure, outweighed by what is reprinted, yet together the old and the new provide a line of argumentation that cannot be gleaned from the journal literature.

Each of the main experiments reported here was conducted while I was a student, first as an undergraduate at Brown University during 1972–73 and then as a graduate student at the Massachusetts Institute of Technology during 1973–75. Throughout this period, I enjoyed the help of a number of persons—professors, fellow students, editors, and perhaps most helpful of all, anonymous reviewers, only some of whose names I can guess. At Brown University, Professor Peter D. Eimas introduced me to the technique of selective adaptation. Professor Eimas's enthusiasm and dedication were contagious, and under his supervision the first of the experimental studies was completed. After enrolling in M.I.T.'s Department of Psychology, I took part in stimulating discussions with a number of people at both the department and the Research Laboratory of Electronics (RLE). At RLE, Professor Kenneth N. Stevens listened with interest and never failed to give me a slightly different picture from my current one. Dr. Dennis H. Klatt took on the difficult job of training me to use computerized techniques for speech synthesis and analysis. In addition, Dr. Klatt and Dr.

A. W. F. Huggins provided computer programs that were essential for carrying out this work. At the Department of Psychology, I received advice and encouragement from Professors Jerry A. Fodor, Merrill F. Garrett, Richard M. Held, and Hans-Lukas Teuber. Visiting Professor Alvin M. Liberman provided an additional source of engaging discussion. Two fellow graduate students—Anthony E. Ades and William F. Ganong, III—sharpened my ideas during many a hallway conversation. The three of us typically disagreed, but we seldom parted without an improved idea of our own or one another's positions.

Five of the experimental reports on which this book is based originally had co-authors, colleagues who deserve special thanks. They contributed much to the overall task, and in addition, gave their permission to reprint portions of original journal articles. They include Professor Sheila E. Blumstein, Professor Ronald A. Cole, Robert R. Ebert, Marc R. Lauritsen, Richard M. Nager, and Georgia Nigro. In addition, I thank Dumont Billings and Steven Lapointe, who collaborated on work cited here, as well as John M. Sorensen, and Janet McCabe for helping with the book during its final stages.

Doctors Blumstein, Ganong, and Stevens read an earlier version of the monograph and provided many helpful suggestions. Finally, thanks go to Professor John R. Ross of the M.I.T. Department of Linguistics and Philosophy. Professor Ross had no direct hand in this project until its final stages, yet his ongoing collaboration on another project made it possible for me to gain some measure of distance from this work, needed to pursue it refreshed.

This research was supported by the National Science Foundation (NSF-URP Harvard University, 1972; NSF-URP Brown University, 1973; NSF Graduate Fellowship, M.I.T., 1974-75), the National Institutes of Health (Grants GM-01064, HD-05168, MH-26612, NS-04332, NS-07615, and NS-13028), the Sloan Foundation, the Spencer Foundation, and the M.I.T. Research Laboratory of Electronics.

chapter one
INTRODUCTION

A student about to embark on his first research project faces a number of difficulties, many of which stem from a lack of experience. Yet, the beginner holds one major advantage over many a senior scientist—he is not bound by a vested interest in previous research. In speech science, the beginner may ask questions like "How do I talk?" or "How do I understand your speech?" in much the same way a child asks "How do trees grow?"

A child's questions are often a parent's undoing, and so it is with the questions raised about speech. An adult may reply that the workings of the vocal tract and the ear allow us to produce and perceive speech. The adult may even be able to explain in some detail the intricate movements of the tongue, the larynx, and other structures that play a role in speech production, and he may explain how the ear acts as a mechanical transducer to transmit acoustic properties of speech to levels of neural processing. But, if the child is unsatisfied with these replies—if he persists in asking *how* and *why*, as he most assuredly will—then the adult must finally admit his own lack of understanding about basic psychological processes that underlie both speech production and perception.

A child asks questions largely because he is innately curious, and this curiosity is not entirely lost in adulthood. In addition to curiosity, understanding speech processes is pursued here with an eye toward certain practical applications. The study of speech in normal adults should, for example, provide help in efforts to build a machine that can communicate verbally with us. Transmitting information in numerous businesses and services would be much more efficient with the advent of man-machine speech communication. In addition, research with normal adults may help in the diagnosis and treatment of certain language pathologies. Such potential goals are a long way off, but reaching them depends on progress in basic research.

To approach this line of study, it is necessary to review something about what we currently know (and do not know) about speech. Our interest at this point lies more with general principles than with a large array of facts. Accordingly, the discussion is centered around the problem of how we produce and perceive a single consonant + vowel syllable. This syllable is represented by phonetic symbols as [bæ], pronounced as in the word *bat* (see Pike, 1948, for a discussion of phonetic symbols used in this book).

SPEECH PRODUCTION

The primary focus of this book lies with the problems of the listener rather than the speaker, yet we begin by reviewing aspects of speech production. The reason is that our task is defined in part by the restricted set of acoustic signals that the human vocal tract can produce.

Traditional observers of speech distinguished two parts of the syllable [bæ], a consonant [b] and a vowel [æ]. The distinction between consonant and vowel is basic in all natural languages, and in speech production, this distinction is represented by a difference in the relative constriction of the portion of the vocal tract which lies above the larynx (hereafter referred to as the *supralaryngeal* tract; see Figure 1). The tract is relatively constricted for a consonant in comparison with a vowel (for a discussion, see Stevens, 1971, and references cited therein).

The consonant [b] is produced by placing the two lips together and then separating them. From the lungs, air is forced through the larynx, a complex throat cavity, or pharynx. Just above the trachea lies the larynx, a complex structure containing a triangular cavity—the glottis—bordered by the vocal cords. For [bæ], the vocal cords are set into vibration either before, or shortly after, the lips are separated. The tongue assumes a relatively flat and low position for the following vowel [æ] as the lips are released, with the highest point of the tongue low in the mandible, nearer to the tongue tip than the velum. The velum is a flaplike structure lying at the back of the mouth cavity near the pharynx (see Figure 1).

One way to learn about the essential properties of [b] is to contrast it with other consonants. This was the research strategy adopted by linguists in early work on speech production. In particular, [b] was studied by asking how it differed from its closest neighbors [pʰ] (as in *pat*), [m] (as in *mat*), and [d] (as in *dad*). If an observer watches a speaker say [bæ], [pʰæ], [mæ], and [dæ], without being able to hear these syllables, he is able to distinguish only [dæ] from the remaining three syllables as a group. This simple demonstration tells us that the distinctions among [bæ], [pʰæ], and [mæ] are not to be found in the

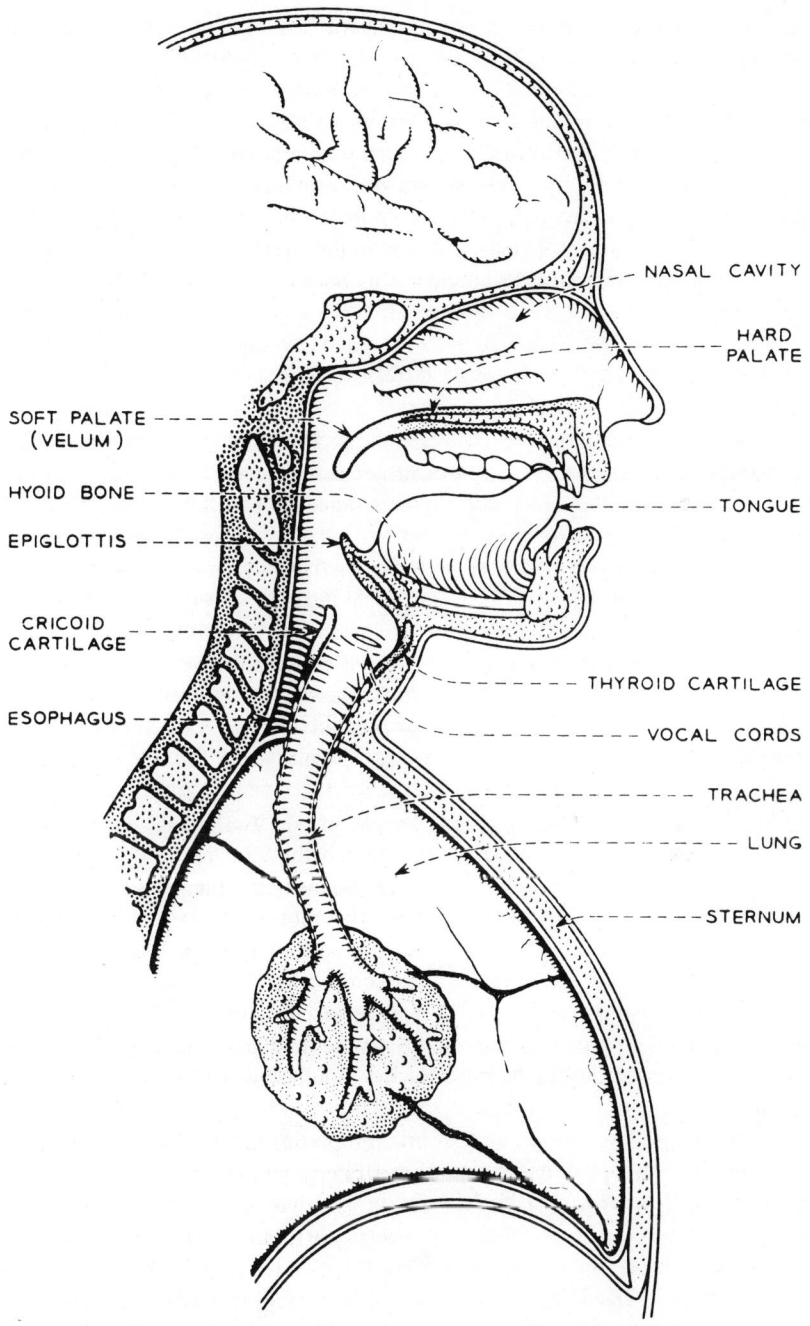

Figure 1. The human vocal apparatus. Reprinted with permission from Flanagan (1972).

observable place in the mouth at which the consonants are released, the so-called *place of articulation*. In all three cases, the place of release is at the two lips. Rather, the differences among these consonants must be a product of unobservable activity, either in the larynx or in the rear portion of the supralaryngeal tract.

First, consider the difference between [bæ] and [pʰæ]. By placing a fingertip on the skin overlying the larynx while uttering these syllables, a speaker may notice that the larynx begins to vibrate sooner in the case of [bæ], relative to the release of the lips. Speech scientists have confirmed and quantified this relation with modern optical techniques that afford a clear view of the larynx. For [bæ], the vocal cords begin to vibrate either before the lips are released or within about 20 msec after the release. For [pʰæ], the vocal cords typically do not begin to vibrate until about 50 msec or more following the release. This difference in the timing of vocal cord vibration relative to oral release is a primary means of signaling the contrast between [bæ] and [pʰæ] in many natural languages, including English (Lisker & Abramson, 1964).

Now consider the difference between the syllables [bæ] and [mæ]. Here, the laryngeal activity is virtually the same for the two syllables, so we must look elsewhere for a major distinction. A clue is found when a speaker says [bæ] and [mæ] while completely closing off the nasal passage. If successful in blocking the air through this passage (as when the speaker suffers from a bad head cold), he will notice that [mæ] but not [bæ] is distorted from its usual sound quality. In fact, a [mæ] spoken under such circumstances sounds very similar to a normal spoken [bæ] (with the [æ] heavily nasalized, however). We can infer from this demonstration that air passes freely through the nostrils during the production of [mæ], but not [bæ], in normal speech. Direct evidence favoring this inference can be obtained by measuring the airflow at the nostrils during speech production. Another source of evidence comes from X-ray motion pictures of the vocal tract. These pictures show that the velum, which controls the opening of the nasal passage (see Figure 1), is lowered to open this passageway during the production of [mæ].

Finally, consider the difference between [bæ] and [dæ]. As noted earlier, the difference between these two syllables can be detected by simple visual inspection, indicating that these syllables are distinguished by the place of articulation at which the consonants are released. For [bæ], the release occurs at the two lips, whereas for [dæ], it occurs just behind the upper teeth, at the alveolar ridge. The tongue tip moves downward from this ridge at the [d]–release.

We have now provided a way of distinguishing [b] from each of its close neighbors [pʰ], [m], and [d]. In a similar vein, we could go on to show how [b] is distinguished for all other consonants. In characterizing the distinctions among consonants, linguists observed that a relatively small number of articulatory properties sufficed. These properties, or *features,* included *place of articulation* (distinguishing [b] from [d]) *voicing* ([b] vs. [pʰ]), *nasality* ([b] vs. [m]), as well as other features to be discussed. By representing the consonants of

English by these articulatory features, as shown in Table 1, one can determine the extent to which any pair of consonants are contrasted in speech production. A feature representation also characterizes English vowels, but we do not discuss vowels here because the main focus throughout this book resides with consonants. This focus is adopted because consonants carry a much greater load of information in speech communication (Denes, 1963).

Table 1
A Feature Representation of English Consonants

	Voiced				Voiceless			
Manner	Labial	Alveolar	Alveo-palatal	Velar	Labial	Alveolar	Alveo-palatal	Velar
Stop	b	d		g	p^h	t^h		k^h
Nasal	m	n		ŋ				
Fricative	v	ð z	ž		f	θ	s	š
Affricate		ǰ				č		
Liquid		r,l*						
Glide	w	j						

*The two liquids are distinguished by tongue shape; for [r], the tongue is grooved with the lowered portion in the middle; for [l], the lowered portion is at the sides.

The feature complex *manner of articulation* divides the consonants into a number of smaller classes. Consonants produced with a complete blockage of airflow at some point in the supralaryngeal tract include the *stop* consonants (also termed *plosives*) [b], [p^h], [d], [t^h], [g] ([g] as in *gas*, not *gin*), [k^h], and the *nasal* consonants [m], [n], and [ŋ] ([ŋ] as in *sing*).

Consonants produced with an incomplete closure include the *fricatives* [v], [f], [ð] (as in *that*), [θ] (as in *thin*), [z], [s], [ž] (as in *azure*), [š] (as in *shin*), the *liquids* [r] and [l], and the *glides* [w] and [j] (as in *yard*). Affricate consonants, [ǰ] (as in *jive*) and [č] (as in *chieve*), are produced like a sequence of a stop and a fricative. The affricate [ǰ] is produced like a sequence of [d]–[ž], whereas [č] is produced like a sequence [t]–[š].

Within each of these manner classes, distinctions are provided by the features of place of articulation and voicing. With the stops, for example, individual members of the triads [b]–[d]–[g] and [p^h]–[t^h]–[k^h] are separated from one another by place of articulation. Members of the pairs [b]–[p^h], [d]–[t^h], and [g]–[k^h] are separated by voicing.

Linguists have devised a number of alternative feature systems to account for the relationships described here. We shall consider some of these in later chapters when discussing experimental findings.

The distinctions among consonants provide us with some information about the essential properties of [b]. To a linguist, such information is important for providing an adequate account of a language's sound system. To a psychologist, this information is useful but far from complete. The distinctions provide only a background for seeking answers to the child's questions about how a syllable like [bæ] is actually produced and perceived. In short, we know from the foregoing discussion that [bæ] is produced by closing and then separating the two lips as the vocal cords are set into vibration, but we are left with questions about *how*, for example, the timing of the lip release is controlled with respect to the onset of vocal cord vibration, or *how* the rate of tongue movement is controlled in approaching its target position for the steady state vowel. Anyone who has viewed X-ray motion pictures of the articulators is amazed at the orchestration of tongue, jaw, and lip movements during speech production, yet we know very little about how this orchestration is controlled. Although this book will not give primary emphasis to such problems of speech production, the problems to be faced in studying speech *perception* have grown out of a similar research tradition, involving a preoccupation with describing minimal distinctions among speech sounds.

SPEECH SOUNDS

The acoustic signal produced by a speaker, like any acoustic signal, can be described in terms of three major components: time, frequency, and amplitude. Variations in one or more of these components suffice to cue differences among the consonants and vowels of a language. A number of means have been devised for displaying these components of speech visually, and we shall review three display forms as background for discussing some of the salient acoustic properties of speech.

The most common visual displays include the *oscillogram,* the *spectrogram,* and the *short-time amplitude-frequency spectrum.* Each of these representations has certain advantages over the others, depending on the task at hand. The oscillogram displays a continuous trace of the speech amplitude as a function of time. The frequency of the periodic portions of the waveform can be determined, using the equation (period $= \frac{1}{\text{frequency}}$). An example of an oscillographic display of the syllable [bæ] is shown in Figure 2.

This representation is useful in studying time and amplitude components of speech when information about frequency is of lesser interest. Digitized oscillogram traces are particularly useful in modern work, allowing computer-controlled marking of locations on the display. We use this type of display in some of the experiments reported in Part II of this book.

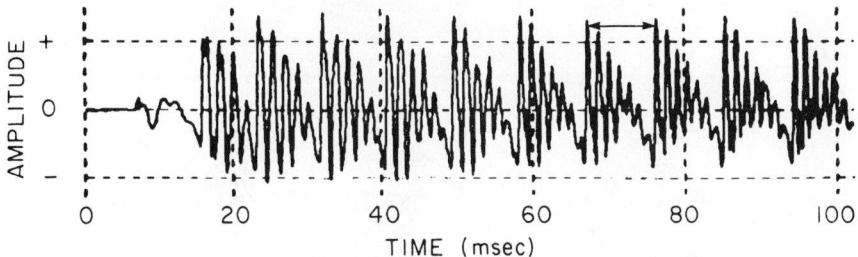

Figure 2. Oscillogram showing the first 100 msec of the syllable [bæ].

The sound spectrogram displays frequency information as a function of time, with amplitude represented grossly by the relative blackness of the trace. The sound spectrogram is the most widely used visual display form in speech research, and it is no exaggeration to say that the invention of the spectrograph (Koenig, Dunn, & Lacey, 1946) heralded the modern era of work in this field. Without this invention, it is unlikely that much progress could have been made toward understanding speech perception.

Let us consider how some of the more prominent aspects of speech are represented by the oscillogram and spectrogram. First, consider the vibration of the vocal cords. This aspect of speech production is represented by the quasi-periodic character of the speech signal, shown directly in the oscillogram of Figure 2. The peak-to-peak period can be measured from this trace, and given the period, the fundamental frequency of the voice can be derived. For an adult male speaker, the fundamental frequency typically ranges from about 100 to 160 Hz (signifying that the vocal cords move through 100 to 160 vibration cycles per second); for an adult female, the average fundamental frequency is nearly twice as great.

On the spectrogram in Figure 3, the individual cycles of vocal cord vibration are represented by vertical striations. Each dark line represents the peak amplitude during one vibration cycle. By measuring the distance between two adjacent lines, one can derive an estimate of the fundamental frequency, as in the case of the oscillogram.

The acoustic consequences of activity above the larynx can best be illustrated by the spectrogram. The dark bands of energy, concentrated in certain frequency regions for vowels, represent the primary resonances of the vocal tract. Each band is called a *formant,* with different bands being referred to conventionally by number, starting with the lowest frequency band. At successively higher frequency regions, the intensities of the formants typically decrease, and their bandwidths increase. The first three formants generally contain enough information for highly intelligible speech; in some cases, the first two formants are sufficient.

8 SPEECH PERCEPTION AND PRODUCTION

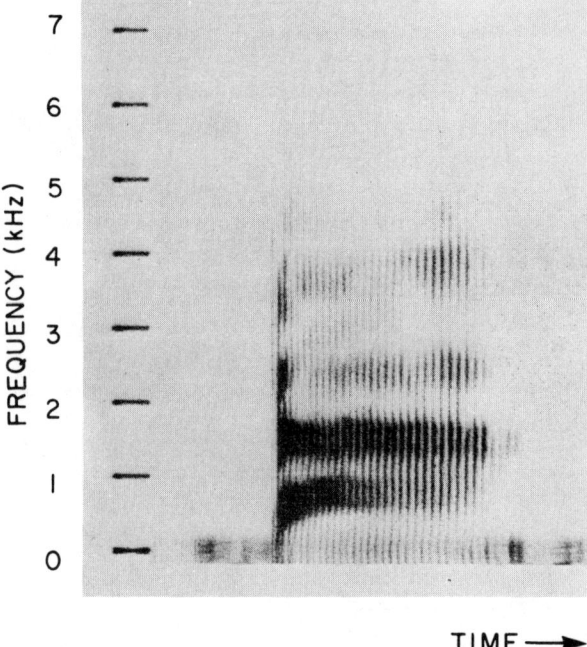

Figure 3. Spectrogram of [bæ].

The formant pattern for a syllable like [bæ] can be subdivided into steady-state and transition portions. During the first 40 msec or so, the lips are being separated as air is pushed through the vocal tract, and the acoustic consequence of this continuous motion is a continuous change in the formant frequencies (since the formants are the primary resonances of the vocal tract). The motions of the formants during this period are referred to as *formant transitions*. The movements of the articulators from consonant to vowel differ, depending on the specific consonant + vowel combination, and as we shall see, the acoustic information contained in the formant transitions provides the listener with a good clue about the identity of the syllable.

A third type of acoustic display, the short-time amplitude-frequency spectrum, provides a plot of the speech amplitude as a function of frequency during a specific time period, or *window*. An example of such a spectrum, taken during the steady-state portion of [æ] in [bæ], is shown in Figure 4. This display is useful for determining amplitude-frequency information over a short time span. One part of the speech signal which may be profitably studied by this means is the release burst of a stop consonant. The *release burst* is a brief, aperiodic signal at the onset of the syllable whose spectrum is dependent on the place of articula-

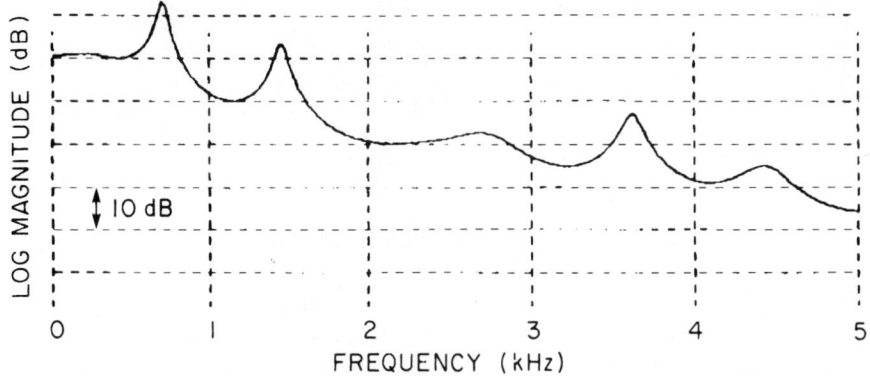

Figure 4. Computer-generated short time spectrum of a 50 msec window for the vowel [æ] in [bæ]. This time window corresponds to the interval from 30 to 80 msec on the oscillographic display for the same stimulus in Figure 2. Note how the relative height of the spectral peaks in this figure corresponds to the darkness of the format bands in the spectrographic display in Figure 3. For the chosen window, the spectral peak for the fourth formant is slightly higher than for the third formant, for example, and the darkness of the spectrographic trace is also greater for the fourth vs. third formant during this interval.

tion. Differences in the burst spectrum provide the listener with a clue about the stop's place of articulation, as do differences in the formant transitions (see Liberman, Cooper, Shankweiler, & Studdert-Kennedy, 1967; Dorman, Studdert-Kennedy, & Raphael, 1977; Just, Suslick, Michaels, & Shockey, 1978).

The relation between articulation and speech acoustics has been studied in detail by Chiba and Kajiyama (1942) and Fant (1960). Recently, Stevens (1971) has emphasized the relevance of this topic to psychology. Following earlier work on the relation between speech and acoustics, Stevens observed that there exist certain portions of the vocal tract where a change in the position of the tongue produces a relatively slight change in the acoustic output. Such regions are referred to as *plateau regions* of acoustic stability. Other portions of the tract show much less stability, with small changes in tongue position yielding quite large changes in the acoustic output.

Since a speaker (particularly a young language-learner) makes small errors in reaching articulatory targets, it would be advantageous for the speaker to use speech sounds which are produced in places of relative acoustic stability. Thus, we might suspect that languages would generally tend to incorporate such sounds in preference to those for which small articulatory errors produce a perceptibly different acoustic output. For vowels, this general hypothesis has been confirmed. Stevens noted that the articulatory positions for [i], [a], and [u] are particularly stable, and these vowel targets appear in natural languages with the greatest occurrence. In Stevens's account, their widespread use is not accidental but reflects a general tendency for speakers to minimize acoustic error. Related observations have been made for consonant distinctions involving place of articulation (Stevens, 1971; Blumstein & Stevens, 1977).

SPEECH PERCEPTION

We have touched briefly upon speech production and its relation to speech acoustics. For present purposes, we need not go into more detail, although the interested reader may pursue an in-depth treatment by reading Fant (1960), Flanagan (1972), and Stevens (1971). As noted, the foregoing topic provides necessary background for any discussion of speech perception because the problems that arise in perception are a consequence of the nature of the set of acoustic signals that the vocal tract can produce.

We may begin to ask questions about speech perception by considering what we already know about the properties of speech signals, since such signals represent the input to the perceptual system. We know, for example, that speech sounds can be described uniquely in terms of their frequency, time, and amplitude characteristics, and we might ask whether and how these parameters are extracted from the speech signal during speech perception. Beyond the earliest stage(s) of auditory processing, we should like to know whether, for example, filters exist for detecting particular frequency bands, and if so, over what time window they operate and how their detection of frequency might depend on the signal's amplitude. We should also like to know how this frequency information is used by later stages of processing in reaching a decision about the identity of a particular consonant, in terms of the inventory of possible phonemes in the language.

Early Modern Work

The questions that naturally arise during this discussion were not, however, of primary interest in the beginning phase of work on speech perception. Like traditional work on speech production, early studies of perception, with few exceptions, focused not on the problem of how we perceive a given speech sound but rather on the problem of how we *distinguish* one speech sound from another. The early concern with distinctions probably stemmed from the assumption that information obtained with this strategy might be useful in guiding later, more elaborate attempts to study the *how* of speech perception. In fact, the work on distinctions did provide some clues about which aspects of the speech signal were most important to perception.

The research strategy on distinctions typically involved the following steps: first, a speaker produced tokens of two syllables, say [bæ] and [pʰæ]; these syllables were then examined by means of spectrograms for possible acoustic differences; when a reliable difference was found, it was hypothesized that this difference might be a sufficient cue for distinguishing the two syllables in perception. A test of the hypothesis was designed by constructing a series of synthetic speech syllables which differed only in the distinctive cue; these sounds were played to listeners in a randomized sequence for identification as [bæ] or [pʰæ]. If listeners could reliably classify the syllables into two distinct categories, the hypothesis was confirmed.

This strategy was used extensively during work on speech perception from about 1950 to 1965, particularly at Haskins Laboratories, where much of the pioneering work on perception was conducted. The synthetic syllables were constructed by using a pattern playback machine, a device which converted handpainted spectrograms into sound (Cooper, Liberman, & Borst, 1951). The studies with synthetic speech allowed the Haskins researchers to identify a number of perceptually relevant properties of the speech signal. In addition, this line of research yielded two bonus findings which provided hints about the general nature of the perceptual process. Many specific findings about the speech cues will be discussed in later chapters as the need arises, but the two bonus findings are mentioned here, since these exerted a strong influence on modern work.

One finding was the phenomenon of *categorical perception,* observed in experiments in which listeners were asked to identify and discriminate synthetic speech sounds differing only in their syllable-initial consonants. In an identification test for a continuous series of sounds spanning the distinction between, say, [bæ] and [pʰæ], listeners show a sharp shift in their responses from one category to the other, as shown in Figure 5. When listeners were asked to discriminate stimuli from the same series, a peak in the discrimination function was obtained at the location of the *phoneme boundary,* the stimulus value for which the responses to [ba] and [pʰa] were equally distributed in the identification task. The subjects were able to discriminate two speech sounds quite well if these sounds had been categorized as belonging to different phoneme categories. Discrimination was relatively poor, however, for two sounds that had been identified as belonging to the same category, even though there was an apparently equal acoustic difference between adjacent stimuli in the series.

The difference between discriminability within and across phoneme boundaries was sufficiently pronounced to prompt the Haskins researchers to suggest that perception of these syllables was nearly categorical—that subjects could discriminate stimuli only so far as they categorized the stimuli as belonging to different phonemes (Liberman, Harris, Hoffman, & Griffith, 1958; cf. Pisoni & Lazarus, 1974; Hanson, 1977). It was argued further that categorical percep-

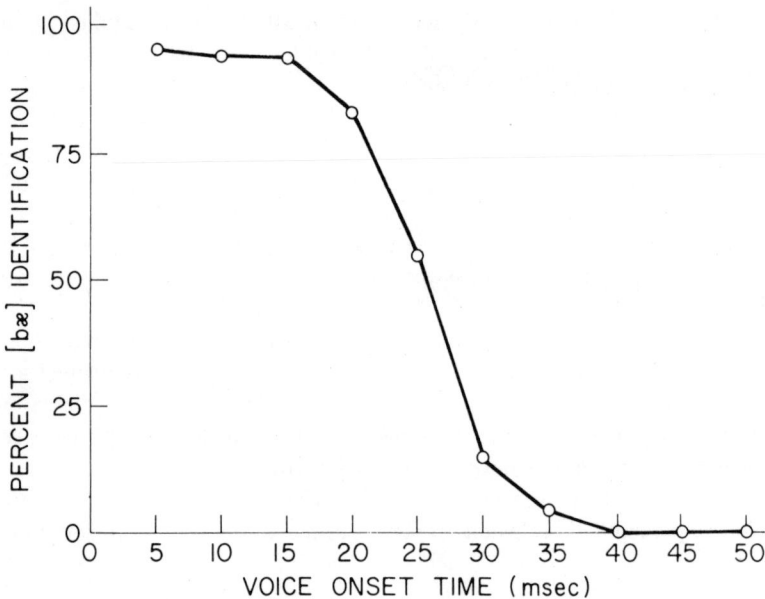

Figure 5. Listener identification function for a series of [bæ]–[pʰæ] synthetic stimuli.

tion was a distinguishing property of speech perception, in contrast to the perception of nonspeech auditory signals. This latter conclusion, however, is no longer considered valid, in light of the recent finding that categorical perception is obtained for certain nonspeech auditory signals of comparable complexity (e.g., Cutting & Rosner, 1974; Cutting, Rosner, & Foard, 1976). Categorical perception appears to reflect a stage of short-term memory in which listeners remember speech sounds in terms of the phoneme categories of their language (Pisoni, 1971).

The other finding of early modern work which purportedly shed light on the nature of the perceptual process concerned a *noninvariance* between the acoustic signal and the listener's percept. A classic case of such noninvariance was provided by the synthetic syllables [di] and [du]. As shown in Figure 6, two-formant versions of these syllables could be synthesized in which only the transitions of the second formant differed. The F_2 transitions for these syllables differed in their direction of frequency change as well as in the particular frequency region traversed. For [di], the transition started above 2100 Hz and rose to about 2700 Hz toward the steady-state vowel [i]. For [du], the same transition fell from about 1200 Hz to 700 Hz toward the vowel [u]. A theory of speech perception must be able to explain why a listener perceives the same phoneme

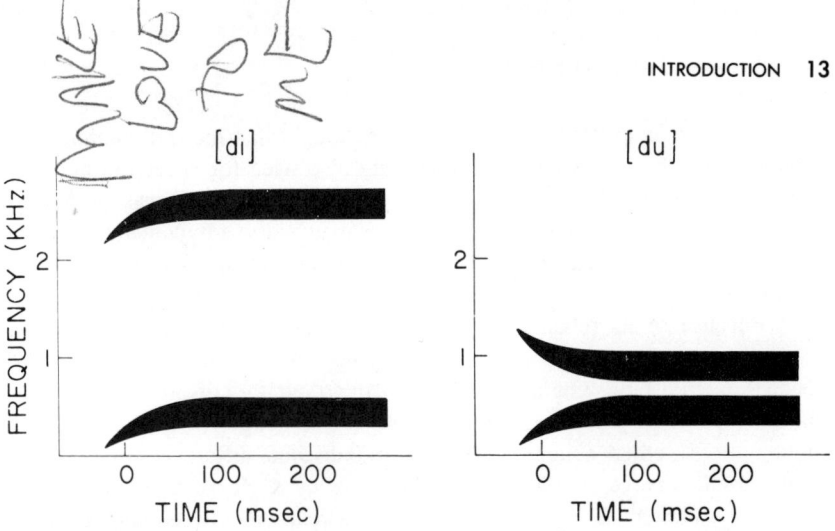

Figure 6. Schematic spectrograms of two-formant patterns for [di] and [du]. (After Liberman, Cooper, Shankweiler, & Studdert-Kennedy, 1967).

[d] in these two diverse acoustic signals. Similarly, in a converse case, involving the three syllables [pʰi]–[kʰa]–[tʰu], the theory must explain why a listener perceives distinct phonemes carried by very similar acoustic signals (Liberman, Delattre, & Cooper, 1952).

Clearly, we cannot resolve the present dilemma for [di]–[du] by referring either to the particular direction of the F_2 transition or to its region of frequency excursion. We are left with three possibilities: (a) at some level of perception analysis, the two F_2 transitions are detected by the same broad-band filter; (b) invariance is not to be found in the acoustic signal at all, but rather in a more abstract relation between the acoustic signal and some representation internally generated by the listener; (c) acoustic invariance is to be found not by studying the formant transitions in isolation but by considering these transitions in relation to other acoustic cues contained in the speech sound. The first possibility can be effectively ruled out, since the kind of broad-band filter required for [di] and [du] would be so broadly tuned for frequency region and direction of frequency change that it would not be able to distinguish [d] in these syllables from [b] and [g]. We know from other experiments with the F_2 transition that the information contained in this transition *is* sufficient to cue the [b]–[d]–[g] distinction when the vowel environment is fixed. So we are left with the second and third possibilities. The second was adopted by the Haskins researchers (Delattre, Liberman, & Cooper, 1955). They suggested that an invariant cue for the percept [d] in both [di] and [du] lay in the *locus* to which the F_2 transitions point, if the transitions are extended backward, hypothetically, from their onset. The locus principle is not an *ad hoc* formula but reflects the fact that, in speech production, all syllables beginning with [d] are initiated at the same place of articulation. The locus computation required of the listener was imagined to be accomplished with reference to speech production; it was thought that the information in the speech signal reached a level of processing also used for speech motor commands. At this level, an operation of analysis-by-synthesis was performed, whereby the transformed acoustic signal was matched to a hypothetical acoustic signal, internally generated by the speech motor system (see also, Stevens, 1960).

Because of its reliance on an abstract relation between perception and production, this hypothesis was not easy to test. Some researchers sought evidence through establishing a relation between articulatory disorders and perceptual difficulties in children (Haggard, Corigall, & Legg, 1970; Monin & Huntington, 1975); others sought evidence from individual differences in the speech production and perception of normal adults (Bailey & Haggard, 1973). In some cases, such indirect tests provide support for a relation between perceptual and productive capacities; in others, the results were ambiguous. But, in fact, such studies did not bear on the analysis-by-synthesis hypothesis, but rather on the weaker, though still interesting, hypothesis that perceptual and productive processors function independently but have evolved to be well-matched to one another (Lieberman, 1975). To test the hypothesis that a unitary processor is involved during some stage of ongoing speech production and perception, it was necessary to involve perception and production in the same experiment. (In Part II, we discuss some recent attempts in this direction.)

As noted earlier, the analysis-by-synthesis approach is not the only means of accounting for perceptual invariance in the face of acoustic noninvariance. Another possibility, becoming of major interest in current research, is that acoustic invariance does exist, but that it is to be found not by considering, for example, the formant transitions in isolation, but by considering the general shape of the short-term spectrum at the release of the consonant (e.g., Blumstein & Stevens, 1977). At present, it is not possible to determine whether this approach will provide a solution to the issue of whether acoustic invariance exists in a manner that is relevant to perception, but the initial results along this line seem promising.

Current Work in Speech Perception

Given the pioneering work on distinctive speech cues, conducted during the 1950s and early 1960s, the way was paved for testing questions about *how* speech perception occurs. A number of experimental techniques were borrowed from other branches of psychology to deal with these questions, including, among others, the methods of choice reaction time, perceptual masking, dichotic listening, and selective adaptation (for a review, see Lass, ed., 1976). Each of these methods has its virtues and shortcomings as a tool for studying a particular set of issues, but the methods have in common a use in exploring three main questions about speech processing: (a) What stages are involved in speech perception? (b) How is information processed within a given stage of the perceptual system? (c) How is information transferred from one stage of the system to another?

Let us consider one plausible model of information-processing for speech perception which provides a framework for discussing these questions.

A MODEL OF SPEECH PERCEPTION[1]

It is assumed that the speech perception system does not process information instantaneously, but in stages, whose operations are distributed over some short time interval. This view has served as the basis for a number of general and specific models of speech perception (e.g., Liberman, 1970; Studdert-Kennedy, 1976; Pisoni & Sawusch, 1975; Summerfield, 1974; Cooper & Nager, 1975). In addition, the view has been explored in some detail by communication engineers in constructing programs for computer recognition of speech (e.g., Reddy, Erman, & Neely, 1973; Rovner, Nash-Webber, & Woods, 1975). To describe the context of the present work, let us consider the model of speech information-processing shown in Figure 7.

As the speechwave enters the ear, it is mechanically transduced into a representation which preserves most of its frequency-time-amplitude information. This initial representation is transformed by successive neural stages to derive increasingly abstract properties from the input. Unless otherwise indicated, the transmission of information from one level to others proceeds in series. At the first of these levels (Level A), a large number of filters code frequency, amplitude, and time information. The specification of separate filters for each of these parameters at Level A is not meant to imply that each filter operates completely independent of information contained in other parameters. For example, individual frequency filters are amplitude-dependent to some extent and operate over specified time-windows. A more precise model of speech perception must include the frequency-response characteristics of these filters and the degree to which the response ranges of separate filters overlap. Studies in auditory psychophysics, physiology, and speech recognition by machine permit some inferences to be made about these details (e.g., Kiang *et al.*, 1965; Tobias, 1970; Bibikov, 1974; Houtgast, 1974; Kiang & Moxon, 1974; Vartanian, 1974; Searle, 1979; Searle, Jacobson, & Rayment, 1979). Up to this point, the processing involved in perception does not also serve speech production, but starting with Level B, it is believed that some aspects of the processing machinery used in perception are used also in production (the information-flow for the *speaker* will not be discussed until Chapter 5).

---

[1]The term *perception* is used throughout this book as a coverall term to include all levels of information-processing normally involved in speech understanding. Thus, by referring to *perception*, I do not exclude some stages which might be more narrowly defined as stages of short-term memory.

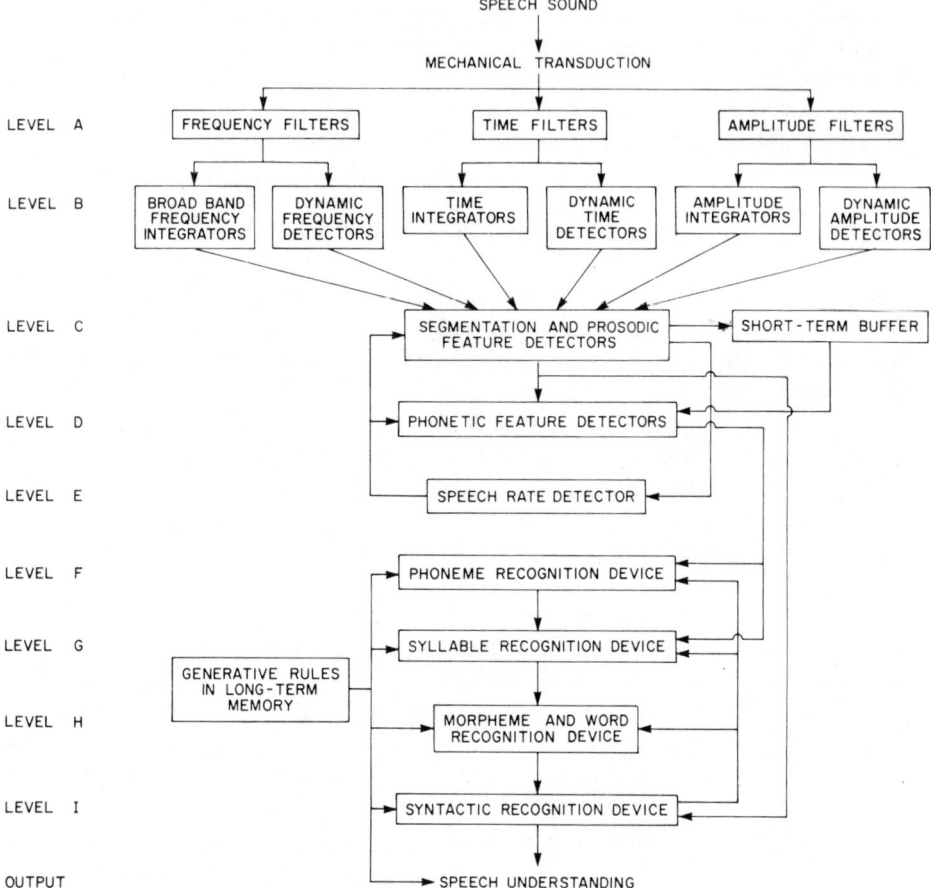

Figure 7. One possible model of information-flow during speech perception. Note that a number of levels may exist within each of the processing stages identified here.

At Level B, the output of each set of Level A filters is integrated by a broader band filter. Here, some degree of frequency, amplitude, and time resolution is lost for the sake of obtaining a more abstract representation. At this level, for example, the outputs of a number of filters for frequency information are pooled to yield a representation resembling a formant frequency, such as that shown in the spectrogram in Figure 3. A variety of possibilities exists for how such formant frequencies are actually computed. Programs for machine recognition of speech may rely on the processing of zero-crossing of an oscillogram-like trace, computing the peak in amplitude for a given broad frequency region, or on more sophisticated procedures, including linear-prediction (based on analysis-by-synthesis) or cepstral analysis (cf. Flanagan, 1972 for a description of these methods). Whether any of these methods provides a useful analog to formant processing in humans remains to be determined.

At Level B, the system also detects information about *changes* in the output of the previous stage over time. At this stage, for example, a rise or fall in the frequency of a particular formant is detected. Again, it is not known how extraction of this information occurs. One possibility is by lateral inhibition among separate formant frequency filters, analogous to a network proposed in the visual system for detecting motion (Barlow & Levick, 1963).

At Level C, segmentation is performed to break down the incoming speechwave into syllablelike chunks. This segmentation process may proceed by computing the average number of times that an oscillogram-like trace crosses zero amplitude. The output of each segmentation pass is stored in a short-term buffer. In addition, the detection of prosodic features, including significant influctions of fundamental frequency and rhythm, is carried out at this level.

At level D, the output signals from Level C are processed to derive information about individual phonetic features, such as manner and place of articulation. A decision regarding the value of any feature is based on inputs from a number of auditory filters. Again, many details are unknown. It is plausible that the manner features are extracted first, since these are the most reliably coded in the speech signal and would be most useful in guiding later hypotheses about phoneme identity.

At Level E, a decision about the speaker's rate of speech is made on the basis of an average of how many segments occurred over a given time interval at Level C. The judgment of speech rate is fed back to Level D where initial hypotheses about phonetic features may be revised (cf. Summerfield, 1974, for another model).

The initial and revised outputs of Level D are transmitted to a phoneme recognition device at Level F, where hypotheses are made about the identity of each phoneme (cf. Oden & Massaro, 1978). The outputs of Level D are also transmitted in parallel to a syllable-recognition device at Level G, where hypotheses are made about the identity of the whole syllable-sized chunk segmented at Level D.

Levels F and G also receive input from a set of generative rules stored in long-term memory. These rules aid the listener in making decisions about phoneme and syllable identity, as well as in computing the probability that the decisions made at Level G and H are correct. Decision-making about phonemes and syllables proceeds independently, and both types of units are accorded an important status as input to later stages of processing (cf. Healy and Cutting, 1976 for discussion). A probability score is derived by assessing the match between the preliminary output of these levels and an internal representation of the phoneme or syllable in question. In this way, the system can decide when sufficient information is available about phoneme and syllable identity to serve as useful input to later stages of processing.

In Level H, larger chunks, such as morphemes (minimal meaning-bearing units) and words are identified, using generative rules for lexical look-up as a guide (Forster, 1975; Cole, Jakimik, & Cooper, 1979). At the same time that lexical information is being extracted, a syntactic processor (Level I) is beginning to make hypotheses about the probable locations of phrase and clause boundaries. This processor receives primary input from auditory filters which compute the fundamental frequency contour (Lea, 1973) and duration of speech segments (Klatt & Cooper, 1975; Cooper & Cooper, 1979) as well as from information based on lexical items whose identity has already been determined. The output of the syntactic processor feeds back to levels F, G, and H to derive revised phoneme, syllable, and word hypotheses as necessary.

In constructing such a model, one is struck by the scarcity of available data on which to base major assumptions about the number of stages, the operations conducted at each stage, and the transfer of information from one stage to another. This model, like all current models of speech perception, lacks the kind of high degree of falsifiability needed to test its validity with respect to competing alternatives. It appears that the model's inadequacy stems as much from a lack of basic data as from poor modeling. The model's primary virtue is in exposing the critical need for experimental data on issues about how information is transmitted and decoded by the perceptual system. As such, this model provides a framework for introducing and interpreting the experiments of later chapters.

Some major areas of uncertainty in the model can be easily identified. For one thing, many substages no doubt operate within the major stages outlined here, and the way in which information is processed among such sub-stages remains largely unexplored. Another source of uncertainty involves the interplay between data- and knowledge-driven sources of information. In this case, data-driven information is provided by aspects of the acoustic signal, whereas knowledge-driven information is provided by systems of generative rules stored in long-term memory. If our model is to be applicable to conversational listening, it must surely incorporate both sources of information (e.g., Norman, 1979), yet the manner in which these sources interact has yet to be studied systematically. Finally, very little is known about the overall temporal control of switching operations within the model. It is believed, however, that the switching times between some of the serial stages are so fast (within 10–15 msec) that the model could accommodate experimental findings that are otherwise considered to provide evidence in favor of a system involving more fully parallel processing (e.g. Marslen-Wilson, 1975; Marslen-Wilson & Tyler, 1975).

In this book, we shall try to examine in detail some aspects of the preliminary, data-driven stages of the model, particularly Levels A and B, involving the early processing of acoustic information. It will be shown in the concluding chapters, however, that this work can also be extended to probe other components of the perceptual system.

The selective adaptation method applied here is designed to tell us something about the way in which information is processed at a given stage or stages of processing. But we also want to know *which* stages (within the context of our model) are being tapped. The problem to be faced at the outset is that independent motivation for these stages of processing is hard to come by. Thus, when an adaptation effect suggests that a particular level of processing operates according to some specific principle, there is no assurance that this knowledge will help in identifying the particular stage itself. We must hence be prepared to make guesses and revise them as the work proceeds, as in any serious study of a relatively unknown system.

Selective Adaptation

The method of selective adaptation, as used in speech research, can be illustrated with reference to the visual system, where the technique was originally applied. Selective adaptation as used in vision was based on a phenomenon known as the *negative afterimage*. If an observer looks at a green circle for a prolonged time (the *adapting* stimulus) and then looks at a white circle (the *test* stimulus), the observer reports that the test circle appears reddish. Two questions may be asked about the outcome of this experiment. First, why did the white test circle appear nonwhite? And second, why did this circle appear reddish, as opposed to any other color? The answer to each of these questions tells us something about the way in which the visual system is organized to process information about color.

The reply to the first question is as follows: prolonged viewing of a colored stimulus produces a decline in the perceptual system's responsiveness for detecting the presence of that color with respect to some opponent color; normally, a white test circle contains a perfect balance of the two colors, but after prolonged viewing of the green circle, the white circle appears nonwhite because this balance has been destroyed. In effect, the answer to the first question provides evidence for some type of *opponent-processing* between color detectors in the visual system.

The answer to the second question provides evidence about what particular colors are processed in opposition. If the answer to the first question is correct, the white circle appears reddish after prolonged viewing of a green circle because red and green are processed by opponent channels. What we require is some independent evidence in support of the red-green opponent relation. One source of evidence comes from experiments in color mixing (Jameson & Hurvich, 1955; Larimer, Krantz, & Cicerone, 1974). Given either a green or red stimulus, we can obtain a neutral white by adding the opposite color in sufficient quantity. This piece of evidence suggests that green and red are opponently processed, whereas, say, green and blue are not, since no mixture of green and blue can yield white. A second source of evidence concerns visual pathologies. In rare cases of color blindness, the colors red and green may be impaired as a unit, whereas pairs such as red-yellow or blue-green are never selectively impaired (Hurvich, 1972). This fact suggests that color detectors for red and green funnel information to a single detector at a later stage of processing (see Hurvich & Jameson, 1957, for a discussion).

Selective adaptation, as it is commonly termed, refers to a systematic extension of experiments on afterimages in which a simple color reported by the observer is supplemented or replaced by a quantifiable measure of the aftereffect. Using our present example, the observer might be asked, in addition to reporting the color of the test stimulus, just how reddish this stimulus is, by being required to add amounts of green to the stimulus until it is perceived as a neutral white or grey. The amount of green added would provide an estimate of the magnitude of the effect.

Visual studies in selective adaptation have been conducted with a variety of variables in addition to hue, including luminance, tilt, motion, curvature, and spatial frequency, among others. The technique has been useful in determining which features of the visual system are processed in opponent-process fashion, and in addition, has provided information about the bandwidth and peak sensitivity properties of perceptual filters for such features.

Selective Adaptation to Speech. The first study of speech adaptation was akin to the work with visual afterimages, yet it differed from the latter in one important respect. The speech adaptation effect, reported by Warren and Gregory (1958), was observed in listeners' reports of changes in the percept of an adapting syllable rather than of some neutral test stimulus. The finding that presentation of a repeated syllable produced dramatic changes in the listener's percept to the same syllable suggested that the adaptation method might be usefully applied. As in the case of visual studies, however, progress awaited the use of a quantifiable measure of the adaptation effect. In the case of speech work, synthetic syllables varying in small acoustic steps provided appropriate test stimuli.

The first systematic studies of selective adaptation with speech were begun by Eimas and Corbit in 1971 (later published in 1973) and, independently, by Bailey (1972). The procedure involved a series of synthetic speech syllables as test stimuli. Listeners were asked to identify the test syllables before adaptation and again after adaptation. A comparison of the pre- and post-adaptation responses provided a measure of the effect's direction and magnitude.

In its simplest form, the adaptation technique is not of much help in uncovering aspects of the speech system. Yet, relatively powerful tests can be provided by considering three extensions of the technique. One of these extensions, used by Eimas and Corbit in their original study, involves the use of an adapting stimulus which is not contained in the test series, a method referred to as *crossed-adaptation* or *transfer*. This procedure not only encompasses the use of different acoustic signals as adaptors and test stimuli but also encompasses different modes of presenting these stimuli, such as presenting the adapting and test stimuli to different ears or from different spatial locations.

The presence of a crossed-adaptation effect suggests that, despite their differences, the adapting and test stimuli share some property which is detected by the perceptual system. To take an example from vision, the crossed-adaptation technique can be used to determine whether an aftereffect taps a detector which receives input from one or both eyes. To test this possibility, an observer is asked to view the adapting stimulus with one eye and, after prolonged exposure, to judge a test stimulus with the other, unadapted eye. If an aftereffect is observed under such circumstances, the effect appears to operate at a processing site that receives input from both eyes. Similarly, the cross-adaptation technique is used in visual work to determine whether certain stimulus parameters, such as hue, motion, and luminance, are extracted independently during some stage of perceptual analysis. In the research to be reported in Part I, we find numerous occasions in which crossed-adaptation is used to test the extent to which consonant features are extracted as such from the speech signal. As in the case of visual research, however, we shall see that the interpretation of such tests is not as straightforward as it first appears.

A second major extension of the selective adaptation method is termed *contingent adaptation*. This procedure represents a complement to crossed-adaptation in that it measures the extent to which two stimulus parameters are processed jointly, or dependently. The origins of this procedure are again to be found in the literature on vision. McCollough (1965) attempted to test whether the stimulus variables of color and tilt are processed jointly by using the following test procedure: observers adapted to an alternating stimulus consisting of a blue field with vertical bars and a yellow field with horizontal bars; after adaptation, the observers were presented a white field with either vertical or horizontal bars; the observers reported that the white field with vertical bars appeared yellow; the field with horizontal bars appeared blue. A simple color adaptation account of the results could not be maintained, since equal amounts of blue and yellow were presented during adaptation. If the blue and yellow colors were processed independent of edge information provided by the bars, then no adaptation effects should have been observed for both test patterns, since blue and yellow are processed in opponent fashion and cancel each other's effect, as noted above. Rather, McCollough suggested that these results indicate the presence of detectors in the visual system that process specific color-edge combinations.

Since the early work on contingent effects in vision, a variety of contingencies have been observed, and some researchers have called into question the notion that these various effects reflect the adaptation of built-in perceptual analyzers (cf., Murch, 1976; McCarter & Silver, 1977; Murch, 1977). Instead, the effects may reflect the system's plasticity to repeated stimulation in terms of classical conditioning. In Chapter 5, we consider evidence for alternative accounts of the contingent effects, but for now, it is sufficient to remark that, regardless of the *adaptation* vs. *conditioning* accounts of the effect, the outcome of experiments with this method are of interest in studying the perceptual system to the extent that results show systematic constraints of direction and magnitude.

The third extension of the adaptation method, *perceptuo-motor adaptation,* is in actuality a subtype of *crossed-adaptation,* yet it differs markedly from other crossed-adaptation procedures used in this book because, as its name implies, it involves adapting or testing speech *production* in order to examine its relation to perception. One kind of perceptuo-motor adaptation involves testing a subject's speech production after prolonged listening; the other involves testing perception after prolonged articulation, either with or without auditory feedback. These extensions of the adaptation method offer the potential of providing a direct means of testing the possibility that a unitary processing site serves perception and production.

We set out with the hope that these extensions of the adaptation method would provide a fair amount of new information about how speech perception is accomplished. But before proceeding, it is useful to consider some reservations.

First, the child might ask, will the results of the adaptation experiments provide valid reflections of the speech processing system? This objection can take at least two forms. According to one, the results might reflect the operation of a conscious strategy on the part of the subject, a strategy particular to the task at hand which does not play a role in normal speech perception. Many of the results to be discussed militate against this possibility. This is not to say that the procedure is free from the effects of bias, but rather that such bias effects, so far as they are present, are overshadowed by effects that reflect a stage or stages of processing that operate automatically, without the listener's awareness or conscious control (see Chapter 4).

But, the child might still object that the results with adaptation, using simple syllables, have no bearing on speech perception as it normally occurs in conversation. We pare down the stimuli to syllables for the sake of providing experimental rigor. But in so doing, do we reduce the problem to triviality? The answer to this question does not, of course, reside in the armchair (or highchair) of the questioner, but rather in the kind of data ultimately yielded by the technique. At the onset of the study, we might reply, following a well-established tradition of Western science, that, in the absence of knowledge, "we have to start somewhere," and that generalization to more complex situations must await controlled study in simple ones. Fortunately, this strategy has been partly vindicated by experimental results. Rudnicky and Cole (1977) have shown very similar adaptation effects for syllable test stimuli using either syllables or full sentences and paragraphs as adapting material. Their results indicate that the adaptation effects do not vanish when a listener is required to process higher-order semantic and syntactic information, as in normal speech contexts. There is some reason to believe, then, that the results obtained here for syllables will find a place within a model of the perceptual system as it operates during conversational listening. (A fuller discussion of extensions to continuous speech will be presented in Chapter 7.)

A final criticism, unreleated to those just stated, concerns the typical magnitude of selective adaptation effects. As noted in the following chapters, adaptation effects for speech are small, in terms of the amount of shift in the phoneme boundary. The small magnitude is not surprising, given the biological need for stability in the perceptual system for speech. Yet, working with small-magnitude effects presents a difficulty in interpreting the presence of a valid effect, as opposed to random fluctuation. To resolve this difficulty, statistical tests of significance have been applied for a large data base in each of the present studies. Such tests are designed to determine whether an effect is highly improbable by chance, based on three factors—the magnitude of the effect, the amount of data, and the data's variability. The statistic used most frequently in these studies is the well-known *t-test for matched pairs* (also known as *t-test for correlated observations*), in which the same listener's pre- and post-adaptation responses are compared. Beginning readers are referred to Ferguson (1959) or Harnett (1975) for an introductory discussion of this statistic and the assumptions on which it is based.

If an effect is considered to be statistically significant according to the preceding test, it must be accounted for by a model of speech processing, regardless of its magnitude. Occasionally, someone may incorrectly assume that the magnitude of an experimental effect is directly proportional to its theoretical importance. Examples from speech research and from other sciences indicate that this assumption is unwarranted. In speech, for example, the technique of dichotic listening has served as a major tool for studying the lateralization of speech perception (e.g., Studdert-Kennedy & Shankweiler, 1970), yet the magnitude of dichotic effects is typically quite small. In physics, chemistry, and biology, there exists a long history of major theoretical insights which have depended crucially on the discovery of small but significant effects. In interpreting the present work, therefore, we focus primarily on the criterion of statistical significance rather than on the magnitude of effect. When a result is found to be statistically significant, and when this effect is replicated in independent work at other laboratories, then it must be reckoned with in a theory of speech processing.

Part One
SPEECH PERCEPTION

It has been observed in Chapter 1 that English consonants can be described in terms of a relatively small number of articulatory features. We can now ask whether such features, or acoustic properties resembling them, are detected at some stage of the listening process. In the next three chapters, the selective adaptation method is applied to this issue.

chapter two
PLACE OF ARTICULATION

Study 1*

INTRODUCTION

As noted in Chapter 1, much of the initial work with the adaptation technique was focused on the consonant feature *voicing,* which in English serves to distinguish voiced from voiceless stop consonant pairs (i.e., [b] from [p^h]; [d] from [t^h]; [g] from [k^h]). In word-initial position, voicing contrasts can be signaled by Voice Onset Time (VOT), defined articulatorily as the time interval between the consonant release burst and the onset of laryngeal pulsing. Acoustically, VOT is specified for synthetic speech as the onset time of the first formant relative to the onset times of the second and third formants, with the second and third formants being excited by a noise source rather than by a periodic source when the first formant is absent (Lisker & Abramson, 1970). Eimas and Corbit (1973) reasoned that, because the VOT dimension is perceived in nearly categorical fashion by adults, as well as by infant listeners (Eimas, Siqueland, Jusczyk, & Vigorito 1971), and is furthermore used to mark phonemic distinctions in virtually all natural languages (Lisker & Abramson 1964), VOT-sensitive detector mechanisms might exist and function as the means by which categorical perception of this feature dimension is achieved.

In the Eimas and Corbit study, subjects' perception of *voicing* contrasts

*Portions of this study are reprinted with permission from *Journal of the Acoustical Society of America,* 1974, 56, 617–627.

was first tested by means of a consonant identification task for two series ([b–pʰ] and [d–tʰ]) of 14 synthetically produced stimuli, varying in small steps of VOT. For all stimuli, the steady-state formants were identical and signaled the vowel [a]. The identification functions were obtained for listeners in the unadapted state and after adaptation with both voiced and voiceless stop consonants that had been selected from the extreme ends of the VOT continua.

It was found that when a full minute of repetitive listening to the voiceless bilabial stop [pʰ] preceded each stimulus-to-be-identified, the locus of the phonetic boundary for a VOT series consisting of either bilabial [b–pʰ] or alveolar [d–tʰ] stop consonants shifted toward the voiceless end of the VOT continuum; thus, a greater number of identification responses were now assigned to the voiced, unadapted category, with most of the increase accruing to stimuli with VOT values lying near the original identification boundary. Adaptation with a voiced stop produced a significant shift in the opposite direction, the phonetic boundary in this case being displaced toward the voiced end of the continuum.

A second experiment showed that the peak in the VOT discriminability function, located at the region of the phonetic boundary (see Liberman, Harris, Hoffman, & Griffith 1957), could also be altered following adaptation. The direction and magnitude of this alteration were in agreement with the direction and magnitude of the displacements found previously in the identification task.

The results as a whole indicated that perception along a feature dimension (the VOT dimension, in this case) could be systematically altered by a selective adaptation procedure. More importantly, the alterations seemed to arise from the adaptation, or fatiguing, of a mechanism specialized for the extracting of feature information. Since the shifts in identification could be produced along the alveolar series ([d–tʰ]) by adaptation with a bilabial stimulus, as well as by adaptation with a stimulus from the same alveolar series, the adaptation shifts could not readily be attributed to the influence of simple contrast; i.e., the tendency for subjects to categorize stimuli as having a phonetic value other than that assigned to the adapting stimulus. In addition, the crossed-series shifts obtained in the identification task seemed to rule out the possibility that adaptation operated primarily on the consonantal sound as a unit. It thus seemed reasonable to conclude that a feature-specific effect had been produced.

Based on a consideration of the stimulus dimension along which perception had been altered, Eimas and Corbit assumed that the effective site of adaptation was at the level of VOT cue analysis. Postulating the existence of two VOT-sensitive detectors, each responsive to a specific range of VOT values, they sought to provide a general account for the obtained shifts found in both the identification and discrimination tasks. According to their hypothesis, the response ranges of VOT values to which each of the two detectors is sensitive partially overlap, such that there exists an equilibrium point at which the two detectors are equally responsive. All other factors being equated, this equilibrium point is assumed to correspond to the locus of the phonetic boundary. The repetitive presentation of a VOT stimulus that excites a single detector is assumed to decrease the sensitivity of that detector across its entire response range, thereby producing a shift in the locus of the equilibrium point, and in turn, producing a shift in the locus of the phonetic boundary. Whether feature adaptation in fact operates on detectors which are sensitive to invariant acoustic cue information, as originally proposed in the case of VOT, or rather on higher-level extractors of *phonetic* information (i.e., feature information which is not necessarily traceable to a single, invariant acoustic cue) will be considered in part of the present study.

This set of experiments is concerned with perception of what has proved to be a highly complex feature dimension for consonants, *place of articulation*. This dimension was chosen for investigation for a variety of reasons. First, as in the case of VOT, the acoustic consequences of variation in *place* are perceived in nearly categorical fashion by adults (Liberman et al., 1957; Pisoni, 1971) as well as by infants (Eimas, 1974). Second, and unlike the feature *voicing,* the *place* dimension is tri-valued for the stop consonants in English, accounting for distinctions among [b]–[d]–[g] and among [pʰ]–[tʰ]–[kʰ]. Thus, with the *place* dimension, it will be possible to study the effects of adaptation on more than a single phonetic boundary within the same experiment. Third, and most important, a major acoustic cue for the perception of *place* distinctions among the stop consonants, namely variations in the second- and third-formant transitions, has been found to be highly subject to contextual variation, being particularly dependent on differences in vowel environment (Cooper, Delattre, Liberman, Borst, & Gerstman, 1952; Harris, Hoffman, Liberman, Delattre, & Cooper, 1958).

In Chapter 1, we cited an example of this contextual variation. A listener readily perceives the phonetic category [d] in both the synthetic syllables [di] and [du], yet the acoustic cue for *place* information contained within these two syllables differs to a substantial extent. For [di], the second-formant transition rises, starting at about 2100 Hz and terminating at 2700 Hz; whereas in the case of [du], this same transition falls from about 1200 Hz to 700 Hz. In effect, *acoustic* information signaling *place* differs considerably for the two syllables, yet the perceived *phonetic* feature information remains invariant.

The question of immediate concern is whether the selective adaptation procedure will produce alterations in perception along this acoustically noninvariant *place* dimension—in particular, whether the adaptation procedure will produce shifts in the loci of phonetic boundaries comparable to those found previously in the case of VOT. In the first two experiments of the present study, selective adaptation for the *place* dimension is evaluated using both identification and discrimination response measures, with the adapting consonant and test consonants always being paired with the same vowel [æ]. If significant adaptation effects are obtained within these two experiments, it becomes of further interest to test whether pairing one of the original adapting consonants with a different vowel (thereby changing the acoustic form of the *place* feature cue) also yields perceptual shifts along the original *place* dimension. In addition to providing a basis for narrowing our definition of the primary site of feature adaptation, the experimental findings, in particular the direction and magnitude of the phonetic boundary shifts, are likely to provide information about other characteristics of the processing mechanism for the feature *place*.

EXPERIMENT 1—IDENTIFICATION

Method

Subjects. Seven undergraduate students at Brown University served in the experiment. All were paid volunteers who had no prior experience in listening to synthetic speech. The subjects were native speakers of English and had no known hearing impairments.

Stimuli. The test stimulus series consisted of 13 synthetic speech CV syllables, constructed by means of a parallel resonance synthesizer (Pisoni, 1971). Stimuli varied from one another only in the starting frequency and direction of the second- and third-formant transitions, which together provide a sufficient cue for perceived distinctions along the *place of articulation* dimension. Table 1

Table 1
Starting Frequencies of the Second- and Third-Formant Transitions for the Synthetic CV Stimuli

Stimulus No.	Starting frequencies (in Hz)	
	F_2	F_3
1	1232	2180
2	1312	2348
3	1386	2525
4	1465	2694
5	1541	2862
6	1620	3026
7	1695	3195
8	1772	3026
9	1845	2862
10	1920	2694
11	1996	2525
12	2078	2348
13	2156	2180

The fixed steady-state formants were centered at: 743 Hz (F_1), 1620 Hz (F_2), and 2862 Hz (F_3) [after Pisoni (1971)].

displays the different starting frequencies of F_2 and F_3, as well as the steady-state frequencies to which these formant transitions rose or fell.

Voicing was produced for each consonant by beginning the syllable pattern with a 40-msec low-amplitude F_1 centered at 150 Hz. This 40-msec period was followed immediately by the formant transition period, also lasting 40 msec. The transitions were in turn followed by the steady-state formants corresponding to the vowel [æ], yielding an overall syllable duration of 300 msec. The stimulus series thus consisted of 13 CV patterns varying from one another in small steps to yield a continuum for the perceived syllables of [bæ], [dæ], and [gæ]. Good exemplars of the three-syllable types are shown schematically in Pisoni (1971) (Fig. 1).

Procedure. To obtain baseline functions of identification, subjects in the unadapted state were presented randomized sequences of the 13 syllable patterns during the first test session. The subjects listened binaurally to the output of an Ampex AG-500 recorder and speaker system, the gain being set at a fixed comfortable listening level. Each of the 13 stimuli was presented 20 times for identification in this manner, with an interstimulus interval of 2.5 sec. The subjects were instructed to identify each stimulus as [bæ], [dæ], or [gæ] by writing the appropriate consonant letter on answer sheets provided.

On the day following this unadapted identification test, a series of three adaptation sessions was begun, each session lasting about one hour and taking place at approximately 24-h intervals. Three different adapting stimuli were used, one in each session. These stimuli consisted of the following Table 1 values: No. 1 ([bæ]), No. 7 ([dæ]), and No. 13 ([gæ]). Four of the subjects were presented the three adaptation tests in the order; [bæ] adaptation, [dæ] adaptation, and [gæ] adaptation; the remaining three subjects were presented these same tests in the reverse order.

Each of the three adaptation sessions was conducted in the manner used by Eimas, Cooper, and Corbit (1973). Listeners were first presented with 2 min (180 presentations) of the selected adapting stimulus ([bæ], [dæ], or [gæ] for a given session), each repetition of the adapting stimulus being separated by 350 msec of silence. Next, 35 adaptation trials were administered. For each trial, the adapting stimulus was first presented for 1 min (90 presentations), followed by 1.5 sec of silence, and then four randomly selected stimuli from the series of 13 stop consonants. Subjects were instructed to identify each of these four stimuli during a 2.5-sec silent period that separated adjacent stimuli-to-be identified. After the fourth stimulus was presented for identification, 5 sec of silence intervened before the onset of the next adaptation trial. Using this procedure, each stimulus in the series was presented a total of ten times within a single, hour-long adaptation session. Throughout each of the tests, stimuli-to-be-identified were played on the Ampex AG-500 recorder and speaker system; the adapting stimuli were played by means of tape loops on a Sony TC-630 recorder and speaker system.

Table 2
Individual and Mean Loci of Phonetic Boundaries for Each Test Condition

(a) b–d Phonetic boundary

Subjects	Without adaptation	Adaptation with		
		[bæ]	[dæ]	[gæ]
(1) A.B.	5.19	2.61	5.02	4.07
(2) B.C.	6.23	3.92	5.77	7.53
(3) E.E.	4.68	3.99	7.08	5.70
(4) L.M.	4.14	4.19	6.79	6.90
(5) B.M.	4.69	3.32	6.41	6.07
(6) C.S.	5.15	2.47	5.84	6.11
(7) A.F.	6.65	2.55	6.63	7.14
$\bar{X}$	5.25	3.29	6.22	6.22

(b) d–g Phonetic boundary

Subjects	Without adaptation	Adaptation with		
		[bæ]	[dæ]	[gæ]
(1) A.B.	10.11	10.22	9.50	12.29
(2) B.C.	8.67	9.63	8.55	10.33
(3) E.E.	10.48	9.50	8.63	10.87
(4) L.M.	8.31	9.89	8.52	10.78
(5) B.M.	9.93	9.56	8.97	10.50
(6) C.S.	10.26	9.55	8.19	12.44
(7) A.F.	9.73	8.07	8.66	12.00
$\bar{X}$	9.64	9.49	8.72	11.32

Note: The locus of the phonetic boundary in each case was determined by first assigning to each stimulus an arbitrary number, ranging from 1 to 13, and then performing a least-mean-squares analysis.

Results and Discussion

The results appear in Table 2, where individual and mean phonetic boundary loci are computed for each test condition. The boundary locus was determined in each case by first assigning to each stimulus a number ranging from 1 to 13 and then performing a least-mean-squares analysis (Ferguson, 1959) on the

Table 3
Tests of Significance for Shifts in Phonetic Boundary Loci Between the Unadapted Condition and Each Condition of Adaptation

(a) b–d Phonetic boundary

Adaptation with:	[bæ]ₐ	[dæ]ₐ	[gæ]
p-value:	$p < 0.01$	$p < 0.05$	$p > 0.05$

(b) d–g Phonetic boundary

Adaptation with:	[bæ]	[dæ]	[gæ]ₐ
p-value:	$p > 0.20$	$p < 0.05$	$p < 0.01$

ₐDenotes one-tailed test.
[*Note:* The direction of each significant shift was toward the category of the adapting stimulus.]

transformed percentages of identification responses. The numbers assigned to the stimuli correspond to the numbers assigned in Table 1.

Table 3 shows the results of tests of significance for the shifts in the loci of phonetic boundaries. One-tailed tests of significance were applied in cases where the phonetic boundary bordered the category of the adapting stimulus (e.g., the b–d phonetic boundary for [bæ] adaptation). Based on the model of the adaptation process proposed by Eimas and Corbit (1973), the predicted direction of the boundary shifts in such cases was toward the category of the adapting stimulus. Inspection of this table indicates that, in comparison with the baseline test of identification, a significant shift occurred in the locus of each phonetic boundary that bordered the adapting stimulus category.

For the [bæ] adaptation condition, a significant shift occurred in the b–d phonetic boundary locus. In a similar manner, for [gæ] adaptation, a significant shift occurred in the d–g boundary locus. Within both of these adaptation test conditions, the direction of the significant shift was toward the phonetic category to which the particular adapting stimulus belonged; thus, after adaptation, listeners assigned fewer identification responses to the adapting stimulus category. These shifts in the phonetic boundary bordering the category of the adapting stimulus occurred uniformly for each of the seven subjects within the [gæ] adaptation test and for six of these same subjects within the [bæ] adaptation test. The shifts were thus comparable in direction and consistency to those found previously for the VOT dimension (Eimas & Corbit, 1973; Eimas et al., 1973). In addition, the magnitude of the obtained shifts averaged close to two stimulus

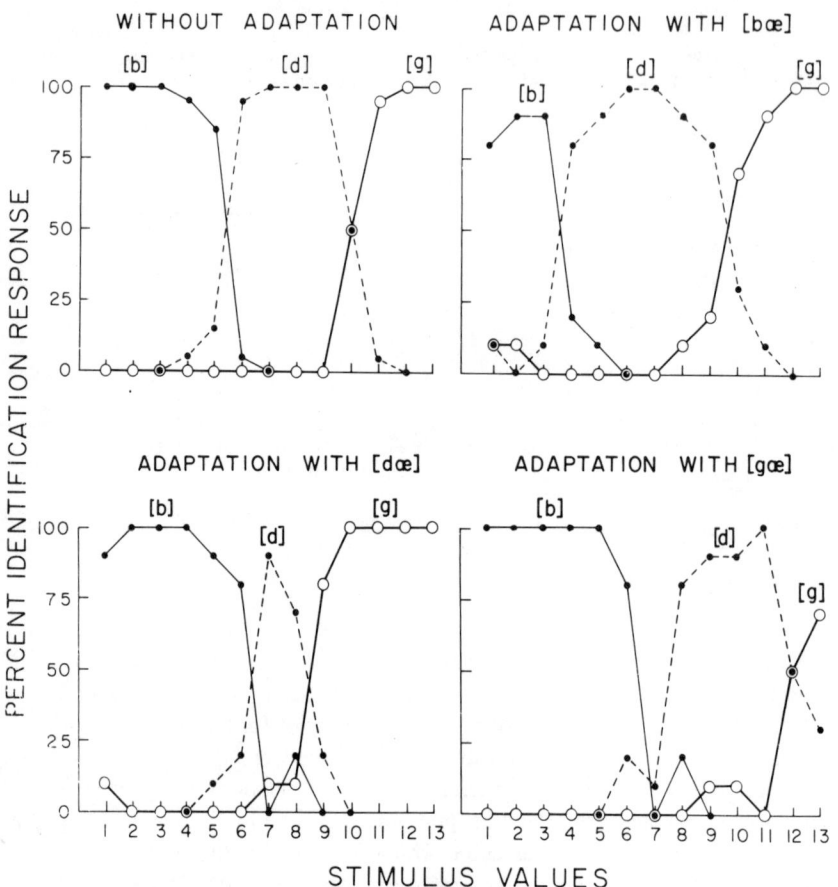

Figure 1. Percentages of identification responses ("b," "d," or "G") obtained for a single subject in the unadapted state after adaptation with [bæ], [dæ], and [gæ].

values. Note that it is impossible to make a direct comparison between this obtained magnitude and that found in the case of the VOT dimension because of the very different nature of the two continua.

For the [dæ] adaptation test condition, both the b–d and d–g phonetic boundaries shifted to a significant extent. These shifts, like the displacements in the single boundary that were obtained for the [bæ] and [gæ] adaptation tests, were in the direction toward the phonetic category of the adapting stimulus, indicating in this case that, after adaptation with [dæ], fewer responses were assigned to the [d] category. These results provide initial support for an acoustically non-invariant type of adaptation, since the [dæ] adapting stimulus, which contained slightly falling F_2 and F_3 transitions, affected the perception of stimuli near the b–d boundary, having rising transitions, as well as stimuli near the d–g boundary with falling transitions (cf. Tables 1 and 2).

Figure 1 depicts the identification data for each test condition for a single subject, C.S. For each of the subjects, shifts in the loci of phonetic boundaries were not accompanied by a significant decline in the magnitude (i.e., steepness) of the slopes of the response functions.

The results of this experiment indicate first that a selective adaptation effect can be induced along the tri-valued feature dimension *place of articulation*. The results also suggest, at least in part, that adaptation operates on stable feature modes (e.g., [bilabial], [alveolar], [velar]) rather than on hypothetical *relative* feature modes (e.g., [relative frontness], [relative backness]). If adaptation were for the most part affecting a purely relative feature analyzing system, it would be expected that, since [b] lies at one extreme end of the b–d–g dimension, adaptation with [bæ] should produce significant shifts of equal magnitude in *both* the b–d and d–g phonetic boundaries, such that both boundaries are displaced in the direction toward the adapting stimulus category. Such relative shifts did not in fact occur to a significant extent in the present experiment when two-tailed tests of significance were applied (cf. Table 3); however, a one-tailed test did show a significant shift for the b–d boundary within the [gæ] adaptation test ($p < 0.05$). Since a shift of similar magnitude did not occur in the d–g boundary with the [bæ] adaptation test, interpretation of the [gæ] adaptation shift should await the results of the next experiment, in which the same adaptation procedure is employed using a response measure of discrimination.

EXPERIMENT 2—DISCRIMINATION

As noted in Chapter 1, listeners' ability to discriminate along a consonantal feature dimension is constrained by their ability to assign differential phonetic labels to stimuli contained within that dimension. Consequently, it was reasoned that the identification shifts found in the first adaptation experiment should be matched by corresponding shifts in the peaks of discriminability functions. To test this prediction, the listeners who had served in Experiment 1 were now presented a discrimination task to be performed in the unadapted state and after adaptation with the syllables [bæ] and [gæ].

Method

Subjects. All seven of the original subjects served in Experiment 2.

Stimuli. The stimuli consisted of the 13 synthetic CV syllables used in Experiment 1.

Procedure. Discriminability was measured by the *ABX* method. For a given trial, three test stimuli were presented: the first two (*A* and *B*) always differed; the third stimulus (X) was identical to etiher A or B. Discrimination triads were prepared by pairing each stimulus in the *place* series with the stimulus two steps removed (e.g., No. 1 with No. 3; No. 2 with No. 4). There were eleven such pairs, four permutations of each pair (*ABA, ABB, BAB,* and *BAA*), yielding a total of 44 triads in a set.

Listeners in the unadapted state were presented three different sets of 44 triads, each set containing a different random order. Each of the three sets was presented twice, yielding a total of 24 responses to each of the eleven stimulus pairs. Listeners were instructed to write "*A*" or "*B*" on their answer sheets to indicate whether they thought the third stimulus of a given triad matched either the first or the second stimulus of that triad.

For the adaptation sessions (12 in all, each lasting about one hour), listeners were presented the adapting stimulus (either [bæ] or [gæ]) repetitively, as in Experiment 1. In these tests of discrimination, subjects responded to a single *ABX* triad following each minute of adaptation. Within a given session, each of the 11 stimulus pairs were presented for discrimination four times. Six sessions were thus required to obtain the 24 total responses to each stimulus pair. All subjects were presented the unadapted test of discrimination first, then the six sessions of discrimination with [bæ] adaptation, and finally the six sessions of discrimination with [gæ] adaptation. For all test conditions, the individual members of each triad were separated from each other by 1.5 sec of silence. The remaining procedural details were identical to those used in Experiment 1.

Results and Discussion

Figure 2 shows the mean discriminability functions obtained for each test condition. Figure 3 depicts the discriminability functions for a single subject, C.S. Within each of the adaptation tests, one and only one of the two discrimination peaks shifted. This situation held true for the group data and, with minor variation, for the individual data as well. The displaced peak in each case was the peak corresponding to the phonetic boundary that bordered the category of the adapting stimulus, and, in each case, the peak was displaced in the direction toward that category. Thus, after adaptation with [bæ], a shift occurred at the b–d boundary peak, whereas after adaptation with [gæ], a shift occurred at the d–g peak. The former shift was in the direction toward the [b] category; the latter shift was in the direction toward the [g] category. The magnitude of each of these shifts was approximately two stimulus values.

We now turn to compare the peak shifts obtained in the present experiment with the phonetic boundary shifts obtained in Experiment 1. For the phonetic boundaries and corresponding peaks of discriminability that bordered the category of the adapting stimulus, the obtained shifts were very similar for the two tasks, with respect to both direction and approximate magnitude of shift. On the other hand, for the phonetic boundaries and peaks of discriminability that did not

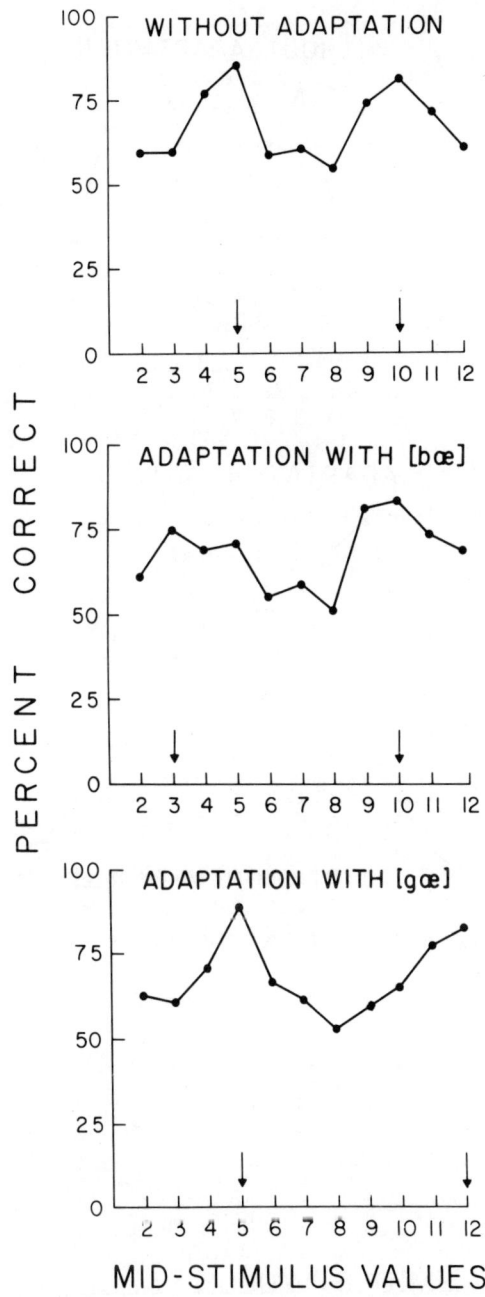

Figure 2. The group discriminability functions for each test condition. The "midstimulus" values plotted on the abscissa are those values lying midway between the two stimulus values being discriminated. Arrows indicate the loci of the peaks in the discriminability functions.

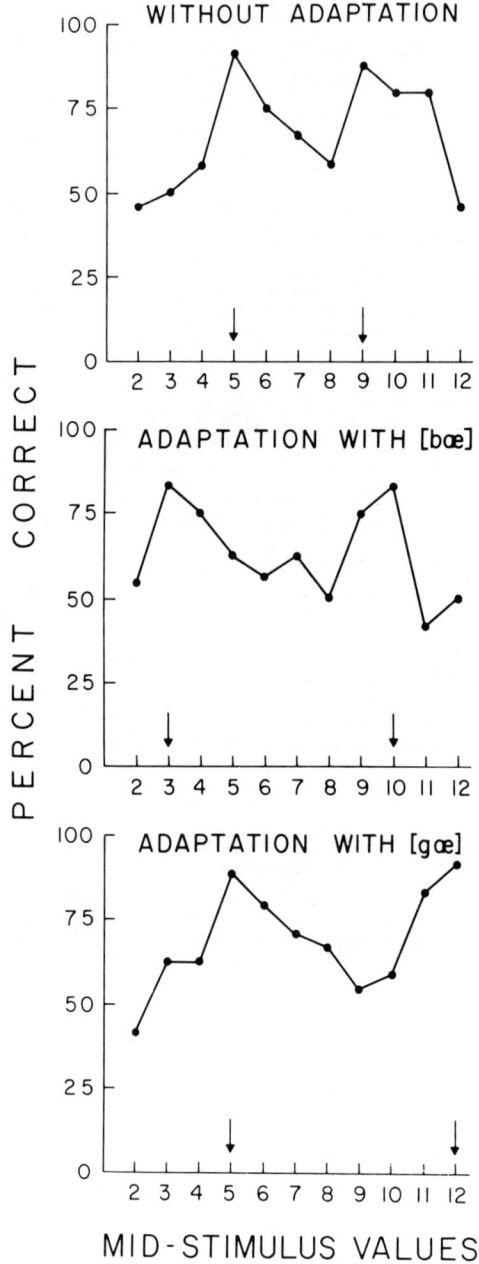

Figure 3. The discriminability functions of a single subject for each test condition.

border the adapting stimulus category, an interesting discrepancy was found in comparing the results of the two tasks.

The discrepancy concerns the b–d phonetic boundary, for the [gæ] adaptation test. In Experiment 1, it was found that a shift occurred in the locus of this boundary, the shift being directed toward the category of the adapting stimulus. However, the discrimination results of the present experiment show that no such shift occurred in the corresponding b–d peak of discriminability. A refined account of this discrepancy between tasks is difficult to formulate, particularly so in light of the fact that within the identification task (cf. Experiment 1), the b–d boundary shift found for the [gæ] adaptation test was not accompanied by a d–g boundary shift in the [bæ] adaptation test. The most that can be suggested at present is that subjects' response criteria might be generally more susceptible to alteration within the identification task than within the discrimination task because of the response-based factor known as "simple contrast," or the tendency for subjects to *overtly* categorize stimuli as belonging to a category unlike that assigned to preceding stimuli, independent of any true adaptation effect that involves the fatiguing of a perceptual analyzing mechanism (see Chapter 4).

Taken as a whole, the discrimination data of the present experiment provide further demonstration of the presence of selective adaptation effects along the feature dimension of *place of articulation*. Additionally, the data provide support for the hypothesis that feature adaptation operates on stable modes of analysis, not on hypothetical relative modes, since within each of the adaptation conditions, consistent shifts occurred for one and only one of the two peaks of discrimination.

EXPERIMENT 3

Given the results of the first two experiments, it was now of interest to begin to determine the extent to which the adapting stimulus could be varied (while holding the mode of the *place* feature constant), without incurring a complete loss of adaptation effects along the original bæ–dæ–gæ test dimension. In one condition of the present experiment, a "crossed-consonant" adaptation test was conducted, using a voiceless bilabial stop for the adapting stimulus (i.e., [pʰæ]) and the bæ–dæ–gæ series as test stimuli, in order to determine whether the phonetic boundary shifts are indeed a function of feature-specific adaptation or are instead based on adaptation of the consonantal sound as a unit. Additionally, a test was conducted to determine whether varying the vowel context of the adapting stimulus would eliminate the presence of the phonetic boundary shifts. It was reasoned that an elimination of the shifts would occur within the "crossed-vowel" test if adaptation operates primarily on acoustic-invariant cue detectors (Level B in the model of Chapter 1), whereas these shifts would be

Table 4
Frequency Values of the Second and Third Formants for the Three Real Speech Adapting Syllables

Syllables	Starting frequency		Steady-state center frequency (in Hz)	
	F_2	F_3	F_2	F_3
[bæ]	1050	2100	1500	2550
[bi]	1575	1950	1800	2625
[pʰæ]	(see Note)		1650	2550

[Note: Frequency values were estimated by examining wide-band spectrograms of the real speech syllables. Since the F_2 and F_3 starting frequencies of a voiceless stop are not easily observable in spectrograms of real speech (due to the obscuring effect of aspiration as well as the weak energy of the formant transitions themselves), measurements of the starting frequencies for the syllable [pʰæ] were less precise than the measurements included in the table. To the best of our ability to estimate the starting frequencies for [pʰæ], the values obtained were the same as those obtained for the real speech [bæ] stimulus, namely, F_2 starting at 1050 Hz and F_3 starting at 2100 Hz.]

preserved if adaptation operates on analyzers which extract feature information at a later, phonetic level of processing (Level D in the model of Chapter 1).

Method

Subjects. Eight subjects, six of whom had served in the first two experiments, participated in Experiment 3. The two new subjects had no prior experience in listening to synthetic speech. In addition, they were native speakers of English and had no known hearing impairments.

Stimuli. The stimuli-to-be-identified consisted of the series of 13 synthetic CV syllables used in Experiments 1 and 2. In addition, three real speech adapting stimuli were recorded for use, all by a male speaker. One stimulus each was recorded for the syllables [bæ], [pʰæ], and [bi]. These three stimuli were edited to the standard 300-msec duration by removing segments at the end of the steady-state formants. The frequency values of the second- and third-formant transitions and steady states are presented in Table 4. The three adapting stimuli were dubbed and then formed into tape loops, each containing an interstimulus interval of 350 msec.

A final control adapting stimulus consisted of the steady-state vowel [æ] in isolation, cut from one of the original synthetic speech adapting syllables; the duration of the isolated vowel stimulus was approximately 220 msec. This stimulus, like the three real speech adapting stimuli, was prepared for repetitive presentation by means of a tape loop, containing an interstimulus interval of 350 msec.

Procedure. Baseline, or unadapted, functions of identification were obtained for all listeners, including those who had served previously in Experiments 1 and 2. On the day after this baseline test, a series of five adaptation sessions was begun, one session being administered per day on consecutive days. Four of the subjects were presented the following test order: synthetic speech [bæ] adaptation, real speech [bæ] adaptation, real speech [pʰæ] adaptation, and real speech [bi] adaptation; the remaining four subjects were presented these same tests in reverse order. All eight subjects were presented the isolated vowel [æ] adaptation test during the final test session. The procedural details for an individual adaptation session was identical to those used in Experiment 1.

Results and Discussion

The individual and mean boundary loci for each test condition appear in Table 5. Among the three real speech adaptation tests ([bæ], [pʰæ], and [bi] adaptation) it is noteworthy that a significant shift in the locus of the b–d phonetic boundary was obtained for each of these conditions, as compared with the baseline, or unadapted test and the control condition (adaptation with the vowel [æ]) ($p < 0.05$). These shifts, like the shift obtained after adaptation with the synthetic syllable [bæ] (replicating Experiment 1 results), were systematically directed toward the *b* category of the test series, indicating that subjects assigned fewer responses to the category of the adapted *place* mode following adaptation. For the d–g phonetic boundary, only the boundary locus for [pʰæ] shifted significantly from the unadapted test ($p < 0.01$).[1]

The shift is the b–d phonetic boundary produced by the real speech syllable [pʰæ] indicates that one component of the adaptation effect is feature-specific, not merely a function of adaptation of the consonantal unit as a whole. The similar shift obtained after adaptation with the syllable [bi] suggests that the feature-specific component operates primarily at a phonetic, as opposed to an acoustic-invariant, level of processing. Since the formant transitions cue for *place* contained within the adapting stimulus [bi] differed at virtually each point in time from the corresponding cue contained in the bæ members of the bæ–dæ–gæ test series, the occurrence of a significant shift along the test series after adaptation with [bi] cannot be readily attributed to an adaptation component that operates on a single acoustic-invariant *place* detector (but see later).

---

[1]The shift for the [pʰæ] adaptation condition was in the direction *away* from the *place* value of the adapting stimulus. A general account of this shift cannot be proposed at present, since similar shifts did not occur in the case of other bilabial adapting stimuli.

Table 5
Individual and Mean Loci of Phonetic Boundaries for Each Test Condition

(a) b–d Phonetic boundary

Subjects	Without adaptation	Adaptation with synthetic [æ]	Real [bæ]	Real pʰæ]	Real [bi]	Synthetic [æ]
(1) A.B.	4.33	3.54	4.34	3.66	4.83	4.90
(2) B.C.	5.34	3.82	4.87	5.33	5.03	5.10
(3) E.E.	4.71	3.18	3.60	4.34	4.45	5.35
(4) L.M.	5.00	4.10	3.63	4.55	4.63	5.11
(5) B.M.	5.46	3.83	3.83	4.14	4.17	4.38
(6) C.S.	4.86	3.00	3.63	4.93	4.69	5.07
(7) J.L.	3.94	2.97	2.97	2.05	1.46	4.27
(8) A.H.	5.24	2.79	4.07	5.00	4.31	5.00
$\bar{X}$	4.86	3.40	3.87	4.25	4.20	4.90

42

(b) d–g Phonetic boundary

Subjects	Without adaptation	Adaptation with synthetic [bæ]	Real [bæ]	Real [pʰæ]	Real [bi]	Synthetic [æ]
(1) A.B.	10.45	10.44	10.50	11.31	10.33	9.39
(2) B.C.	10.94	10.69	11.44	12.00	11.17	11.34
(3) E.E.	10.14	10.44	9.78	10.89	10.00	9.50
(4) L.M.	10.20	9.83	9.89	10.33	9.41	8.83
(5) B.M.	9.56	9.83	9.61	10.79	10.15	9.65
(6) C.S.	10.35	9.69	10.00	10.89	9.27	9.33
(7) J.L.	9.78	10.03	9.93	10.11	9.42	9.39
(8) A.H.	9.91	9.46	10.27	11.44	9.63	9.50
$\bar{X}$	10.17	10.05	10.18	10.97	9.92	9.62

[Note: The locus of the phonetic boundary in each case was determined by first assigning to each stimulus an arbitrary number, ranging from 1 to 13, and then performing a least-mear-squares analysis.]

Aside from the feature-specific component of adaptation, the data of the present experiment indirectly reveal the presence of at least two other components. One component is required to provide a general account for the significant difference in shift magnitude between the synthetic and real speech [bæ] adaptation conditions, for the b–d phonetic boundary. The smaller shift was obtained for the real speech syllable, perhaps because this syllable contained more acoustic information that was irrelevant to the task of perceiving phonetic distinctions based solely on differences in the second- and third-formant transitions.

An additional component is required to account for the significant difference in shift magnitude between the real speech [bæ] and [pʰæ] adaptation conditions, again for the b–d phonetic boundary. Since the larger shift occurred for the adapting stimulus [bæ] (the syllable whose consonant was represented directly in the bæ–dæ–gæ test series), it is reasonable to attribute the present increment in shift magnitude to a "phonetic unit" component of adaptation. The phonetic unit component, which operates not on individual distinctive features but on the consonantal sound as a unit, can account for analogous differences in shift magnitude obtained previously with the VOT dimension. It should be pointed out that postulating this and other components of adaptation, in addition to the feature-specific component, involves no logical inconsistency, as long as it is assumed that the processing of speech sounds takes place at more than one level of analysis and that more than one such level is capable of being adapted.[2]

It is of interest, finally, to note the finding that adaptation with the vowel [æ], having a + *front* place of articulation, produced no highly systematic effect on perception of the b–d–g continuum. This result suggests that there exist separate channels of *place* feature analysis for each of the two major speech sound classes; that is, for consonants and vowels. The suggestion here must be tempered, however, by the fact that the traditional feature description of [æ] as a low front vowel is much less precise than is the description of place of articulation in the stop consonants (cf. Ladefoged, 1971).

GENERAL DISCUSSION

It has been shown in the present experiments that the selective adaptation procedure yields significant shifts in the loci of phonetic boundaries for the consonant dimension *place of articulation*. For the most part, the shifts occurred in a systematic fashion, such that test stimuli lying near a phonetic boundary, normally perceived as having the same *place* value as the adapting stimulus, were perceived after adaptation as having a different *place* value.

An important component of these shifts can be accounted for by the fatigu-

[2] A third component, a "syllable unit" factor, might be needed to account for the difference in shift magnitude between the real speech [bæ] and [bi] adaptation conditions, for the d–b phonetic boundary. The larger shift in this case occurred for the syllable [bæ].

ing of a specialized analyzing mechanism, organized to process *place* distinctions along a single dimension of analysis. This single dimension is assumed to contain three separate analyzer modes, designated here as the *B*, *A*, and *V* modes. At present, the pattern of cues to which these analyzer modes respond is not known; thus, the adequate stimulus of each analyzer must remain unspecified and will simply be referred to at present as a range of *place stimulus values*. For the *B* mode, these stimulus values yield a perceived bilabial consonant; for the *A* mode, they yield a perceived alveolar consonant; and, for the *V* mode, they yield a perceived velar consonant, all other factors being equal.

It can be inferred from the present data that the response ranges of the three analyzer modes are arranged in a specific order, *B–A–V*, such that the response ranges partially overlap for the adjacent modes *B–A* and *A–V*.[3] Within each of the two overlapping ranges of response, there exists a point of equilibrium, defined as the *place* stimulus value to which the adjacent modes of analysis respond with equal strength. All other factors equated, this equilibrium point corresponds to the locus of the phonetic boundary.[4]

During selective adaptation, it is assumed that the sensitivity of one analyzer mode is decreased across its entire response range, such that any equilibrium point bordering the adapted mode is displaced in the direction toward that mode. The displacement in the point of equilibrium is manifested as a shift in the phonetic boundary locus.

The foregoing model of the *place* feature analyzing mechanism, which shares many attributes with that of the analyzing mechanism proposed for *voicing*, differs from the latter model in one very important respect. Unlike the model proposed for *voicing*, the *place* feature model contains no well-specified stimulus to which the analyzer modes respond. Rather than simply detecting the presence of an invariant acoustic cue, the analyzer modes for *place* appear to operate in a more complex fashion.

One manner in which the analyzers for *place* might operate is to compare the second- and third-formant transitions of incoming speech signals with fea-

[3] If the response ranges for the two adjacent modes did not overlap, a decrease in sensitivity of one analyzer would presumably lead to much inconsistency in response to the stimulus values to which neither analyzer is now sensitive. However, consistency of response was generally maintained after adaptation—shifts in loci of phonetic boundaries occurred, but decreases in the magnitude of the slope of the response functions did not occur. Maintaining consistent response after adaptation suggests that the response ranges for adjacent modes must overlap. In psychological terms, the response of adjacent modes mutually inhibit one another.

[4] The *B A V* model has been proposed to provide a general account of the perceptual analyzer modes utilized by English-speaking listeners in decoding place information. Extensions of the model, perhaps even gross modification, will be required if any differences are found to exist between the perceptual capabilities of English listeners and those listeners whose native languages contain phonemic place distinctions other than those found in English (e.g., Arabic contains a place distinction between velar and post-velar stops). Since the perceptual capabilities of such non-English-speaking listeners has not yet been determined, extensions of the model, as well as the important and closely related matter of whether the feature analyzer modes are innate to the human organism, cannot be evaluated at present.

tures of internally *generated* signals (cf. Stevens, 1960; Liberman, Cooper, Shankweiler, & Studdert-Kennedy, 1967). Since the neural commands that presumably control the internal generation of speech sounds are nearly invariant for a given *place* value, this analysis-by-synthesis method of decoding *place* information seems able to account for the perceived invariance of consonants contained in differing vowel environments. This same means of operation must be fully internalized, however, if it is to be able to account for the perception of *place* distinctions demonstrated for very young infant listeners, who have not achieved control of their articulatory movements at time of testing (Eimas, 1974).

Another possibility is that, instead of relying on an analysis-by-synthesis routine, the analyzing mechanism utilizes complex acoustic *pattern* detection schemes for decoding *place* information directly from the speech signal (cf. Wickelgren (1969) for some discussion of these two major possibilities as they relate to feature storage). Such pattern detection schemes might include, for example, an analysis of the second- and third-formant transitions in which the frequency ratios between these transitions are computed at various moments in time.

The present results offer no help in deciding between these two major types of operation. The results do indicate that there remains the need to look for mechanisms of this degree of complexity (i.e., of greater complexity than acoustic-invariant cue detectors) in order to account for how the consonant feature *place* is analyzed. The possibility remains that mechanisms of such complexity will be required to account for the perceptual analysis of other consonant features as well, including the feature *voicing*.

It is of importance, finally, to contrast the proposed uni-feature, trimodal analyzing mechanism for *place* with a major plausible alternative—namely, a mechanism which processes *place* information in terms of two separate features, each containing two modes. Such a mechanism might be set up to process *place* information in terms of the features *grave* and *compact* (cf. Jakobson, Fant, & Halle, 1963; Halle, 1964), with each of these two independent dimensions containing the modes [+] and [−]. If this hypothetical processor were the actual site of the adaptation effects, it would be expected that when, for example, [gæ] serves as the adapting stimulus, a decrease in identification response should occur to [b] as well as to [g], since the analyzer mode for + Grave (strongly responsive to both [b] and [g]) is being fatigued. But such a result was not usually obtained in the present experiments. It is thus tentatively concluded that, in comparison with the dual-feature model of *place* analysis, the proposed uni-feature model provides a better characterization of the mechanism adapted here.[5]

[5]The present data do not, of course, rule out the possibility that feature dimensions such as *grave* and *compact* are processed at some stage of analysis not tapped by the selective adaptation procedure.

Postscript to Study 1

REINTERPRETATION

The crossed adaptation observed in Experiment 3 of this study led to the suggestion that the effects operate in part on a stage of processing that codes a *phonetic* representation of the place feature. This stage corresponds to Level D in the model presented in Chapter 1. But an auditory detector at Level B could, in fact, account for the crossed-adaptation results, as pointed out by a number of authors, most convincingly by Bailey (1975). Such a detector could respond to a specific pattern of formant trajectory (for example, sharply rising for [b], slightly rising or falling for [d], and sharply falling for [g]) within a relatively broad frequency region. This interpretation is adopted in later discussions.

RELATED STUDIES

A number of other studies have been reported for the place feature. One series of experiments was conducted by Bailey (1975), who began work independently and concurrently with this study. A particularly relevant set of experiments engaged a series of synthetic syllables ranging from [ba] to [da]. The stimuli varied from one another in the starting frequency and direction of the second- and third-formant transitions, like the [bæ]–[dæ]–[gæ] stimuli used here. In a first experiment, Bailey obtained adaptation effects using [ba] and [da] endpoint adaptors, replicating the effects found here for the adaptors [bæ] and [dæ]. Crossed-adaptation tests were then conducted in an attempt to test whether the effects operate on an auditory or phonetic site of processing. In one set of experiments, this issue was tested by examining whether the adaptation effects were restricted to a particular formant. Two series of [ba]–[da] stimuli were used, one varying only in F_2 transition with no F_3 present, the other varying only in transitions of F_3. The second series included the same F_2 for all stimuli, and this F_2 contained a slightly rising transition. Crossed-adaptation tests with the endpoint members of both series showed effects in the expected direction for most conditions, indicating that the adaptation effects were not restricted to a single formant. This set of results provided evidence against the simplest auditory account of the adaptation effects. Bailey, however, chose to emphasize another aspect of the results, namely, that the crossed-adaptation effects were considerably smaller in magnitude than the within-series effects. On this basis, he favored a formant-specific auditory account of the results. In fact, one of the crossed-adaptation tests, involving an adapting stimulus with both F_2 and F_3 on the series with no F_3, could be interpreted in terms of either of the preceding accounts. But an effect using an adapting stimulus with F_2 but without F_3 on the series varying only in F_3 suggests that some portion of the effect taps detectors of at least the complexity of responding to a pattern of rising vs. falling formant transitions, operating regardless of the frequency region or the formant number to which the transitions belong.

Bailey also attempted to test the auditory-phonetic issue by conducting crossed-adaptation studies in which the adaptors and test series contained different vowels, using a procedure like that of Experiment 3. Crossed-adaptation effects were obtained using test series of [ba]–[da] and [be]–[de] (with the endpoint members as adaptors), and these effects, like the effects reported here, could be accounted for in terms of either the acoustic or phonetic similarity between the adaptor and test series. Using series of [bi]–[di] and [bu]–[du], no crossed-adaptation effects were obtained. In this case, the formant transitions for the adaptor and test series differed more markedly in both direction and region of frequency excursion; the lack of crossed adaptation here represents Bailey's strongest piece of evidence favoring an auditory site of adaptation.

In yet another series of tests, Bailey studied adaptation effects using a three-category series of test stimuli, including [ba]–[da]–[ga]. He obtained an asymmetry like that found in Experiment 1 of this study. Adaptation with [b] produced an effect restricted to the [b]–[d] boundary, whereas adaptation with [g] produced an effect for both [d]–[g] and [b]–[d] boundaries. Bailey provided a possible account for this otherwise curious set of findings in terms of the spectral separation between the formant transitions of the adaptor and test stimuli. The spectral separation was defined in terms of two components: (a) the mean frequency difference between the same-numbered formants of the adaptor and test stimulus during the formant transitions period, (b) the formant trajectory pattern. The spectral similarity was greater between the [ga] adaptor and the [b]–[d] boundary stimulus than between the [ba] adaptor and the [d]–[g] boundary stimulus. This acoustic asymmetry was also present in this study. Bailey's interpretation may indeed be correct; it should, however, be recalled that the asymmetry in adaptation noted in Experiment 1 of this study was not found in the discrimination data of Experiment 2.

Many other investigators have studied adaptation effects for place of articulation, including Diehl (1974), Tartter and Eimas (1975), Ades (1974 a, b), Ganong (1975), Blumstein, Stevens, and Nigro (1977), Pisoni and Tash (1975), Sawusch (1976a,b, 1977a,b), Keating and Blumstein (1978), and Wolf (1978). Most of these studies included a test replicating the general findings of Experiment 1. In addition, crossed-adaptation tests revealed a number of interesting effects which permitted further inferences about the nature of the site of adaptation. Diehl (1974), for example, attempted to assess the extent to which adaptors differing in the initial burst portion of the stop consonant would affect the identification of [bɛ]–[dɛ] test stimuli, varying in the second- and third-formant transitions. As noted in Chapter 1, both the burst and transitions provide information about the place cue in normal speech. Diehl obtained significant cross-adaptation effects, which were attributed to a phonetic site of adaptation. The evidence for this interpretation is not yet compelling, however, since the effects could be accounted for by a stage of integrative auditory detection like that proposed by Stevens (1975). At this level, information would be extracted from a combined representation of the burst and formant transitions to determine whether the spectral pattern contains a sharply rising or falling frequency excursion.

Ganong (1975) conducted cross-adaptation tests in a similar vein to test whether adaptors containing burst and/or transition cues to place of articulation would affect listeners' perception of a series of stimuli varying only in the second- and third-formant transitions, from [bæ] to [dæ]. A key test involved [sæ] as an adaptor. This syllable contains cues to place of articulation that are like those for [dæ]; the second- and third-formant transitions for [sæ] and [dæ] are quite similar; in addition, the fricative noise at the beginning of [sæ] provides a sufficient cue to place of articulation, though this noise is much higher in frequency than the onset burst of a normally spoken [dæ]. Ganong tested whether a [sæ] with high-frequency fricative noise and optional formant transitions would produce adaptation effects of the [dæ] members of the [bæ]–[dæ] test series. Adaptation effects were obtained for [sæ] with and without the formant transitions, though the magnitude of the effect was larger for the transition-bearing adaptor. The effect with the transitionless [sæ] suggests that a portion of the adaptation effects for place taps a level of processing that can integrate information for frication noise and transitions over a broad frequency range, in this case amounting to more than 1200 Hz. As with the crossed-adaptation findings reported by Diehl (1974), it is not yet possible to determine whether this stage of processing should be viewed as part of the auditory system or as a specialized processor of phonetic information.

Another study examining adaptation effects for bursts and transitions was conducted by Blumstein, Stevens, and Nigro (1977). The test stimuli in their experiments included a [ba]–[da]–[ga] series which varied in the second- and third-formant transitions, similar to the series used in this study. Also like the stimuli used here, their syllables contained no onset bursts. For adapting stimuli, however, Blumstein et al. used some syllables which contained initial bursts as well as formant transitions. By comparing the magnitude of adaptation effect for adapting stimuli which contained both bursts and transitions with adaptors containing transitions but not bursts, they hoped to test whether the adaptation effects occurred at a stage of processing which detects the burst and transition information separately or as a single integrated cue. A sizeable increase in the magnitude of the adaptation effect with the burst + transition adaptors would support an integrative site. Only a slight increase in the magnitude of effect was obtained for the burst + transition adaptors, however, and since the effect did not reach statistical significance, the issue remains open. The experimental design used by Blumstein *et al.*, however, is in principle a useful method for testing the presence of integrative stages of processing, and it may be profitable to apply the method to similar situations with other speech features.

Adaptation effects for a test series of syllables varying in place of articulation have also been studied using *non*speech sounds as adaptors (Ades, 1973; Tartter & Eimas, 1975; Pisoni & Tash, 1975; Sawusch, 1976a). Tartter and Eimas (1975), for example, conducted experiments in which individual spectral components of a [bæ] syllable were used as adaptors. The presence of adaptation results using such isolated components indicated that adaptation with a speech stimulus was not a necessary requirement for obtaining adaptation effects for a speech test series. The magnitude of the effects, however, was small compared with the effects of speech adaptors.

Another type of nonspeech adaptation test was conducted by Pisoni and Tash (1975), who constructed an adapting stimulus in which the formant transitions appropriate for a syllable-initial [b] were located *after* a vowel. Following adaptation to this stimulus, listeners assigned fewer [b] responses to a [ba]–[da] series. This result appeared to indicate that adaptation operated on a detector that responds to formant transitions of a particular pattern regardless of whether they appeared at the onset of the syllable or at the end—see Ades (1976) and Sawusch (1976a) for further discussion.

The experiments with nonspeech adaptors provide some evidence that the adaptation effects tap a level or levels of processing that function automatically in speech perception and do not tap conscious strategies on the part of the listener. In some cases, as with the stimuli used by Pisoni and Tash, the relation between the adaptor and test stimuli was quite subtle, yet systematic effects were obtained.

Generally, it can be said that the growing number of studies on adaptation for place of articulation have begun to provide constraints on the inferences that can be made about the detection of place information. Further work mentioned in Chapter 7 is yielding additional information regarding the following issues: the detectors' frequency bandwidths, their regions of maximal sensitivity, their time windows of operation, and the degree to which different detectors overlap in their responses.

Study 2*

This study extended the work on place adaptation to test whether the adaptation effects observed for the [bæ]–[dæ]–[gæ] test series would be restricted to the use of adaptors that also contained stop consonants. If instead, adaptation effects for the stop series could be obtained using adaptors whose consonants contained

*Portions of this study are reprinted with permission from *Perception & Psychophysics,* 1974, *15,* 591–600, Sheila E. Blumstein, coauthor.

separate manners of articulation (e.g., nasal, fricative), we would have evidence that information about place of articulation is extracted by a single detector for different manners. This question could be asked and answered independently of the auditory-phonetic distinction, but our data in fact provided some information on the latter issue, too, favoring a site of adaptation that involved auditory rather than phonetic detectors.

Five different real speech syllables were selected as adapting stimuli in this experiment. The five adapting syllables included [bæ], [pʰæ], [mæ], [væ], and [wæ]. All contain a labial initial segment and thus represent likely candidates as adaptors of the [bæ] members of the bæ–dæ–gæ test series.

Attention should be paid to the rationale for our choice of the adapting syllables [mæ], [væ], and [wæ], the three adapting syllables whose initial segments do not belong to the class of stop consonants. The phonetic segment [m], a voiced nasal consonant, is articulated like [b] except that the velum is lowered to permit airflow through the nasal passages, as noted in Chapter 1. The location at which the airflow is obstructed for both [m] and [b] is at the lips. Because this closure of the lips accompanies the production of both consonants, their place of articulation is traditionally termed *bilabial*. By using [m] as an adapting consonant, we could begin to assess whether the adaptation effect along the bæ–dæ–gæ series is restricted to the class of stop consonants or whether it is more general in scope, involving both stops and nasals.

The phonetic segment [v], a voiced fricative consonant, is distinguished from both [m] and [b] by virtue of the fact that at no point in the oral cavity does a complete obstruction of airflow exist. Rather, a partial obstruction of the airflow accompanies the production of [v], this partial closure being made by the front upper teeth and the lower lip. The place of articulation for [v] is thus termed *labio-dental*, distinguishing it from bilabial consonants such as [m], and [b]. In addition to providing a further test of the scope of the adaptation effects across different consonant classes, employing [v] as an adapting stimulus was of interest here because it allowed us to test whether a strict sharing of place of articulation by the adapting and test stimulus members is a necessary condition for obtaining the adaptation effects.

In linguistic feature descriptions of the phonetic structure of English, the three consonants [b], [m], and [v] share all feature values for place of articulation. In the feature system devised by Jakobson *et al.* (1963), these three consonants share values for the two place features, *grave* and *compact*, all three being described as [+*grave*] and [−*compact*]. In the feature system proposed by Chomsky and Halle (1968), the same consonants share feature values for each of five *place* features, being marked as [+*anterior*], [−*coronal*], [−*high*], [−*low*], and [−*back*].

Although the classes of stop, nasal, and fricative consonants are distinguished acoustically by the presence of noise bursts, nasal resonance bands, and frication, respectively, the syllables [bæ], [mæ], and [væ] all contain rising and sharply sloping second- and third-formant transitions. These transitions have been found to be sufficient cues for the perception of place of articulation in these consonants (cf. Cooper, Delattre, Liberman, Borst, & Gerstman, 1952; Malecot, 1956; Harris, 1958; Sharf & Hemeyer, 1971). Because of the acoustic similarity in the formant transitions for [bæ], [mæ], and [væ], as well as the articulatory and abstract phonetic similarity already mentioned, it was predicted that any adaptation effects obtained for [mæ] and/or [væ] would be like the effects obtained previously for [bæ] and opposed to the effects obtained previously for either [dæ] or [gæ].

Unlike the consonants [b], [m], and [v], the phonetic segment [w] is represented linguistically as a semiconsonant. This classification reflects that, in linguistic systems, [w] functions in part like a consonant and in part like a vowel (cf. Jakobson, Fant, & Halle, 1963). Although [w] is not a consonant and contains no significant zeroes in its spectrum, [w] does share some acoustic and articulatory characteristics with the consonants [b], [m], and [v]. The production of [w] contains a bilabial component in that it is accompanied by considerable lip-rounding. In addition, [wæ] is acoustically similar to [bæ] in that both syllables contain rising second- and third-formant transitions. The difference between these two syllables is signaled by the duration and slope of the transitions (cf. Liberman, Delattre, Gerstman, & Cooper, 1956). By employing [wæ] as an adapting stimulus, we attempted further to define the extent of the adaptation effects for *place*.

Method

Subjects. Eight paid volunteers, primarily students enrolled at Boston area universities, served as experimentally naive listeners in this study. All Ss were native speakers of American English and had no known hearing impairments. No S had had any prior experience in listening to synthetic speech.

Stimuli. The test stimuli consisted of a series of 13 synthetic CV syllables. These stimuli were the same bæ–dæ–gæ test stimuli used in the prior study of *place* adaptation.

Synthetic stimuli were used in the test series in order to obtain a series of syllables varying only in the second- and third-formant transitions, allowing a quantitative measure of adaptation to be obtained. The adapting stimuli, on the other hand, consisted of five real speech syllables, all produced by a male speaker of American English (W.E.C.). The five stimuli represented exemplars of the syllable types [bæ], [pʰæ], [mæ], [væ], and [wæ]. Each stimulus was judged by the authors to be a good representative of its syllable type as spoken in American English. All five syllables were edited to a duration of 300 msec, and, in addition, the peak amplitudes of the five stimuli were equalized. The starting frequency and steady state center frequency of the second and third formants for

Table 6
Starting Frequencies of the Second- and Third-Formant Transitions for the Synthetic CV Stimuli

Stimulus Number	Starting Frequencies (in Hz)	
	F_2	F_3
1	1232	2180
2	1312	2348
3	1386	2525
4	1465	2694
5	1541	2862
6	1620	3026
7	1695	3195
8	1772	3026
9	1845	2862
10	1920	2694
11	1996	2525
12	2078	2348
13	2156	2180

Note: The fixed steady state formants were centered at 743 Hz (F_1), 1,620 Hz (F_2), and 2,862 Hz (F_3) (after Pisoni, 1971).

each syllable were measured spectrographically; these frequency values are presented in Table 7. Spectrographic analysis also showed that the duration of the formant transitions for [bæ], [pʰæ], [mæ], and [væ] was approximately 30 msec, whereas for [wæ] the duration of these transitions was about 65 msec.

Procedure

Two baseline functions of identification were obtained for all listeners in the unadapted state. The first was obtained prior to the series of adaptation tests, and the second was obtained after the series of adaptation tests had been completed. In each of the baseline tests, listeners were presented randomized sequences of the 13 test syllable patterns, with an interstimulus interval of 2.5 sec. The Ss listened to the output of a Tandberg 1200X tape recorder and Advent speaker, the gain on the tape recorder being set at a fixed comfortable listening level. Each of the 13 stimuli was presented 20 times for identification in this manner. The Ss were instructed to identify each stimulus as [bæ], [dæ], or [gæ] by writing the appropriate consonant letter on answer sheets. The listeners were instructed to make their responses as soon as possible after hearing each identification stimulus.

On the day after the initial baseline test, a series of five adaptation tests was conducted, each test lasting about 1 h and taking place at approximately 24-h intervals. In order to make certain that each adaptation test was begun with the S in the unadapted state, a minimum of 20 h separated any two adaptation tests (cf. Eimas & Corbit, 1973).[6] Five different adapting syllables were used, one in each test. These adapting stimuli were the real speech syllables [bæ], [pʰæ], [mæ], [væ], and [wæ]. Four of the Ss (B.S., D.D., S.T., and W.N.) were presented the five adaptation tests in the order: [bæ] adaptation, [pʰæ] adaptation, [mæ] adaptation, [væ] adaptation, and [wæ] adaptation; the remaining four Ss were presented these same tests in the reverse order.

Each of the five adaptation tests was conducted in the manner used previously. Listeners were first presented with 2 min (180 presentations) of the selected adapting stimulus ([bæ], [pʰæ], [mæ], [væ], or [wæ] in a given session). Each repetition of the adapting stimulus was separated by 350 msec of silence. Following this 2-min "warm-up" period of adaptation, 35 adaptation trials were administered. On each trial, the adapting stimulus was first presented

Table 7
Frequency Values of the Second and Third Formants for the Five Real Speech Adapting Syllables

Syllable	Starting Frequency		Steady State Center Frequency (in Hz)	
	F_2	F_3	F_2	F_3
[bæ]	1000	2000	1400	2400
[pʰæ]	(See Note)		1500	2500
[mæ]	1000	1975	1500	2500
[væ]	1000	2000	1500	2400
[wæ]	800	2000	1500	2500

Note: The frequency values were estimated from wide-band spectrograms of the real speech stimuli. Since the F_2 and F_3 starting frequencies for pʰæ are not readily observable in spectrograms of real speech (due to the obscuring effect of aspiration and the weak energy of the formant transitions themselves), measurements of the starting frequencies for pʰæ were less precise than the measurements included in the table. To the best of our ability to estimate the starting frequencies for pʰæ, the values obtained were F_2 starting at 1100 Hz and F_3 starting at 2000 Hz.

[6]The assumption that recovery from adaptation would be complete after 20 h was substantiated by the results of the second baseline test, administered about 20 h after the fifth adaptation test (cf. Tables 9 and 12).

Table 8
Individual and Mean Loci of Phonetic Boundaries for Each Test Condition

S_s	Without Adaptation	Adaptation with			
		[bæ]	[pʰæ]	[mæ]	[væ]	[wæ]

Table 3a: b-d Phonetic Boundary

S_s	Without Adaptation	[bæ]	[pʰæ]	[mæ]	[væ]	[wæ]
W.N.	4.85	0	4.10	2.55	4.10	5.03
A.S.	4.92	3.72	3.47	1.44	2.50	3.34
E.B.	3.32	3.32	2.48	1.72	0	2.92
B.S.	4.25	0	0	0	0	1.85
S.T.	4.19	1.02	1.96	3.29	3.73	5.43
D.D.	5.44	4.44	6.00	5.67	5.45	6.39
J.M.	5.36	3.13	4.33	4.04	2.87	2.72
Mean	4.33	2.23	3.19	2.67	2.66	3.95

Table 3b: d-g Phonetic Boundary

S_s	Without Adaptation	[bæ]	[pʰæ]	[mæ]	[væ]	[wæ]
W.N.	10.23	9.32	9.92	10.50	10.41	10.41
A.S.	9.33	9.11	8.34	9.65	9.54	9.07
E.B.	10.38	9.65	9.68	10.00	10.00	10.46
B.S.	10.74	10.73	10.73	11.08	9.96	10.41
S.T.	8.98	9.11	8.96	10.04	10.33	9.96
D.D.	10.47	10.55	10.61	10.46	10.45	10.20
J.M.	8.56	9.45	9.94	10.00	9.67	8.39
Mean	9.81	9.70	9.74	10.25	10.05	9.84

Note: The locus of the phonetic boundary was determined in each case by first assigning to each stimulus an arbitrary number ranging from 1 to 13, and then performing a least mean squares analysis. The loci of the phonetic boundaries for the "without adaptation" condition are based on the pooled results of baseline functions obtained before and after adaptation testing (see text).

for 1 min (90 presentations), followed by 1.5 sec of silence, and then four randomly selected stimuli from the series of 13 stop consonants. The Ss were instructed to identify each of these four test stimuli during a 2.5-sec silent interval separating adjacent stimuli to be identified. As in the baseline tests of identification, the listeners were instructed to respond as soon as possible after hearing each test item. After the fourth stimulus was presented for identification, 5 sec of silence intervened before the onset of the next adaptation trial. Using this method, each stimulus in the series of 13 synthetic test syllables was presented a total of 10 times within a single, hour-long adaptation session. Throughout each of the five adaptation sessions, the stimuli to be identified was placed on a Tandberg 1200X tape recorder and Advent speaker, while the adapting stimuli were played on a Tandberg 12-41 tape recorder and the same Advent speaker. The two speaker outputs were matched in peak amplitude by means of a General Radio sound-level meter (Type 1565-A). On the day after the last adaptation test, Ss were presented the second baseline test of identification.

Table 9
Individual and Mean Loci of Phonetic Boundaries for the Two Baseline Tests

Ss	Without Adaptation	
	First Test	Second Test
b-d Phonetic Boundary		
W.N.	5.28	4.80
A.S.	4.93	5.28
E.B.	3.01	3.66
B.S.	4.51	4.03
S.T.	3.16	4.99
D.D.	5.03	6.11
J.M.	3.48	3.27
Mean	4.20	4.59
d-g Phonetic Boundary		
W.N.	9.86	10.31
A.S.	9.10	9.47
E.B.	10.83	10.24
B.S.	10.79	10.52
S.T.	9.27	9.41
D.D.	10.52	10.41
J.M.	8.36	9.33
Mean	9.82	9.96

Note: The locus of the phonetic boundary was determined in each case by first assigning to each stimulus an artibrary number, ranging from 1 to 13, and then performing a least mean squares analysis.

Results

The results for seven Ss appear in Table 8. The data for the eighth S, D.M., were analyzed separately on the basis of his initial baseline function, which did not show the sharply sloping contours found for all listeners in this experiment as well as for the listeners in experiments conducted previously with the bæ-dæ-gæ test stimuli (cf. Pisoni, 1971; Study 1). For all eight Ss, the loci of the b-d and d-g phonetic boundaries were determined for each test condition by first assigning to each test stimulus a number ranging from 1 to 13, and then performing a least-mean squares analysis (Ferguson, 1959) on the transformed percentages of identification responses. The numbers assigned to the test stimuli for the purpose of this analysis correspond to the numbers assigned in Table 7.

To assess the amount of baseline variability for each S in the pre- and postadaptation baseline tests, we determined the loci of the phonetic boundaries for each of the two baseline tests separately. These results appear in Table 9. An inspection of this table reveals that the loci of both the b-d and d-g phonetic boundaries were very similar overall for the two baseline measures. A statistical test of this difference was found to be nonsignificant ($p > 0.20$, two-tailed t-test for correlated observations) for both the b-d and d-g phonetic boundaries. Note, however, that the individual baseline functions obtained before and after adaptation testing are more variable for some Ss than for others. Three of the Ss, W.N., A.S., and B.S., showed a minimal baseline disparity (less than 0.5 units) in both the b-d and d-g phonetic boundary loci.[7]

We reasoned that a better estimate of the Ss' baseline during the course of the study would be provided if the baseline functions obtained before and after adaptation testing were pooled than if either of these individual baseline functions were considered alone. The phonetic boundary loci for the baseline test which appear in Table 8 were thus determined for each S by pooling his responses from the pre- and postadaptation baseline tests and then performing a least-mean squares analysis on this pooled identification function.

Table 10 shows the results of statistical tests of significance (t-tests for correlated observations) for shifts in the loci of the phonetic boundaries after adaptation. One-tailed tests of significance were applied in cases where the phonetic boundary bordered the category which shared its *place* mode with the adapting stimulus (i.e., the b-d phonetic boundary for [bæ], [pʰæ], [mæ], [væ], and [wæ] adaptation). Based on the model of the selective adaptation effect proposed in Study 1, the predicted direction of the boundary shifts in these cases was toward the category having the same *place* mode as the adapting stimulus (i.e., toward the [b] category). The results of Table 10 show

---

[7]It may well be that baseline fluctuations account for the inability to obtain predicted shifts in the case of some Ss. Evidence in support of this view is derived from the fact that the three Ss showing minimal baseline variability, S.B., B.S., and W.N., showed the most clear-cut and consistent shifts in the predicted direction, whereas the performance of other Ss was less uniform across the various adaptation test conditions.

Table 10
Tests of Significance for Shifts in Phonetic Boundary Loci between the Unadapted Test Condition and Each Adaptation Condition

	Adaptation with				
	[bæ]*	§pʰæ]*	[mæ]*	[væ]*	[wæ]*
			b-d Phonetic Boundary		
t Value	2.82	1.72	2.40	2.67	0.76
p Value	p < .025	p > .05	p < .05	p < .025	p > .20
	Adaptation with				
	[bæ]	[pʰæ]	[mæ]	[væ]	[wæ]
			d-g Phonetic Boundary		
t Value	0.47	0.24	1.85	0.83	0.19
p Value	p > .20	p > .20	p > .10	p > .20	p > .20

*Denotes one-tailed test, the direction of shift being toward the [b] category.

that, in comparison with the baseline measure of identification, a statistically significant shift occurred in the locus of the b-d phonetic boundary after adaptation with each of the syllables [bæ], [mæ], and [væ], the shift in each instance being directed toward the [b] category. Overall, a somewhat greater magnitude of shift was obtained after adaptation with [bæ] than with [mæ] or [væ], although this difference was not systematic across Ss. After adaptation with each of the three syllables [bæ], [mæ], and [væ], listeners made a smaller percentage of [b] responses than in the baseline test. A statistically nonsignificant shift in this same direction was obtained for the syllable [pʰæ] ($0.10 > p > 0.05$) and for the syllable [wæ] ($p > 0.20$). For the d-g phonetic boundary locus, no significant shift occurred for any of the five adaptation conditions.

Figure 4 depicts the identification functions for each test condition for a single listener, B.S. For the group of seven Ss, shifts produced by selective adaptation were usually not accompanied by a decline in the steepness of the response function slopes. In addition, for each S showing a shift in the b-d phonetic boundary locus after adaptation, the decrease in the percentage of [b] responses was accompanied by an increase in the percentage of [d] responses, while the percentage of [g] responses remained virtually fixed.

The results of the eighth S, D.M., appear in Tables 11 and 12 and in Figure

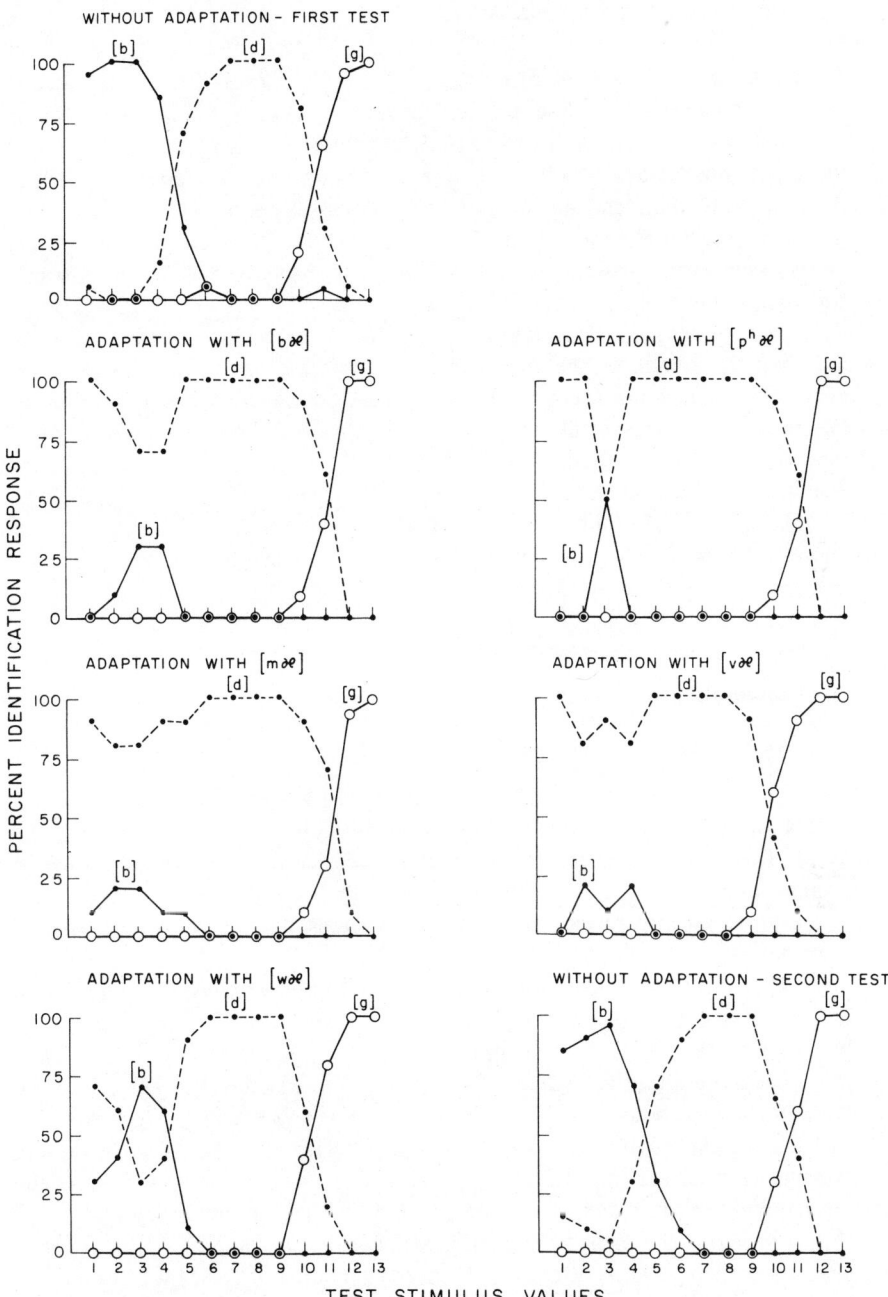

Figure 4. Percentages of identification responses ([b], [d], or [g]) obtained for the single listener B.S. in the unadapted state and after adaptation with [bæ], [pʰæ], [mæ], [væ], and [wæ].

5. The shape of the baseline functions for this S (cf. Fig. 5) differs dramatically from the shape of the baseline functions obtained for B.S. (cf. Fig. 4) and for the other listeners as well. Unlike these Ss, D.M. identified only a small portion of the 13 stimulus values as belonging to the same consonant category on all trials. Despite this marked tendency toward probabilistic, as opposed to absolute, identification, the baseline function obtained for D.M. before adaptation testing closely matches his baseline function obtained after the series of adaptation tests had been completed (cf. Table 12 and Figure 5).

For the adaptation test conditions, D.M. showed a systematic shift in the b-d phonetic boundary. The direction of this shift was *away* from the [b] category, in contrast to the direction of shift obtained for the other seven Ss. Whereas the group of seven Ss made fewer [b] responses after adaptation with each of the syllables [bæ], [pʰæ], [mæ], [væ], and [wæ], D.M. made more [b] responses after adaptation with each of these syllables. For the d-g phonetic boundary, D.M. showed no systematically directed shifts in the locus of the phonetic boundary after adaptation, similar to the results obtained for the other listeners.

Discussion

Ss A.S., E.B., W.N., B.S., J.M., S.T., and D.D.

The results for the group of seven listeners were very similar for the adaptation tests conducted with the adapting stimuli [bæ], [pʰæ], [mæ], and [væ]. The results obtained after adaptation with the syllable [bæ] replicate the findings of Study 1. That is, after adaptation, the b-d phonetic boundary shifted in the direction toward the [b] category, whereas the d-g phonetic boundary remained fixed.

The results obtained with the adapting syllable [pʰæ] are in only partial agreement with the data obtained in the earlier *place* study. For the b-d phonetic boundary, both studies showed some shift in the direction toward the [b] category, in accord with the findings obtained with the adapting syllable [bæ]. For the d-g phonetic boundary, however, a discrepancy between the results of the two studies exists. In the prior study, a shift occurred in the locus of the d-g boundary toward the [g] category. This shift was unexpected on the basis of the results obtained after adaptation with [bæ]. In the present study, no systematic shift occurred in the locus of this boundary, consistent with the results obtained after [bæ] adaptation. A different real speech exemplar of [pʰæ] was used in the two studies (different exemplars of [bæ] were used as well), and it is possible that an acoustic difference between the two [pʰæ] stimuli can account for the observed discrepancy. The exemplar used in the earlier study was more heavily aspirated and had a stronger initial burst than the one used here. This heavy aspiration coupled with a high-energy burst may have rendered the former

Table 11
Individual Loci of Phonetic Boundaries for Each Test Condition

		Adaptation with				
S	Without Adaptation	[bæ]	[pʰæ]	[mæ]	[væ]	[wæ]
		b-d Phonetic Boundary				
D.M.	4.98	5.93	5.20	6.84	6.60	6.47
		d-g Phonetic Boundary				
D.M.	8.57	6.85	9.50	9.45	10.21	8.28

Note: The locus of the phonetic boundary was determined in each case by first assigning to each stimulus an arbitrary number, ranging from 1 to 13, and then performing a least mean squares analysis. The loci of the phonetic boundaries for the "without adaptation" condition are based on the pooled results of baseline functions obtained before and after adaptation testing (see text).

stimulus somewhat [k]-like (cf. Cooper *et al.*, 1952), even though Ss reported hearing both stimuli unambiguously as [pʰæ].

The results obtained with the adapting stimuli [mæ] and [væ] show that both these stimuli exert a reliable influence on the perception of certain members of the bæ-dæ-gæ. For both these syllables, significant shifts in the locus of the b-d phonetic boundary occurred, the shifts being in the direction toward the [b] category. For the d-g phonetic boundary, on the other hand, no significant shifts occurred. The data for the adapting stimuli [mæ] and [væ] are thus akin to the results obtained with the adapting syllable [bæ].

The adapting stimulus [wæ] showed a slight mean shift in the d-b phonetic boundary, in the direction toward the [bæ] category. This stimulus was certainly less effective as an adapting syllable than any of the other adapting stimuli, however.

S D.M.

For the S showing an atypical baseline function, we found, surprisingly, that repetitive listening to each of the adapting syllables produced an effect of facilitation. Because D.M.'s systematic tendency to make a greater percentage of [b] responses after adaptation was not shared by any other S, either in this study or in Study 1, it is important to try to rule out any trivial explanation of D.M.'s atypical performance. Since the second baseline test function for this S was in remarkably close agreement with his baseline function, the possibility of a gen-

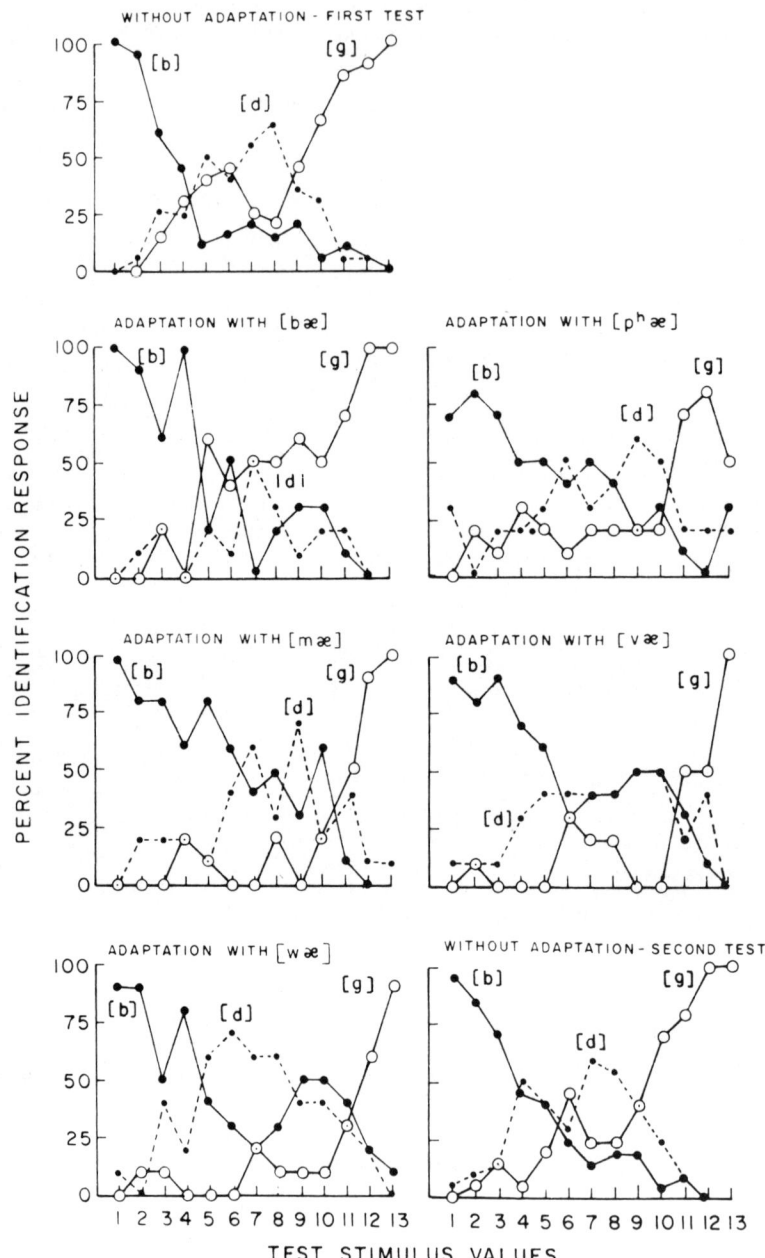

Figure 5. Percentages of identification responses ([b], [d], or [g]) obtained for the single listener D.M. in the unadapted state and after adaptation with [bæ], [pʰæ], [mæ], [væ], and [wæ].

eral shift in baseline criterion or the possibility of random responding can be discarded as explanations of either the usual baseline function or the facilitation effects. The S himself reported after all testing had been completed that he had used no unusual strategies in making his response choices, and that he, like the other Ss, reported each stimulus as he heard it. As in the case of the other listeners, D.M. was able to identify correctly each of the adapting syllables and consistently heard all the adapting and test stimuli as speech. Both the atypical baseline function and the effects of facilitation thus seem to be valid perceptual phenomena for this S. Each of these two phenomena, as well as their possible relation, deserves to be studied further. Although facilitation effects have previously been reported for the sensory modalities of taste (cf. Mayer, 1927; Dallenbach & Dallenbach, 1943; Meiselman, 1968) and smell (cf. Engen & Bosack, 1969; Corbit & Engen, 1971), such effects have been found to be dependent upon certain pairings of the adapting and test stimuli, not dependent on the nature of the Ss' performance in the unadapted state. The case presented here thus differs from the facilitation effects reported previously in the literature.

CONCLUSIONS

The results of the present experiment corroborate and extend the earlier finding that adaptation effects can be systematically produced along the consonant feature dimension *place of articulation*. The previously reported effects were accounted for by the fatiguing of an analyzing mechanism which decodes *place* information unidimensionally in terms of three major place analyzers, named the bilabial, alveolar, and velar analyzer modes.

The results of the present study are readily accommodated by the unidimensional model. The results also provide information about some additional properties of the analyzing system for *place*. First, the perceptual shift obtained after adaptation with the syllable [væ], containing a labio-dental consonant, indicates that the analyzer mode formerly termed *bilabial* actually extracts feature information that is more general in nature. To reflect the fact that [v] and [b] produce similar adaptation effects, we must change the term used to describe this analyzer mode from *bilabial* to *labial*. The results for [væ] show that the adaptation effects do not depend on a strict correspondence between the articulatory values of the adapting stimulus and members of the test stimuli. Rather, the adaptation effects appear to depend on either the sharing of certain invariant acoustic patterns, in particular the sharing of rising and steeply sloping second- and third-formant transition patterns, or on the sharing of more abstract phonetic information.

The acoustic pattern interpretation is certainly favored by the present data. Recall that relatively strong adaptation effects were obtained for the adapting stimuli [bæ], [mæ], and [væ]. The second- and third-formant transitions of these stimuli were of the same pattern as the transitions of the [b] members of

Table 12
Individual Loci of Phonetic Boundaries for the
Two Baseline Tests

	Without Adaptation	
S	First Test	Second Test
	d-b Phonetic Boundary	
D.M.	5.07	4.86
	d-g Phonetic Boundary	
D.M.	8.61	8.13

Note: The locus of the phonetic boundary was determined in each case by first assigning to each stimulus an arbitrary number, ranging from 1 to 13, and then performing a least-mean squares analysis.

the test series (cf. Tables 6 and 7); these adapting stimuli contained strong second- and third-formant transitions that were both rising and steeply sloped. On the other hand, adaptation effects were small for the adapting stimuli [pʰæ] and [wæ]. Unlike the [b] members of the test series, [pʰæ] contained second- and third-formant transitions that were relatively weak in energy, while [wæ] contained transitions that had a gradual, rather than steep, slope.

The perceptual shifts obtained in this experiment indicate further that the feature analyzer sensitive to labial *place* values extracts this information from consonants belonging to any of three different consonant classes; that is, the analyzer extracts information from consonants independent of their particular manner of articulation. Support for this conclusion is derived from the fact that perceptual shifts were obtained for the stop consonant test series after adaptation with [b], a stop consonant, [m], a nasal consonant, and [v], a fricative consonant.

A clue to the operating limit of the labial analyzer was provided by the failure to obtain consistent perceptual shifts after adaptation with the semiconsonant [w]. Further research must be conducted to determine whether this failure is complete (see later). If [w] is indeed inadequate as an adapting stimulus for the stop consonant series, the defining limit of the labial analyzer would appear to be that it extracts *place* information only for the class of true consonants.

Postscript to Study 2

Bailey (1975) had extended the work using glides as adaptors to test for crossed-adaptation effects on a stop consonant [b]–[d] series. Recall that, in this study, we found no significant adaptation effect using a [wæ] adaptor, suggesting that the feature analyzer for place in labials was limited to detecting formant transitions with a relatively sharp frequency rise. Bailey conducted glide-stop crossed-adaptation tests using two synthetic series of syllables, ranging from [bɛ] to [dɛ] and from [wɛ] to [jɛ]. The series differed from each other in the rate and duration of the formant transitions (see Chapter 4 for extended discussion of the acoustic differences between stop and glides). For the [bɛ]–[dɛ] stimuli, the duration of the formant transitions was 30 msec; for the [wɛ]–[jɛ] stimuli, the duration was 126 msec. Bailey found that neither of the glides in [wɛ] or [jɛ] produced an adaptation effect on the [b]–[d] boundary, although, as in the case reported here, small trends in the expected direction were observed.

Bailey did, however, obtain a significant effect on the [w]–[j] test series after adaptation with [bɛ]. He accounted for this result in terms of the spectral overlap (for a time window covering about 100 msec) between the adaptor and test stimuli in the region of the phonetic boundary. In so doing, Bailey abandoned the notion that the cross-adaptation effects reflect a stage of *feature* processing in favor of the suggestion that the effects reflect the degree of spectral similarity between adapting and test syllables as wholes. This view can, like the notion of feature-processing, account for the principled direction of the adaptation effects.

The general problem pointed up by Bailey is an example of a common experience in psycholinguistic work. From linguistic theory we have beed led to believe in the usefulness of some theoretical construct (in this case, the *phonetic feature*), and we ask whether this construct might be processed as a psychological entity. Since our results from cross-adaptation tests have, by and large, been consistent with the view that phonetic features, or auditory features resembling them, are extracted during the listening process, we have adopted this interpretation. It is at least conceivable, however, that adaptation may operate primarily at the syllable level, with various cross-adaptation effects being accounted for in terms of the overall acoustic similarity of adaptor and test stimuli.

This problem of interpretation is not new to experiments in speech perception. Neisser (1967), for example, noted the same problem for interpreting the results of experiments on identifying syllables presented in noise (Miller & Nicely, 1955). In subsequent chapters, we shall stick with the interpretation favoring the processing of independent features, though the ultimate fate of this interpretation remains unclear. It is fortunate, in any case, that a number of other issues to be tested in this study do not rest on the correctness of this view.

More recently, Miller and Eimas (1977) have replicated the findings of this study for adaptation with the nasal [m] on a [b]–[d] test series. In addition, they showed a converse cross-adaptation effect, adapting with [d] and testing a [m]–[n] series. The [d] adaptor produced a shift in the phoneme boundary toward [n] (i.e., fewer [n] responses), consistent with the notion that [d] and [n] share the same alveolar place of articulation. As in our study, the magnitude of these crossed-series effects was somewhat less than the magnitude of corresponding within-series effects (e.g., [d] adaptor with [b]–[d] test series). Miller and Eimas argued on this basis that the feature detectors sensitive to place of articulation are context-dependent on the manner of articulation. As noted above, these results could be accounted for alternatively, by discarding an interpretation in terms of feature detectors altogether in favor of an interpretation involving phoneme or syllable similarity (Neisser, 1967). In any event, it is clear from the results that the perceptual system treats ⌊b⌋ and ⌊m⌋ more alike than, say, ⌊m⌋ and ⌊d⌋, and this difference may be accounted for in a straightforward manner by assuming that the system extracts information about the shared acoustic features of ⌊b⌋ and ⌊m⌋. In our study and in the study of Miller and Eimas, the shared property for place involved the starting frequency and direction of the second- and third-formants.

In conclusion, the studies on place of articulation have helped to establish constraints on possible models of speech perception at early stages of processing. Evidence from a variety of crossed-adaptation studies indicates that listeners process information about a consonant's place of articulation regardless of the consonant's voicing or manner of articulation. Listeners also seem capable of integrating information about place over a relatively broad range of frequencies in the speech spectrum (Diehl, 1975; Ganong, 1975).

The variety of effects obtained in this chapter also points to the possibility that more than a single level of perceptual analysis is tapped by the selective adaptation procedure. In fact, Sawusch (1977a) has recently provided evidence for both peripheral and central effects of adaptation with place of articulation. It is quite possible that the precise interpretation of the array of results reviewed in this chapter will become clearer when the peripheral and central components of adaptation are properly isolated in future work. (We return to this matter in Chapter 7, where Sawusch's findings and their implications are considered in more detail.)

chapter three
VOICING

Study 3*

As noted at the outset of Chapter 2, Eimas and Corbit proposed that their adaptation effects reflected the fatiguing of linguistic feature detectors, each sensitive to a particular range of Voice Onset Time values, one sensitive to short-lag VOT values and one sensitive to longer-lag VOTs, presumed to contain partially overlapping ranges of sensitivity along the VOT dimension. The VOT value at which the two detectors were equally sensitive was taken as the underlying basis of the phonetic boundary locus. According to their model, adaptation with a voiced stop consonant was assumed to decrease the sensitivity of the short-lag VOT detector across its entire range of sensitivity, such that the locus of the phonetic boundary was displaced toward longer VOTs after adaptation. Assuming further that any higher levels of processing attend only to the output signal of the single VOT detector having the greater response, Eimas and Corbit were able to provide a general account of both the categorical nature of perception in the unadapted state (cf. Liberman, Harris, Kinney, & Lane, 1961) as well as the highly systematic and circumscribed effects obtained after adaptation.

However, other interpretations could be advanced to account for these adaptation results. According to one interpretation, the effects do not reflect a lowering of sensitivity in any detector mechanism but rather represent a response contrast effect, operating at the level of the listener's decision rule. The contrast

*Portions of this study are reprinted with permission from *Journal of Phonetics,* 1974, 2, 303–313.

notion, simply put, represents the tendency for listeners to identify stimuli as being unlike the stimulus which has been repeatedly presented beforehand, independent of sensory fatigue. Weak evidence has been cited in attempting to discredit this contrast interpretation. Such evidence includes the presence of the cross-adaptation effects, as well as shifts obtained in the peaks of discriminability functions after adaptation (cf. Eimas & Corbit, 1973). Findings by Sawusch and Pisoni (1973) provide another source of evidence against the contrast account (see Chapter 7 also).

The contrast interpretation rests on the assumption that the phonetic boundary locus is generally malleable as a function of the stimulus presentation schedule. Yet, Sawusch and Pisoni have found that the phonetic boundary locus for stimuli varying in VOT remains remarkably stable despite variations in the stimulus presentation schedule large enough to produce significant anchor effects (cf. Appley, 1972) on the identification functions for nonspeech stimuli. The absence of anchor effects for speech stimuli varying in VOT makes it unlikely that the phonetic boundary shifts obtained in the adaptation experiments represent either response contrast or an effect of Adaptation Level (cf. Helson, 1964).

Another counterinterpretation of the adaptation results is not so easily dismissed. This interpretation, which forms the basis of the present study, supposes that the effects observed along the VOT dimension are not actually due to adaptation of detectors for VOT information but are rather due to adaptation of detectors that are sensitive to variables typically confounded with VOT. One of these additional variables is the phonetic feature *voicing*. It could be argued that the adaptation effects reflect not fatiguing of VOT detectors *per se* but rather the fatiguing of *integrative voicing* analyzers, whose job it is to extract the phonetic feature *voicing* from the speech signal. Any of a number of possible voicing cues would provide adequate input to such integrative analyzers. Another possibility is that the effects are due to analyzers that are sensitive to a weighted combination of the hypothetical cues of VOT and the formant transitions (see later).

Although VOT may well be an important voicing cue in word-initial stops, other relevant cues do exist. Two of these have been studied in some detail, including pitch changes that occur at the onset of voicing (cf. Fujimura, 1961; Haggard, Ambler, & Callow, 1970) and the presence or absence of significant formant transitions at voicing onset (cf. Liberman, Delattre, & Cooper, 1958; Stevens & Klatt, 1974). Taking the existence of these additional cues into account, it is quite possible that the effects observed along the VOT dimension operate on analyzers that extract voicing information rather than VOT information as such.

One of the additional cues for voicing in initial stops, namely the presence or absence of the formant transitions at voicing onset, was directly confounded with absolute VOT in the previous adaptation tests. Thus, it is possible, in addition to, or in lieu of, adaptation of phonetic *voicing* analyzers, that the adaptation effects operate on analyzers for the specific formant transitions cue.

Such analyzers would perform the task of detecting the presence or absence of a rapid spectral change at voicing onset (cf. Stevens & Klatt, 1974).

The present experiment was designed to test the possibility that the adaptation effects observed by Eimas and Corbit (1973) and by Eimas et al. (1973) are attributable to variables other than absolute VOT. It is clearly important to determine the precise factors involved in the adaptation effects, since only when we know this information can we begin to make efficient use of the adaptation technique in exploring properties of the level (or levels) of speech processing being affected.

The present study focuses on the possible role of the formant transitions cue to voicing in accounting for the prior adaptation effects. In normal articulation, the formant transitions cue is always confounded with absolute VOT. This situation can be readily seen on spectrograms of real speech or synthetic syllables which vary in VOT (cf. Abramson & Lisker, 1973, Figure 1). A typical voiced stop is accompanied by a VOT of between 0 and 20 ms as well as significant formant transitions immediately following the onset of voicing. This covariation is a consequence of the fact that, for an initial voiced stop, the supraglottal articulators have not yet completed their movement toward the steady-state position at the time of voicing onset (the duration of formant transitions being on the average about 40 ms; Kent & Moll, 1969). A voiceless stop, on the other hand, is accompanied by a longer-lag VOT (greater than 40 ms for most speakers) and an absence of substantial formant transitions after the onset of voicing. For voiceless stops, movement of the articulators is more nearly or wholly complete at the time of voice onset.

Stevens and Klatt (1974) constructed series of CV syllables ([da]–[t^{h}a]) in which the formant transistors cue and absolute VOT were varied independently. They accomplished this by varying either the slope and duration of the transitions or by varying VOT, and found that differences in the formant transitions cue accounted for as much as a 15 ms displacement in the locus of listeners' normal phonetic boundary, as measured in terms of absolute VOT. For the subjects as a group, there was a significant trading relation between the degree to which identification of the test stimuli was governed by the presence of the transitions or by VOT, and individual listeners differed markedly in the extent to which either of the two cues controlled performance.

Given the findings of Stevens and Klatt, it seemed necessary to find out whether the adaptation effects obtained along the original VOT dimension (in which VOT and the transitions cue always covaried) are independent of the formant transitions cue. If the effects are not independent of this cue, then such adaptation effects alone cannot be taken as evidence for the existence of detector mechanisms selectively sensitive to VOT information. The present adaptation experiment was designed to provide a strong test of the VOT detector hypothesis.

In the experiment, two stimuli were selected from the series constructed by Stevens and Klatt (1974), to be used as adapting stimuli. These stimuli contained the same absolute VOT value (+ 25 ms) but differed in the amount of voiced formant transitions. One adapting stimulus, which is henceforth denoted as "[da]-long," contained significant formant transitions after voice onset. The duration of these transitions was 40 ms. The other adapting stimulus, "[da]-short," contained only slight (10 ms) formant transitions after voice onset. The duration of these transitions was shorter than the average threshold for detection of such a spectral change (cf. Stevens & Klatt, 1974, second experiment, part 2). The [da]-long stimulus was perceived as a good exemplar of [da] by all listeners of the present study; the [da]-short stimulus was perceived as either a "weak" [da] or as being ambiguous between [da] and [t^{h}a].

The purpose of the experiment was to test whether adaptation with these two syllables, [da]-long and [da]-short, would produce different effects on the perception of a typical test series varying in VOT. Since the two adapting stimuli contained different formant transitions but the same VOT information, any difference in the location of the phonetic boundary obtained under the two adaptation conditions could not be attributed to absolute VOT.

Method

Ten M.I.T. undergraduates served as paid volunteers in this experiment. All were native speakers of English and had no known hearing loss. No subject had prior phonetic training.

The *test* stimuli (i.e., the stimuli that listeners were required to identify) included 11 synthetic CV syllables [ba]–[p^{h}a]. The stimuli were five-formant patterns generated on a terminal analog speech synthesizer at the M.I.T. Research Laboratory of Electronics (Klatt, 1972). The range of VOT values was from + 5 to + 55 ms (positive VOT values indicate that voice onset occurred subsequent to the release burst) in five ms steps, sufficient to produce the phonetic distinction between [ba] and [p^{h}a]. In addition to VOT, an important parameter of the test stimuli was the duration of the formant transitions. These transitions were 20 ms long for each stimulus; the 20 ms duration is shorter than the average for spoken CV syllables but within the range of normal speech (cf. Kent & Moll, 1969). Each of the test timuli having VOTs of 20 ms or greater thus contained no formant transitions after voicing onset. Furthermore, since voiced transitions are detectable only when they are about 15 ms or longer in duration (cf. Stevens & Klatt, 1974, Experiment 2, second part), all test stimuli in the present series except the one having a VOT of + 5 ms probably had no perceptible voiced transitions.

The two *adapting* stimuli, [da]-long and [da]-short, each contained a VOT value of + 25 ms. These two stimuli were constructed on the same terminal analog synthesizer as the test stimuli. The two adapting stimuli differed from one another in the slope and duration of the formant transitions after voicing onset. The [da]-long stimulus contained lengthy (40 ms) transitions after voicing onset, whereas the [da]-short stimulus contained only brief (10 ms), and somewhat steeper, transitions. Wide-band spectrograms of the two stimuli are shown in Figure 1. For a more complete description of the adapting stimuli, see Stevens and Klatt (1974). In the Stevens and Klatt paper, the [da]-long stimulus is coded as "A1"; the [da]-short stimulus is coded as "D2."

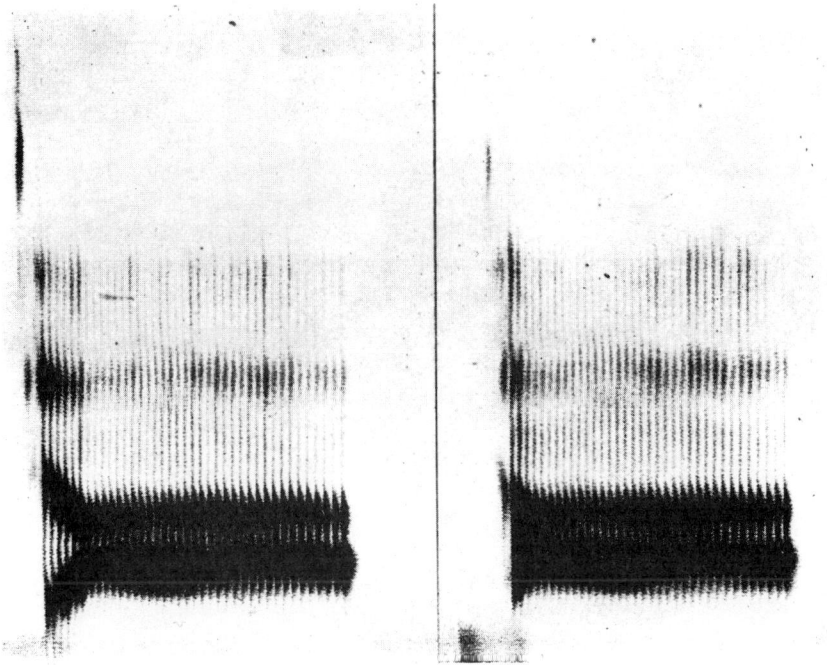

Figure 1. Wide-band spectrograms of the two adapting stimuli [da]-long (left) and [da]-short (right). The [da]-long stimulus contains 40 ms formant transitions after voicing onset; the [da]-short stimulus contains 10 ms formant transitions after voicing onset. Both stimuli have a VOT value of +25 ms. Note that the initial burst for [da]-long is of higher amplitude, due to a randomized factor in the synthesizer configuration. The more intense burst should, if anything, render the [da]-long stimulus somewhat more [tʰa]-like (cf. Stevens, 1977), representing a negative bias in the experiment.

The fundamental frequency contour of the adapting stimuli, as well as other acoustic parameters not directly associated with the voicing or place properties of the consonant, closely matched the parameter values of the test series.

The procedures of the experiment were very similar to those used by Eimas et al. (1973). The 10 listeners were first presented a randomized sequence of items from the [ba]–[pʰa] test series, to be identified as either "B" or "P." Listeners were instructed to write their answers and to make their response as soon as possible after hearing each stimulus item. The test stimuli were played binaurally via Telex headphones on an Ampex PR-10 tape recorder, at a fixed comfortable intensity level. The interstimulus interval for the test items was 2.5 s. Using this procedure, listeners identified each of the 11 test stimuli 10 times in the unadapted state.

After the initial unadapted condition, listeners were presented two adaptation tests, with about 24 h separating the two adaptation sessions. Each of these tests consisted of 28 consecutive adaptation trials. In one adaptation test, subjects listened on each trial to 70 repetitions of the [da]-long stimulus, prior to identifying four stimuli randomly selected from the [ba]-[pʰa] series. In the other test, subjects listened to 70 repetitions of the [da]-short stimulus, prior to identifying four items from the same [ba]-[pʰa] series. The order of presentation of the two adaptation tests was reversed for half the subjects.

Each repetition of the adapting stimulus was separated by 350 ms of silence. A 1.5 s interval occurred between the last repetition of the adapting stimulus and the first stimulus to-be-identified. Each of the four test items were separated by 2.5 s. In addition, 3 s separated the last stimulus to-be-identified from the next adaptation trial. For each subject, 10 responses were obtained at each of the 11 test stimuli in each adaptation condition. The adapting stimuli were played binurally via the Telex headphones on a Tandberg 3000X tape recorder, at the same intensity level as the test stimuli.

Table 1
Individual and Mean Phonetic Boundary Loci for Each Test Condition
(in ms of VOT)

Subject	No adaptation	[da]-long adaptation	[da]-short adaptation
J.F.	29.2	28.7	33.9
D.G.	30.8	28.3	25.5
M.G.	20.3	16.4	20.7
R.G.	26.7	25.2	29.2
E.H.	21.2	19.1	21.1
M.H.	28.1	24.6	27.7
P.K.	19.4	13.6	21.0
K.M.	23.3	17.4	28.2
P.S.	28.6	16.1	29.8
B.S.	24.5	21.6	25.0
$\bar{X}$	25.2	21.1	26.2

Results and Discussion

The results of the experiment are shown in Table 1, where the individual phonetic boundary loci are presented for each test condition. Each phonetic boundary locus was determined by a least-mean squares analysis (Ferguson, 1959). A graph of the pooled identification data appears in Figure 2.

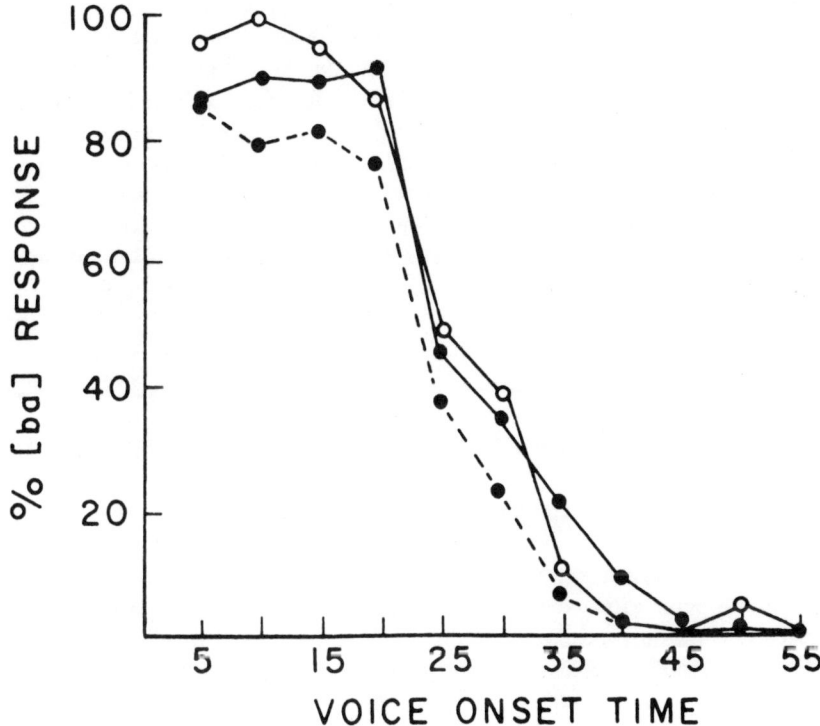

Figure 2. Identification functions of the group of 10 listeners in each of the three test conditions. The solid line with filled circles represents the identification function obtained with listeners in the unadapted state. The dotted line represents the function obtained after adaptation with [da]-long; the solid line with open circles represents the function obtained after adaptation with [da]-short.

Adaptation with the two stimuli [da]-long and [da]-short produced significantly different phonetic boundary loci for the [ba]–[pʰa] test series ($P < 0.01$) (two-tailed t-test for correlated observations). Compared with the phonetic boundary locus obtained in the unadapted state, adaptation with the [da]-long stimulus produced a significant shift in the locus of the phonetic boundary toward the [b] category, signifying that listeners made fewer "B" responses after adaptation. This shift occurred uniformly for each of the ten listeners ($P < 0.01$). After adaptation with the [da]-short stimulus, a shift in the phonetic boundary locus occurred in the opposite direction. This shift, although statistically nonsignificant ($P > 0.20$), was obtained for seven of the 10 listeners. Each of these listeners assigned slightly fewer responses to the "P" category after adaptation with the [da]-short stimulus.

The results cannot possibly be accounted for by an adaptation effect that operates on detectors of absolute VOT information. According to such a hypothesis, since the two adapting stimuli have the same VOT value, these stimuli should have produced the same effect on the phonetic boundary locus of the test stimuli. Yet, the adapting stimuli produced significantly different effects. With this finding, we can effectively eliminate the strong VOT explanation of the adaptation effects. For the same reason we reject the strong VOT explanation of the effects, so too we reject any explanation of the effects based solely on a rate normalization hypothesis, such as the account proposed by Bailey (1972).

On initial inspection, it appears that the present effects can be accounted for in two separate ways. First, the effects may operate on analyzers sensitive to the presence or absence of a rapid spectral change following onset of voicing. Alternatively, the effects may operate on what I have so far loosely referred to as *integrative analyzers,* sensitive to any number of possible voicing cues (cf. Lisker & Abramson, 1970; Haggard *et al.,* 1970; Stevens & Klatt, 1974).

The first alternative can possibly be ruled out upon close inspection of the stimulus series in the present experiment. Recall that most stimuli of the test series contained no formant transitions after voicing onset. If adaptation with the [da]-long stimulus affected an analyzer sensitive to the degree of spectral change after voice onset, irrespective of VOT, then the perception of these test stimuli should have remained unaltered after [da]-long adaptation, contrary to the results. This argument (and the one below) rests crucially on the assumption that the hypothetical detector for long voiced transitions is effectively unresponsive to test stimuli with no voiced transitions, an assumption which seems reasonable but which should be tested if possible in the future.

We are left with the general hypothesis that the present effects arise due to the fatiguing of an integrative analyzer. Two important subtypes of integrative analysis must be distinguished, however. The first, and simpler type, concerns an analyzer sensitive to each of the two hypothetical cues (VOT and the formant transitions) independently, being triggered disjunctively by the presence of either cue alone. Such an analyzer, which may be sensitive to other *voicing* cues as well, such as the pitch skip (Haggard *et al.,* 1970), approximates what has previously been termed an analyzer that performs a *phonetic* analysis (Study 1). Whether such an analyzer exists can be demonstrated by further crossed-adaptation research in which voicing cues in addition to VOT and the formant transitions are played off against one another.

If anything, the present data do not support the existence of such a simple integrator. Consider the test stimulus having a VOT of + 25 ms. This test stimulus, which contains no formant transitions after voicing onset, is identified more often as [ba] after adaptation with [da]-short but more often as [pʰa] after adaptation with [da]-long. Since the two adapting stimuli have the same VOT as this test stimulus, it is difficult to account for the differential effects of the two adapting stimuli, in particular of the [da]-long stimulus with lengthy transitions, given only a simple integrative analyzer that detects VOT and the formant transitions cue disjunctively.

Another important sub-type of integrative analyzer, first pointed out to me by W. Francis Ganong, concerns an analyzer sensitive to a specific weighted combination of the two cues of VOT and the formant transitions. Under this hypothesis, the acoustic information relevant to the perception of voicing distinctions would be neither VOT nor the formant transitions *per se*, but a cue that is in some sense intermediate to both. This cue may correspond to the ratio of the duration of aspiration (a co-variant of VOT) and the duration of the formant transitions after voice onset.

The existence of such a detector derives some support from the data in Stevens and Klatt (1974; Experiment 2). Most subjects in their identification experiments based their judgments neither wholly on VOT nor on the formant transitions, but rather on a combination of both, with individuals varying from one another to the extent that they relied on each cue.

The hypothetical response range of a unitary detector system of the type proposed here is shown in Figure 3, along with a representation of stimuli used in this experiment. Given such a response range, one can predict the present adaptation effects as follows: First, assume that two detectors exist, responsive to partially overlapping ranges of values along the entire range proposed here as represented by the diagonal line in Figure 3 (the exact slope of this line is not crucial to the argument and indeed probably differs from one listener to another to some extent). Assume also that these two detectors operate in an opponent-process fashion, such that the output of one detector inhibits the response of the other. Assume finally that each detector is sensitive to a given stimulus at a point on its response range closest to the stimulus representation in the coordinate space of Figure 3, and that the output of the two detector feeds into a decision system that responds "voiceless" when the output of the detector sensitive to stimuli at the left portion of the diagonal range is greater than that of the alternative detector, *ceteris paribus*. The decision system responds "voiced" otherwise. Repetitive presentation of the [da]-long adapting stimulus selectively decreases the sensitivity of the detector most responsive to cue values on the right portion of the diagonal, whereas presentation of the [da]-short adapting stimulus decreases sensitivity of the detector most responsive to cue values on the left portion. After adaptation with [da]-long, more overt identification responses are thus made to the voiceless category than after adaptation with [da]-short. This

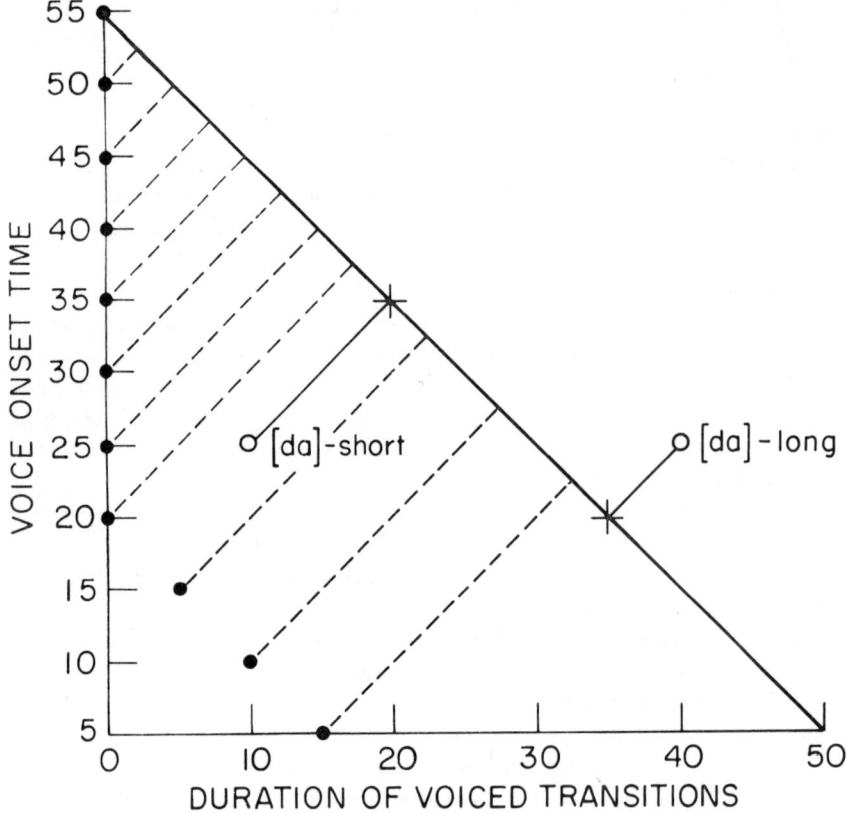

Figure 3. Response range of an integrative analysis system sensitive to a weighted combination of VOT and the formant transitions cue. In this illustration case, the response range is represented by the solid diagonal line. The two adapting stimuli are represented in the coordinated space by open circles; the test stimuli are represented by filled circles.

integrative analyzer, sensitive to a weighted combination of VOT and the formant transitions, can thus account for the present adaptation effects.

In summary, the present results demonstrate the incorrectness of both the strong VOT explanation of speech adaptation effects as well as an explanation based on rate normalization. Rather, the present effects are attributable to an integrative feature analysis system that operates by either (a) responding to any of two or more acoustic cues of voicing disjunctively or (b) responding to a particular weighted combination of the two cues of VOT and formant transition rate after voicing onset. The latter of these two possibilities represents a complex but essentially invariant acoustic detector, whose properties, if known, would enhance our understanding of how the perception of voicing contrasts is accomplished. The work of Summerfield (1974) is of considerable interest in this same regard.

Postscript to Study 3

Additional work on voicing cues has uncovered another cue for voicing which has a bearing on this study. Lisker (1975) and Summerfield and Haggard (1976; 1977) showed that when the F_1 starting frequency was sufficiently low, a stop consonant would be perceived as voiced rather than voiceless, even in the absence of an F_1 transition. In the present test series, as well as in the series of Eimas and Corbit, the F_1 starting frequency covaried with both VOT and the duration of the formant transitions. In this experiment, the two adapting stimuli, [da]-long and [da]-short, differed in the starting frequency of F_1 in addition to differing in the duration of the formant transitions, opening the possibility that adaptation operated directly on a detector which simply extracts information about the F_1 starting frequency. According to this possibility, pointed out by Ades (1976), the [da]-long adaptor's effect on the [b] members of the series would be attributed to the sharing of a relatively low F_1 starting frequency; the [da]-short effect of the [p] members of the series would be attributed to the sharing of a relatively high-starting F_1.

In light of this additional information on voicing cues, it would be appropriate to replicate the present experiment with adapting stimuli that differed only in the duration of the formant transitions. If such adaptors produced effects on a test series which varied only in VOT, or only in the starting frequency of F_1, then we would again be forced to consider the kind of integrative property detector proposed here. Until such a test is designed, however, the conservative interpretation of the results can be stated in terms of adaptation of a detector for the acoustic cue of relatively low vs. high F_1 starting frequency.

Ades (1976) suggests that the identification data obtained in the baseline test of this study provide indirect support for Lisker's position regarding the importance of the F_1 starting frequency cue. Ades notes that Stimulus 4, which contained a VOT of + 20 msec and did not contain any formant transitions, received about 80% voiced responses. Ades goes on to observe that the high percentage of voiced responses can be accounted for by the presence of a relatively low F_1 starting frequency. It should also be noted that, if short VOT values serve as a positive cue for voicing, contra Ades (1976), the presence of a + 20 msec VOT for this stimulus might account for the voiced responses (cf. Chapter 5).

In summary, this study demonstrated that adaptation effects for a test series like that used by Eimas and Corbit (1973) could be obtained for acoustic cues other than VOT. Recently, Diehl (1977) replicated the present results using test stimuli which contained longer formant transitions than those used here. Diehl's results closely matched our data, providing further confirmation that adaptation effect for a voiced-voiceless series can be produced for acoustic cues other than VOT. Further work remains to be conducted before it is known whether adaptation operates exclusively at a level of processing at which each of these cues is detected seperately or at a level at which some degree of integration occurs.

Study 4*

This study was conducted to test whether the perception of voicing in stop consonants is dependent on the context of the following vowel. For the feature place of articulation, early work on speech cues showed a considerable degree of context dependence, as noted in Chapter 1, indicating that perception of the place feature might take into account the following vowel environment. For voicing, however, the early work on speech cues did not reveal such a context dependence (Lisker & Abramson, 1967), so it remained questionable whether a dependency existed in perception. To test this possibility, a contingent adaptation method was used, similar to the procedure reviewed in Chapter 1 for studying dependencies in vision.

Method

Stimuli. The stimuli were five-formant synthetic speech patterns. All stimuli were CV syllables generated on a terminal analog speech synthesizer at the M.I.T. Research Laboratory of Electronics. The test stimuli included 22 syllables, 11 [ba]-[p^{h}a] stimuli and 11 [bi]-[p^{h}i] stimuli. In each series, the 11 stimuli varied from one another in VOT. The VOT variations were in equal stops of 5 msec, covering a range of from +5 to +55 msec of VOT (positive VOT values indicate that the onset of voicing occurred subsequent to the release burst). Relative formant amplitudes were set according to the acoustic theory of speech production (Fant, 1956). The overall amplitudes of the stimuli in the [ba]-[p^{h}a] series were thus approximately 7 dB greater than the amplitudes of stimuli in the [bi]-[p^{h}i] series. The fundamental frequency contour and all other acoustic parameters not directly associated with the formant frequencies and amplitudes were equivalent for the stimuli in the two series. The duration of each stimulus was 255 msec.

In addition to the 22 test stimuli, two adapting stimuli were synthesized, [da] and [t^{h}i]. The adapting syllables contained VOT values of +5 and +55

---

*Portions of this study are reprinted with permission from *Perception & Psychophysics*, 1974, *16*, 201–204.

msec, respectively, and were 255 msec in duration. The fundamental frequency contour, relative formant amplitudes, steady-state formants, and bandwidths of each adapting stimulus corresponded to the parameter values of the test stimuli having the same vowel.

Subjects. Fourteen M.I.T. undergraduates served as naive listeners in the experiment. All were native speakers of English. None had prior phonetic training or any known hearing impairment.

Procedure. To obtain a measure of perception in the unadapted state, Ss were first instructed to identify stimuli from each of the two test series. The stimuli of each series were presented in random order with an interstimulus interval of 2.5 sec. The listeners first identified the stimuli of the [ba]–[p^{h}a] series and then the stimuli of the [bi]–[p^{h}i] series. Ss listened binaurally over Telex headphones to the output of an Ampex PR-10 tape recorder. They were instructed to write "B" or "P" as their response, and to make the response as soon as possible after hearing the stimulus item. For each S, a total of 20 responses was obtained to each of the 22 test stimuli. All baseline testing was conducted during a single hour-long session.

Starting with the day after baseline testing, Ss were presented two adaptation tests, one test per day on consecutive days. In each test, adaptation consisted of listening to repetitions of an alternating sequence of the two syllables [da] and [t^{h}i], each syllable being presented three times in succession before a changeover to the alternate syllable. The interstimulus interval for repetitions of the adapting stimuli was 350 msec. After each minute of adaptation, Ss were presented four randomly selected test stimuli, each stimulus to be identified as either B or P. An interstimulus interval of 1.5 sec intervened between the last repetition of the adapting sequence and the first stimulus to be identifed; adjacent stimuli to be identified were separated by 2.5 sec of silence. After the fourth stimulus was presented for identification, 5 sec of silence intervened before the onset of the next adaptation trial. All timing intervals were specified by computer, and the entire adaptation sessions were recorded onto tape.

In one adaptation test, the stimuli to be identified consisted of the [ba]–[p^{h}a] series, and in the other adaptation test, the [bi]–[p^{h}i] series. Seven Ss were presented the adaptation test with the [ba]–[p^{h}a] stimuli first; the other seven were presented the two adaptation tests in reverse order. Each of the adaptation tests lasted about 1 h. For each S, 10 responses were obtained to each of the 22 test stimuli during the adaptation tests.

Results and Discussion

The results appear in Table 2, where phonetic boundary loci are computed by a least-mean squares analysis for each listener. The baseline results were

Table 2
Individual and Mean Phonetic Boundary Loci for Each Test Condition (in Milliseconds of VOT)

S	[ba]–[pʰa] Series		[bi]–[pʰi] Series	
	No Adapt	With [da]–[tʰi] Adapt	No Adapt	With [da]–[tʰi] Adapt
A.C.	27.4	20.7	28.0	32.3
J.C.	26.1	27.9	31.1	35.4
L.C.	20.1	23.3	21.7	26.7
L.Ch.	23.5	18.8	28.5	25.2
P.F.	22.0	7.4	38.9	36.2
S.G.	31.0	33.8	31.2	30.4
B.H.	20.2	19.3	38.3	32.8
H.H.	30.6	25.5	36.3	36.2
P.H.	29.4	26.1	34.4	35.0
J.I.	26.2	17.3	21.2	31.3
J.K.	36.7	33.6	36.1	39.1
T.M.	27.0	25.8	31.9	37.3
C.S.	29.8	21.2	37.9	40.2
T.S.	16.4	16.0	30.0	36.0
Mean	26.2	22.6	31.8	33.9

similar overall to those obtained by Lisker and Abramson (1970) (see Figure 4). Importantly, the phonetic boundary loci of the two series in the baseline test differed significantly from each other (p < 0.01).[1] This difference provided strong initial evidence that VOT is perceived in a vowel-dependent manner. The fact that the VOT boundary locus for the [bi]–[pʰi] series was greater than that for the [ba]–[pʰa] series is correlated with an interesting finding of Klatt (1973). In contrast to Lisker and Abramson (1967), Klatt has found that VOT values for the production of voiceless stops are significantly greater when these stops are followed by high as opposed to low vowels (e.g., [pʰi] vs [pʰaʸ]).

The vowel-dependent nature of VOT perception was also demonstrated in the two adaptation tests of the present study. Adaptation with the [da]–[tʰi] alternating sequence produced opposite shifts in the identification functions of the [ba]–[pʰa] and [bi]–[pʰi] series. The results for the [ba]–[pʰa] series indicate the presence of a small, but significant, shift in the locus of the phonetic

---

[1] Two-tailed *t*-test of significance for correlated observations. All subsequent tests of significance were one-tailed *t*-tests for correlated observations.

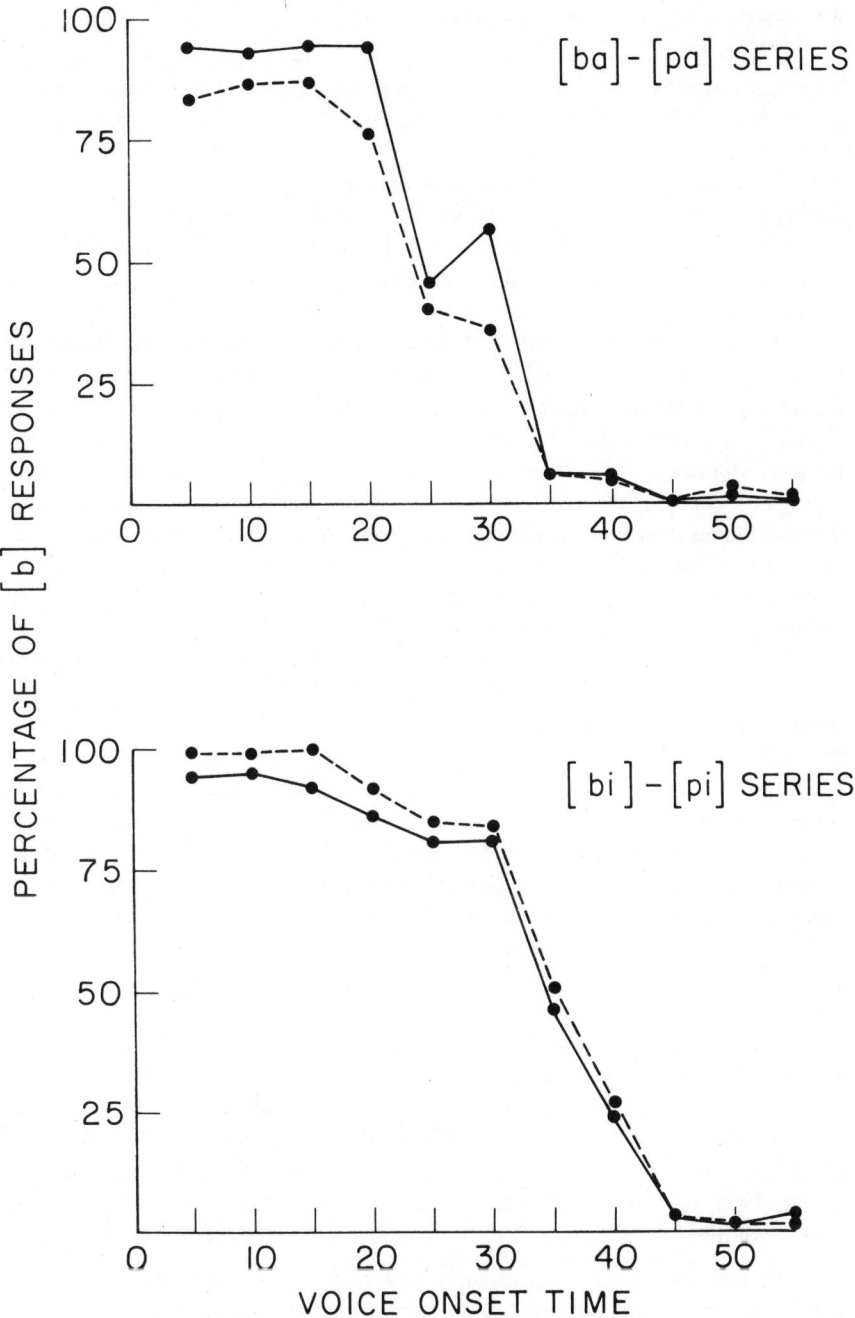

Figure 4. The percentage of "B" identification responses for the group of 14 Ss. Solid lines denote the identification functions obtained in the unadapted state. The dotted lines denote the identification functions obtained after adaptation to the alternating [da]-[tʰi] sequence.

boundary toward the [b] category, as compared with the baseline performance for the same series ($p < 0.01$). Ss thus made fewer [b] responses to the [ba]–[pʰa] stimuli after adaptation with the [da]–[tʰi] alternating sequence. The results for the [bi]–[pʰi] series show an opposite shift in the locus of the phonetic boundary after adaptation with the [da]–[tʰi] sequence. The shift in this case was in the direction toward the [p] category ($p < 0.05$). The difference between the two shifts was highly significant ($p < 0.005$), the net shift for 12 of the 14 listeners being in the same direction.[2]

To account for the obtained shifts, it is proposed that the identification of stimuli in each of the two VOT series was primarily governed by that member of the adapting sequence which contained the same vowel as the test stimuli. In effect, perception of the [ba]–[pʰa] stimuli was primarily influenced by the adapting stimulus [da], while the perception of the [bi]–[pʰi] stimuli was more highly influenced by the adapting stimulus [tʰi]. The differential effectiveness of the two adapting stimuli cannot be accounted for by an adaptation effect presumed to operate on the perception of the consonant feature of *voicing* alone. The effects observed here must rather be attributed to adaptation that operates on *voicing* perception in a vowel-contingent manner.

Further support for this vowel-contingent interpretation was provided in a second experiment. Five listeners, none of whom had served in the main experiment, were presented the [ba]–[pʰa] and [bi]–[pʰi] series for identification in the unadapted state and after adaptation to an alternating sequence of two new syllables [di] and [tʰa]. As predicted by the vowel-contingent hypothesis, it was found that after adaptation with the alternating [di]–[tʰa] sequence, listeners assigned fewer responses to the [b] category of the [bi]–[pʰi] series but assigned more responses to the [b] category of the [ba]–[pʰa] series (mean boundary shift = 3.4 msec VOT). Here, as in the main experiment, the perception of each test series was primarily governed by the adapting stimulus which contained the same vowel as the test stimuli.

It was considered possible that the contingent effects observed in this study share some properties with the contingent aftereffects demonstrated in human vision (cf. McCollough, 1965; Harris & Gibson, 1968; Fidell, 1970; Held & Shattuck, 1971; Mayhew & Anstis, 1972).[3] A similarity apparent from the data of the first two experiments was the relatively small magnitude of the contingent effect compared with simple (i.e., single variable) adaptation effects (cf. McCollough, 1965). A further test was conducted to determine whether the present effect exhibited an unusually long time course of recovery, similar to that ob-

---

[2] As in another study of speech adaptation (Study 2), the failure to obtain shifts in the expected direction for some Ss was highly correlated with a lack of monotonicity in the identification functions obtained in the unadapted state; this was true for Ss S.G. and B.H.

[3] The search for formal similarities between these effects is carried out in the spirit of obtaining more information about speech adaptation. I do not subscribe to the view that a demonstration of similar adaptation effects in vision and speech necessarily indicates the presence of any strong similarity between the mechanisms underlying such effects.

served with the contingent aftereffects in vision which in some cases last for as long as 6 weeks (cf. Mayhew & Anstis, 1972). The experiment involved three listeners (A.C., J.I., and J.K.), each of whom had demonstrated relatively large boundary shifts after adaptation in the main experiment. The contingent adaptation effect on both the [ba]–[pʰa] and [bi]–[pʰi] series was replicated for each of the three Ss (mean boundary shift = 4.7 msec VOT). The listeners were presented another baseline test 5 days after adaptation. For each S, approximately complete recovery from adaptation was obtained. The contingent adaptation effect for speech does not, then, appear to exhibit an extremely long time course, unlike some contingent aftereffects in vision.

To summarize, the results of the main experiment indicated that adaptation to an alternating sequence of [da] and [tʰi] produced opposing shifts in the perception of two CV test series varying in VOT. After adaptation, fewer [b] responses were made to stimuli of the [ba]–[pʰa] series, whereas more [b] responses were made to stimuli of the [bi]–[pʰi] series.

The presence of this contingent adapation effect, as well as the complementary effect obtained with the [di]–[tʰa] adapting sequence, indicates that the analysis of the feature *voicing* in consonants is carried out, at least in part, by detection channels that are vowel-dependent. The present evidence supports this interpretation, but other evidence from our laboratory would appear to support the existence of vowel-independent channels for consonant feature analysis as well (cf. Ades, 1974b; Study 1). Using the selective adaptation technique, both Ades and I have found that partial adaptation can be produced for consonants varying in the feature *place of articulation* when the adapting syllable contains a different vowel from the vowel of the test series. Such data may well indicate the presence of vowel-independent channels; another way to account for these data, however, would be to postulate the existence of vowel-dependent channels only (at the stage of analysis adapted here), each channel responding to a consonant feature best in a particular vowel environment but responding in other vowel regions as well. Tuning in this case would need to be broad enough so that adaptation to C_1V_1 would adapt channels that also detect, to a lesser extent, the features of C_1V_2. Whether such vowel-dependent channels exist can be studied further with the contingent adaptation technique.

Postscript to Study 4

Related Studies

The contingent adaptation effect for voicing obtained here has been replicated by two other groups of investigators (Miller & Eimas, 1976; Pisoni, Sawusch, & Adams, 1975). Miller and Eimas replicated the effect using two series of test stimuli varying from [bæ] to [pʰæ] and from [bi] to [pʰi], with [dæ] and [tʰi] as alternating adaptors. The procedure was quite similar to the one used here; the adaptation sequence consisted of three repetitions of one adaptor followed by three repetitions of the other.[4] Oppositely directed effects were obtained for the two test series after adaptation with this alternating sequence. For the [bæ]-[pʰæ] series, fewer [b] responses were reported after adaptation with the [dæ]-[tʰi] sequence, for the [bi]-[pʰi] series, fewer [pʰ] responses occurred. The average shift in the phoneme boundary was slightly less than 5 msec for a group of 8 listeners, consistent with the results reported here. In addition, the magnitude of effect was slightly larger for the [bi]-[pʰi] series.

Pisoni *et al.* (1975) also replicated the contingent effect, using test series of [ba]-[pʰa] and [bi]-[pʰi], as in this study. The adapting sequence consisted of either [da]-[tʰi] or [di]-[tʰa]. The adaptation effects with the two adaptor sequences on the ⌊ba⌋-⌊pʰa⌋ series replicated the effects reported here.[5] No significant effects were obtained with the adapting sequences for the [bi]-[pʰi] series, unlike our results and those of Miller and Eimas. We shall return to this discrepancy after discussing a reinterpretation of the contingent effects.

Reinterpretation

The contingent effects have been taken to support the notion that the detection of voicing in stop consonants is carried out with reference to the environment of a following vowel. Yet, no auditory basis for the results was provided. Summerfield and Haggard (1974) took an important step in this direction by pointing out a difference in the processing of two voicing cues—VOT and the duration of the formant transitions (cf. Study 3)—in the environment of different vowels like [i] vs [a]. A major assumption underlying their explanation is that a sufficiently long lag in VOT serves as a positive cue to voiceless stops, but that a short lag in VOT does not serve as a positive cue to voiced stops. Similarly, Summerfield and Haggard assume that a sufficiently long duration of formant transitions serves as a positive cue to voiced stops, but that a short duration does not serve as a positive cue to voiceless stops. Both assumptions are quite reasonable a priori, although it must be recognized that a relatively simple system of neural inhibition could be constructed to allow the absence of long

---

[4]In Study 4, the adapting sequence began with one syllable and ended with the other syllable. The starting and ending syllables were the same for all adaptation trials, ruling out a possibility (originally suggested by W. F. Ganong) that separate short-term adaptation effects could be produced on alternate trials for the last adaptor only, yielding the appearance of contingent adaptation effects over a whole test session. It is not known whether Miller and Eimas or Pisoni *et al.* used this particular procedure.

[5]As noted in this report, the location of the phonetic boundaries in the baseline identification data also provides a way of testing for the presence of vowel-condition responses. In the baseline tests conducted by Pisoni *et al.*, the location of the boundary was at a longer VOT value for the series of stops with [i] than with [a], as found in this report and by Summerfield and Haggard (1974). The direction of this difference is in accordance with a similar difference in the VOT values found in speech production, as noted earlier. A difference in the reverse direction was obtained by Miller and Eimas (1976) in their baseline data.

VOTs and formant transitions to serve as positive cues for voiced and voiceless stops, respectively (see Chapter 5 for details).

With these assumptions, one can provide an auditory basis of some of the contingent effects. For a stop before [i], the formant transitions are quite short in natural speech. Summerfield and Haggard showed that listeners used the VOT cue at the expense of this cue in categorizing synthetic stimuli varying in the two cues. For [a], on the other hand, the formant transitions are considerably longer, and here, listeners relied on the formant transitions to a greater extent in making decisions about voicing.

Summerfield and Haggard discussed the possibility that VOT and the formant transitions cue are detected independently at some processing stage and are then weighted for importance depending on the vowel environment, such that greater weight is given to information obtained about VOT in the environment of [i] vs. [a]. With this condition, plus the assumptions already mentioned that long VOTs and formant transitions serve as positive cues to voiceless and voiced stops, respectively, whereas short VOTs and formant transitions do not enter into the decision process about voicing, it is possible to provide an account of contingent adaptation effects with an alternating sequence of [da] and [t^{h}i], in terms of two separable effects. For [da], adaptation occurs for the formant transitions cue; for [t^{h}i], adaptation occurs for VOT. Thus, listeners' identification of stimuli along a [bi]–[p^{h}i] series contains fewer [p^{h}i] responses.

If this account is correct, adaptation with a sequence of [di] and [t^{h}a] should not produce an equal effect on a [bi]–[p^{h}i] series, since the formant transitions for [di] are not heavily weighted. Ades (1976) suggests that the null results obtained for the [bi]–[p^{h}i] series by Pisoni *et al.* (1975) can be accounted for in these terms. The positive results obtained in this report and by Miller and Eimas are at odds with this account, and an auditory basis for the contingent adaptation effects thus remains elusive.

In a more recent paper, Summerfield and Haggard (1977) suggest that the contingent effects may be attributed to the difference in onset frequency of the first formant for [i] and [a] contexts, following Lisker (1975), as discussed in the Postscript to Study 3. On this view, the differential effects in these vowel contexts would be attributed to the fact that voicing is cued by a relatively low starting value of F_1, as in [a] contexts.

Contingent Effects for Place of Articulation

Miller and Eimas (1976) and Pisoni *et al.* (1975) extended the contingent adaptation procedure to the study of place of articulation. Considering the context dependencies already noted for the place feature, it is not surprising that

---

[6] It is important to note that the account of Summerfield and Haggard holds even though the actual range of acoustic values for VOT and the formant transitions were the same for the two test series. According to the interpretation of their data on context effects, a listener applies the weighing of the two cues for these vowel contexts in accordance with their relevance in normal speech, even though this heuristic is not of aid to the perceptual system in this particular test situation.

contingent effects were obtained, Miller and Eimas observed systematic effects using two test series, [bæ]-[dæ] and [bi]-[di], after adaptation with an alternating sequence of either [bæ]-[di] or [pʰæ]-[tʰi]. After adaptation with [bæ]-[di] or [pʰæ]-[tʰi], fewer [b] responses were assigned to the [bæ]-[dæ] test series, while fewer [di] responses were assigned to the [bi]-[di] series. Similar effects were obtained by Pisoni *et al.* using test series [ba]-[da] and [bi]-[di] after adaptation to an alternating sequence of [ba]-[di].

A further test by Miller and Eimas is potentially of considerable importance. The contingent procedure was applied to CVC syllables in which the place of articulation of the initial consonant and final consonant were varied jointly. Two test series were constructed, including [bæb]-[dæb] and [bæd]-[dæd]. Using a [bæb]-[dæd] adapting sequence, Miller and Eimas obtained no significant adaptation effects for the two test series. This finding was not surprising since the acoustic information for place of articulation for a syllable-initial consonant does not appear to depend on the place of value of a syllable-final consonant. This null result may be important, however, because it indicates that the contingent effects observed thus far are probably not produced by associative learning of a relation that is built up during the adapting repetitions (cf. Mayhew & Anstis, 1972; Murch, 1976). If a learning account of the contingent effects were appropriate, then contingent effects should be observed regardless of which elements covary.[7] The restriction on the contingent adaptation effects suggests that the effects are rather produced by the sensory fatigue of analyzers that form part of the normally functional perceptual system.

The contingent effects discussed so far have involved covariation between a consonant and vowel. Contingent effects have recently been demonstrated for place of articulation in the context of variations in amplitude (Ganong, 1976) and fundamental frequency (Ades, 1977). Ganong constructed two series of stimuli varying from [boʷ] to [goʷ]. The two series differed from one another in stimulus amplitude. Contingent adaptation effects were observed after adaptation with a high amplitude [goʷ] and a low amplitude [boʷ], such that fewer [g] responses were assigned to the high amplitude [boʷ]-[goʷ] series, while fewer [b] responses were assigned to the low amplitude series. The contingent effect was not observed systematically under all test conditions, however. The presence of a bidirectional contingency in this case is somewhat surprising, given the results of a study by Hillenbrand (1975), who showed that the magnitude of within-series adaptation effects increases as a function of the amplitude of the adaptor.

---

[7]The argument against a learning account is not yet airtight, however, since it is conceivable that associative pairings of two stimulus properties are built up during the adaptation trials only when such properties are temporally overlapping or contiguous, not separated by a vowel, as in the case studied by Miller and Eimas (1976).

Future Research

One particular extension of the contingent adaptation method has not yet been attempted, but may provide a good deal of useful information in future work. This extension is intended to provide information about the bandwidth properties of the adapted site of processing. The work involves systematically narrowing the difference between the two alternating adaptors in successive adaptation tests in order to find out the limits of the contingent effect. In the first contingent adaptation study, the voicing feature of stop consonants were covaried with two very different vowels, [i] and [a], in order to maximize the chance of obtaining a contingent effect. If the difference between the two vowels in the adapting sequence were narrowed successively, by, for example, using the vowel pairs [ɛ]–[i], [I]–[i], and [i]$_1$–[i]$_2$ (where [i]$_1$ and [i]$_2$ contain slightly different formant frequencies, it would be possible to determine the limiting difference between vowels that is sufficient to produce the contingent effect. In turn, it might be possible to determine whether the stage of processing tapped by the procedure involves a small or large number of distinct vowel-contingent channels and whether these channels are narrowly or broadly tuned to a particular range of vowel formant frequencies. This procedure has been used with some success for studying contingent effects in vision (Fidell, 1970; Held & Shattuck, 1971).

chapter four
STOP CONSONANTS AND GLIDES

Study 5*

As noted in Chapter 1, the class of speech sounds known as *stop consonants* consists of sounds that are produced with a complete obstruction of airflow at some location in the supralaryngeal tract. These sounds carry the greatest informational load in English (Denes, 1963), and it is therefore not surprising that a considerable amount of speech research has been aimed at understanding how the perception of individual stop consonants is achieved. Most of this work has focused on the problem of perceptual distinctions between two or more stop consonants.

Comparatively little work has been conducted on the problem of perceiving distinctions between stop consonants and glides that have similar voicing and place of articulation, such as the distinctions between [b] and [w] and between [g] and [j] ([j] as in "yellow"), although these distinctions are also essential for effective communication. Two noteworthy exceptions are the classic study by Liberman, Delattre, Gerstman, and Cooper (1956) for English listeners and a more recent study by Suzuki (1970) for Japanese listeners. In the study of Liberman *et al.*, perceptual distinctions between [bɛ]–[wɛ] and [gɛ]–[jɛ] were examined using synthetically-produced syllables constructed on a pattern playback device (Cooper, Liberman, & Borst, 1951). Liberman *et al.* (1956) generated series of two-formant speech sounds varying from one another only in

---

*Portions of this study are reprinted with permission from *Journal of Experimental Psychology: Human Perception and Performance*, 1976, 2, 92–104; Robert R. Ebert and Ronald A. Cole, coauthors.

the duration and rate of the first- and second-formant transitions. Because the starting frequency and steady-state center frequency for these two formants were held constant, the rate and duration of the formant transitions were negatively covaried.

Liberman et al. (1956) demonstrated that listeners were capable of perceiving the difference between [bɛ] and [wɛ] and between [gɛ] and [jɛ] on the basis of the rate and duration information alone. However, the data for the labial sounds [bɛ] and [wɛ] differed from the data for the velar sounds [gɛ] and [jɛ] in two important respects. First, listeners were capable of distinguishing [bɛ] from [wɛ] on the basis of a much smaller difference in the rate and duration of the formant transitions than was needed to distinguish [gɛ] from [jɛ]. A second difference, of particular relevance to the design of the present study, involved the actual location of the changeover point in the identification responses from stop to glide. For the [bɛ]–[wɛ] weries, this point was located approximately 35 msec of transition duration, whereas for [gɛ]–[jɛ], the changeover point was located at about 60 msec. This labial–velar difference is of interest here because it provides a means of comparison allowing us to test whether the processing of rate and duration information is carried out by a unitary analyzer at some stage of perceptual decoding.

In this study, listener identification tests of the type used by Liberman et al. (1956) were not sufficient to test for the presence of such an analyzer. An adequate test was possible, however, using selective adaptation procedures, in which listeners' perception of speech sounds is examined before and after repetitive listening to a given syllable.

Although the selective adaptation technique seemed well suited to our present purpose, it was necessary also to consider the possibility that repetitive listening to an adapting stimulus might produce shifts in listeners' criteria for identifying the test stimuli, rather than altering the sensitivity of a perceptual analyzer (Green & Swets, 1966; Helson, 1964). Although a number of results suggest that the adaptation technique as used in speech research produces a primary change in listeners' sensitivity (see Cooper, 1975 for a review), we decided to put this matter to a more direct test in Experiment 3 of this study.

EXPERIMENT 1

Method

Subjects. Sixteen Massachusetts Institute of Technology (M.I.T.) undergraduates served as paid volunteers in this experiment. All were native speakers of English and had no history of hearing impairment. The subjects had little or no training in phonetics.

Stimuli. The stimuli consisted of 14 five-formant patterns generated on a digital terminal analog speech synthesizer at the M.I.T. Research Laboratory of Electronics (Klatt, 1973). These stimuli, 7 in the [ba]–[wa] series and 7 in the [ga]–[ja] series, were chosen from a larger set of stimuli on the basis of pilot work showing that these sounds distinguished the stops from glides reliably for author WEC, especially in the case of [ba]–[wa]. The synthetic patterns for stimuli within each of the two series varied from one another only in the duration and rate of the first-, second-, and third-formant transitions. In addition, the stimuli of the labial series differed from those of the velar series in the starting frequency and direction of the second-formant transition, which rose from 759 Hz to 1267 Hz in the case of the labials and fell from 1897 Hz to 1267 Hz for the velars.[1]

The duration of the formant transitions for the [ba]–[wa] series ranged in 5-msec steps from 15 to 45 msec, whereas the transition durations for the [ga]–[ja] series ranged in 5-msec steps from 45 to 75 msec. As in the Liberman *et al.* (1956) study, the starting frequency and steady-state center frequency of each formant were fixed within each series, such that lengthening the transition duration was accompanied by a decrease in the transition rate.

The values of the acoustic parameters which were held constant for all stimuli during the input phase of synthesis were presented in Table 1. Schematic representations of the labial and velar stimuli appear in Figure 1.

With the terminal analog synthesizer used here, as in real speech, increasing the frequency of the first formant results in an accompanying increase of the intenstiy of the first formant as well as higher formants (Fant, 1973, p. 10). Since the first formant frequency rises to its steady-state value more quickly for the [ba] and [ga] members of the test series than for the [wa] and [ja] members, the [ba] and [ga] members contain faster rise times, that is, faster increases in amplitude as a function of time.

Procedure. The experiment consisted of four 1-hour sessions conducted on separate days. In two of the sessions, the subjects listened to the stimuli of the [ba]–[wa] series, and in the other two sessions, they listened to the stimuli of the [ga]–[ja] series. Ten subjects participated in both the [ba]–[wa] and the [ga]–[ja] tests. Three additional subjects took part in the [ba]–[wa] tests only, and the remaining 3 subjects took part in the [ga]–[ja] tests only. Of the 10 subjects who participated in both sets of tests, 5 started with the [ba]–[wa] tests and 5 with the [ga]–[ja] tests. The order of presentation of the two tests within the [ba]–[wa] and [ga]–[ja] sets was also counterbalanced across the subjects.

[1]The starting frequenices of the second- and third-formants for stimuli of the [ga]–[ja] series were 1897 Hz and 2028 Hz, respectively, sufficiently close to one another to simulate a plosive burst (Fant, 1973, p. 9). Because the simulated burst was the same for all members of the velar test series, its net effect was presumably to bias perception slightly toward the [g] category (see later discussion).

Table 1
Acoustic Parameters for the [ba]–[wa] Stimuli of Experiment 1

Parameter	Time	Value
Fundamental frequency	0– 15	off
	20– 95	122 Hz
	295–	90 Hz
First-formant frequency	0– 20	297 Hz
	50–295	739 Hz
Second-formant frequency	0– 20	a
	50–295	1,267 Hz
Third-formant frequency	0– 20	2,028 Hz
	50–295	2,439 Hz
Fourth-formant frequency	0–295	3,500 Hz
Fifth-formant frequency	0–295	4,500 Hz
Amplitude of voicing	0– 15	off
	20	57 dB.
	55–195	60 dB.
	270	52 dB.
	275–295	off
First-formant bandwidth	0–295	50 Hz
Second-formant bandwidth	0–295	70 Hz
Third-formant bandwidth	0–295	110 Hz
Fourth-formant bandwidth	0–295	170 Hz
Fifth-formant bandwidth	0–295	250 Hz

Note. The time values represent the specific times used for stimuli containing formant transitions of 30 msec. Other stimuli were constructed by altering the onset time of the steady-state portions of the first three formants. All changes in the value of a parameter as a function of time are linear.

aSee text for different values for labial and velar stimuli.

Each test session began with a warm-up period during which the subjects simply listened to a random sequence of the speech sounds. The subjects were then presented—first, a baseline test in which the subjects identified random sequences of the stimuli in the unadapted state, and second, an adaptation test in which the subjects identified the same stimuli after repetitive listening to a single syllable chosen from one of the extreme ends of the test series being identified.

For the [ba]–[wa] tests, the baseline included 10 presentations of each of the 7 [ba]–[wa] stimuli, with an interstimulus interval of 2.5 sec. The subjects identified each stimulus by writing "B" or "W" on their answer sheets. The stimuli were played to the listeners at approximately 70dB re 10 μN/m² via Telex headphones from the output of an Ampex PR-10 tape recorder and an AR amplifier. A rest period was provided after half of the test presentations.

The adaptation subtest of each session consisted of periods of repetitive listening to either [ba] or [wa] end points (the stimuli containing transitions having a duration of 15 msec or 45 msec, respectively), followed by presentation of test sounds taken from the same [ba]–[wa] series, to be identified as in the baseline test. Each adaptation subtest consisted of 18 adaptation trials. On each trial, the subjects were first presented 40 repetitions of the adapting stimulus, with an interrepetition interval of 350 msec. Following this period of repetitive listening, 4 stimuli were presented for identification. These stimuli were chosen randomly from the [ba]–[wa] test series. The first of these 4 stimuli was presented 2.5 sec after the final repetition of the adapting stimulus, and the remaining 3 test stimuli followed at 2.5-sec intervals. Five seconds elapsed between the presentation of the last of the 4 test items and the beginning of the next adaptation trial. A 5-min rest period was provided after 9 of the 18 adaptation trials. With this procedure, a total of 10 identification responses was obtained for each of the 7 [ba]–[wa] test stimuli after adapatation, as in the baseline test. Two extra stimuli were identified in the adaptation tests in order to make a total of 72 test presentations, 4 on each trial.

All timing intervals were specified by computer, and the stimulus presentations for each test session were recorded onto magnetic tape. The procedures of

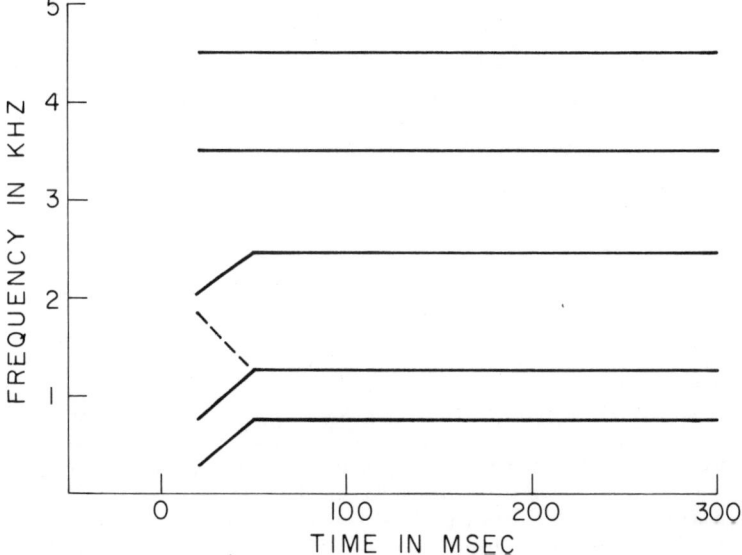

Figure 1. Schematic representations of the labial and velar test stimuli used in Experiment 1. A labial stimulus is represented by the solid lines, denoting the frequency values of the formant transitions and steady-state formants. The difference between the labial stimulus and the velar stimulus is represented by the dotted line, corresponding to the frequency of the second-formant transition for the velar stimulus.

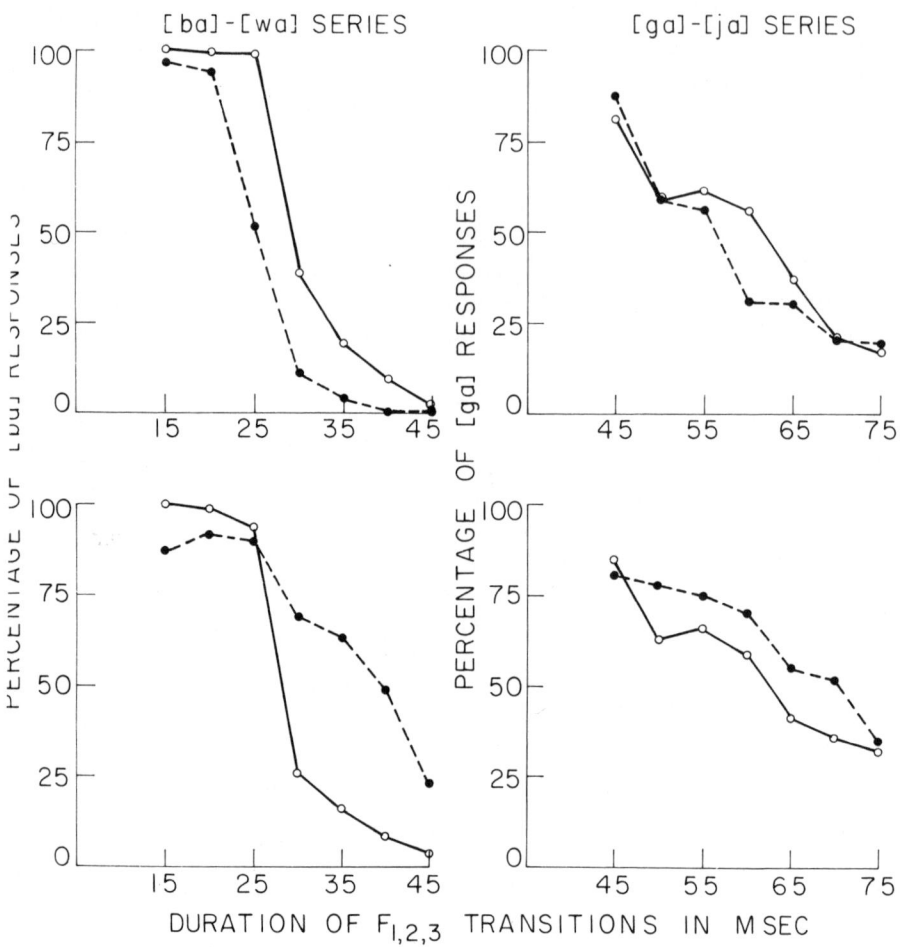

Figure 2. Pooled percentage of [b] and [g] responses in each test condition of Experiment 1. Solid lines denote the identification functions obtained in the unadapted state, whereas dotted lines denote the identification functions obtained after adaptation. The dotted curve on the top left graph represents the function obtained after [ba] adaptation, and the dotted curve on the bottom left graph represents the function obtained after [wa] adaptation. Similarly, the dotted curve on the top right graph represents the function obtained after [ga] adaptation, and the dotted curve on the bottom right graph represents the function obtained after [ja] adaptation.

the [ga]–[ja] sessions were identical to those of the [ba]–[wa] sessions, except for the test series stimuli ([ga]–[ja]) and the adapting stimuli, consisting of the [ga]–[ja] end point members (the stimuli containing transition durations of 45 msec and 75 msec, respectively).

Results and Discussion

The results appear in Figure 2, where the pooled identification responses for the listeners are presented for the baseline and adaptation conditions. In addition, phonetic boundaries were computed by a least-mean squares analysis for each individual listener in each [ba]-[wa] test condition.

The results of the baseline tests indicated that the duration and rate of the formant transitions sufficiently distinguished [b] from [w], as demonstrated in the prior work of Liberman et al. (1956). For the [ga]-[ja] series, listeners were unable to categorize the stimuli as distinctively as for the [ba]-[wa] series, also in accordance with earlier work.

The results of the selective adaptation tests showed the presence of systematic shifts in the listeners' identification of stimuli for both the [ba]-[wa] and the [ga]-[ja] series. For the [ba]-[wa] series, listeners assigned fewer identification responses to the [b] category after adaptation with [ba] in comparison with the baseline measure obtained during the same test session. This effect was obtained for each of the 13 subjects tested with the [ba]-[wa] series, and the effect, as measured in terms of a shift in the phonetic boundary, was statistically significant (mean shift = 5.85 msec; $t(12) = 6.268$, $p < 0.001$; two-tailed t-test for correlated observations). After adaptation with [wa], listeners assigned fewer responses to the [w] category in comparison with the baseline measure obtained during that session. This effect was observed for 12 of the 13 subjects tested, and, as in the case of [ba] adaptation, the effect was statistically significant as measured in terms of shift of the phonetic boundary (mean shift = -7.97 msec; $t(12) = -5.172$, $p < 0.001$; two-tailed t-test for correlated observations). The oppositely-directed shifts in the [ba]-[wa] identification functions after adaptation with [ba] vs. [wa] are like the effects obtained for consonant distinctions in previous adaptation work, in which fewer identification responses were assigned to the category of the adapting stimulus following adaptation. The bidirectionality of the present effects indicates that the effects probably operate on an opponent-process system of perceptual analysis, of the same general type proposed for voiced-voiceless distinctions in Chapter 5.

Systematic effects of selective adaptation were also observed for the [ga]-[ja] stimuli, after repetitive listening to [ga] and [ja].[2] As can be seen in Figure 2, repetitive listening to [ga] resulted in fewer [g] responses in compari-

---

[2]We have noted a strong positive correlation between subjects' identification of the adapting stimulus in the unadapted state and performance following adaptation. For example, subjects who identified the [ga] adapting stimulus as [ga] 100% of the time in the unadapted state produced relatively large effects of adaptation after repetitive listening to this stimulus, whereas subjects who identified the [ga] adaptor as [ga] less than 100% of the time in the unadapted state showed relatively small effects of adaptation. Two subjects identified the [ga] adaptor more often as [ja] in the unadapted state, and both of these subjects showed adaptation effects opposite in direction from the group as a whole. The presence of this correlation, noted also in a recent study of place of articulation for stop consonants (Diehl, 1975), does not, however, provide evidence favoring any particular site of the adaptation effect, as Diehl suggests. Individual differences in the operation of either relatively low- or high-level property detectors may account for the correlation.

son with the baseline results, whereas repetitive listening to [ja] resulted in fewer [j] responses. In the case of both the [ba]-[wa] and [ga]-[ja] series, the magnitude of the shift for each adaptation condition as measured in terms of the phonetic boundary was between 5 and 10 msec of transition duration for most subjects.

Besides calculating the phonetic boundaries for the [ba]-[wa] tests, we also computed the slopes of the least-mean squares fit for each subject in each test condition. The pooled data indicated that the mean slopes before and after adaptation with [ba] were -0.42 and -0.31, respectively, whereas the mean slopes before and after adaptation with [wa] were -0.27 and -0.12, respectively. The slope decline in the case of [wa] adaptation was statistically significant, $t(12) = 3.68, p < 0.01$, and examination of Figure 2 reveals a similar slope change for [ja] adaptation.

Earlier work with the selective adaptation technique revealed no systematic slope changes in the case of voiced-voiceless distinctions among top consonants (Eimas, Cooper, & Corbit, 1973). The theoretical importance of the decline in slope observed after adaptation here remains uncertain. Although the finding may at first glance appear to have some bearing on the issue of whether repetitive listening induces a primary effect of sensory fatigue as opposed to a shift in response criterion, the slope decline can, in fact, be accounted for by either possibility, depending on how the precise form of the fatigue or criterion shift is viewed with respect to the system of perceptual analysis and decision making under consideration. At present we must thus be content to acknowledge that the slope data may provide some information about the nature of the adaptation effect when some other currently unknown properties of the perceptual and decision-making systems are better understood.

EXPERIMENT 2

Given the results of Experiment 1, it became possible to test whether an analyzer exists which processes rate/duration information about the formant transitions for speech sounds having different places of articulation, and, if so, whether the analyzer processes this information for labial and velar sounds in precisely the same fashion. In an attempt to answer the first of these questions, crossed-adaptation experiments were conducted in which velar adapting stimuli were employed in conjunction with labial test stimuli. The subjects listened to repetitions of either [ga] or [ja] and then identified stimuli from the [ba]-[wa] test series. The existence of crossed-adaptation effects in this context would suggest the presence of a unitary rate/duration analyzer.

By careful selection of the acoustic parameters of the [ga] adapting stimuli, it was also possible to determine whether the rate and duration information is processed in precisely the same manner for labial and velar sounds. We chose two [ga] stimuli which contained formant transitions having an absolute duration of 35 msec, identical to the transition duration for one of the [wa] members of the labial test series. If the adaptation effect operates on an analyzer which computes the absolute rate and duration information of the transitions, wholly independent of place of articulation, then the direction of effect for the [ga] adapting stimuli should be in the same direction as that obtained in Experiment 1 for the adapting stimulus [wa]—namely, fewer [w] responses. If, on the other hand, the adaptation effect operates on an analyzer that computes the rate and duration information differently for labials and velars, such that, for example, the velar transitions are computed at a slower clock rate (see the results and discussion section), then adaptation with the [ga] stimuli should produce an effect like that produced in Experiment 1 after adaptation with [ba]—namely, fewer [b] responses. In the following experiment we tested these alternative hypotheses, which, although oversimplified, provide a first approximation to the types of stop-glide analysis we shall need to consider later on.

Method

Subjects. Twenty-eight M.I.T. undergraduates participated in the experiment, including 10 subjects who had participated in Experiment 1. The new subjects had the same qualifications as those who had served previously.

Stimuli. The test stimuli consisted of the seven [ba]-[wa] stimuli used in Experiment 1. Four adapting stimuli were employed, consisting of the [ja] adaptor used in Experiment 1, with transition duration of 75 msec, two [ga] adaptors, with transition duration of 35 msec, and an isolated [a] adaptor, whose steady-state formant frequencies matched those of the stimuli used in Experiment 1. The amplitude of voicing excitation for the isolated vowel adaptor, as for the other stimuli, rose from 57 to 60 dB within the first 35 msec of the stimulus (in terms of the synthesis input parameter value), and the overall duration of the stimulus was 255 msec (see Table 1).

The two [ga] adaptors differed from each other in the starting frequencies of the second- and third-formant transitions and hence differed in the rate of these transitions as well. One [ga] adaptor, which we denote as [ga]$_1$, contained starting frequencies equivalent to those used in the [ga]-[ja] series of Experiment 1. These starting frequencies were 1897 Hz and 2028 Hz for the second and third formants respectively, sufficiently close to one another in frequency to simulate a plosive burst (Fant, 1973, p. 9), since the intensity of each formant increased 6 dB per halving of the distance between them. Examination of short-time spectra indicated the presence of a low-intensity burst for [ga]$_1$ in the Formant$_2$-Formant$_3$ region.

To test the effect of removing this burst, a second [ga] adaptor, [ga]$_2$, was constructed which contained second- and third-formant starting frequencies of

1651 Hz and 2150 Hz, respectively. Although short-time spectra revealed that the intensity in the region of the second and third formants was still higher during the initial portion of the formant transitions for [ga]$_2$ than for members of the [ba]–[wa] series, the intenstiy of this region for [ga]$_2$ was less than for either [ga]$_1$ or the [ja] adaptor.

Procedure. The experiment consisted of four 1-hour sessions. In each session, 2 subtests were conducted—a baseline test for assessing the listeners' identification of the [ba]–[wa] stimuli as in Experiment 1 and an adaptation test in which the [ba]–[wa] stimuli were identified after periods of repetitive listening to one of the four adapting stimuli: [ja], [ga]$_1$, [ga]$_2$, or [a]. Each of these adaptation tests was conducted using the same test format as in Experiment 1. Sixteen subjects participated in the sessions involving adaptation with [ja], [ga]$_2$, and [a], whereas 22 subjects participated in the session involving adaptation with [ga]$_1$.

Results and Discussion

The phonetic boundaries for each test condition were computed for each listener, and statistical tests were then applied to these boundary values to determine the significance of adaptation effects in comparison with baseline performance. The slopes of the pooled identification response functions were equivalent to those obtained previously for the [ba]–[wa] test series in Experiment 1.

After adaptation with [ja], listeners assigned somewhat fewer identification responses to the [w] category (mean boundary shift = 0.79 msec). However, the shift in the phonetic boundary was not statistically significant, $t(15) = -1.23, p > 0.20$. After adaptation with the [ga]$_1$ and [ga]$_2$ adapting stimuli, on the other hand, listeners assigned fewer responses to the [b] category, and statistical analysis of the phonetic boundaries showed these effects to be significant (for [ga]$_1$: mean shift = 2.02 msec; $t(21) = 2.19, p < 0.05$) and for [ga]$_2$: mean shift = 3.10 msec; $t(15) = 2.164, p < 0.02$). The direction of each of the effects for both [ga] adaptors was like that produced in Experiment 1 after adaptation with [ba], and thus opposite in direction from the effect produced after adaptation with [wa].

The results for the [ga] adaptors suggest that adaptation operates on an analyzer which processes rate and duration information for both labial and velar consonants, yet processes this information slightly differently for the two types. Two possible means of operation can be suggested for such an analyzer. On one hand, the analyzer might operate on analysis-by-synthesis principles (Stevens, 1972), whereby speech sounds are identified with reference to the central motor commands utilized for their articulation. This analysis-by-synthesis scheme can account for the longer duration of transitions required for a perceptual changeover with velar stimuli (cf. Experiment 1, Figure 2) and for the adaptation results of Experiment 2 because in speech production the formant transitions are longer for velars than for labials. It is by no means certain, however, that the difference observed in speech production arises at the level of central motor commands, since a difference in the peripheral sluggishness of the labial versus velar articulators may wholly account for the longer transitions accompanying velars.

A second possibility, suggested by Stevens (personal communication), is that the auditory system at Level B (in the model of Chapter 1) clocks the transition durations at a slower rate in the case of the velar stimuli because the formant transitions for these sounds move in different directions along the frequency dimension (see Figure 1), unlike the case for labial sounds. If the clock rate is slower for velar transitions, longer formant transitions would be required for velar than for labial stimuli in order to register the same duration of transitions according to the clock. The present results could be accounted for by assuming that the adaptation effects operate at a level of integrative processing for labial and velar sounds subsequent to this clock computation. The level of analysis that undergoes adaptation would consist of two analyzers, for short and long transition durations, and the sensitivity of the two analyzers would be assumed partially to overlap one another. Although no available psychoacoustic evidence exists to support the basic premise of a difference in clock rate as a function of transition direction in the frequency domain, the present schema does represent one plausible alternative to the analysis-by synthesis routine, and experiments can be conducted to test this schema empirically.

Before leaving the discussion of the [ga] adaptation effects, one other possible account must be considered which involves the analysis of amplitude changes during the formant transition period of the syllables. We noted earlier that a rather abrupt increase in amplitude in the F_2–F_3 region exists for the [ga]–[ja] stimuli and that the amplitude in this region at the onset of the syllable was greater for [ga]$_1$ and [ja] adaptors than for the [ga]$_2$ adaptor in the present experiment. These differences would be unimportant in the present context were it not as noted in the description of the stimuli in Experiment 1, that differences in rise time also exist within the [ba]–[wa] test series, as a consequence of the differences in the rate of the formant transitions of the test series members. Since the first formant changes more rapidly for the [ba] members of the [ba]–[wa] series, the amplitude in the F_2–F_3 region also increases more abruptly, thus opening up the possibility that adaptation with [ga]$_1$ and [ga]$_2$ affects an analyzer sensitive to abrupt amplitude increases in the F_2–F_3 region, rather than affecting an analyzer sensitive to information about rate and duration of the formant transitions. The rise-time account, however, cannot readily explain the results of the [ja] adaptation test. Since the [ja] stimulus contained more energy in the F_2–F_3 region than [ga]$_2$ at syllable onset, it should have been a more effective adaptor than [ga]$_2$ for the [ba] members of the test series, according to the rise-time hypothesis. However, the [ja] adaptor produced a weak effect in the opposite direction from [ga]$_1$ and [ga]$_2$, supporting the view that adaptation operates primarily on an analyzer for rate and duration information rather than rise time in the F$_2$–F$_3$ region. On similar grounds, it is highly unlikely that the present effects can be attributed to adaptation of an analyzer sensitive to information contained in the overall envelope of the syllable (i.e., information concerning amplitude over the entire frequency range as a function of time [cf. Cole & Scott, 1974]).

Adaptation with the isolated vowel [a] also produced a significant effect on the perception of the [ba]–[wa] stimuli, in the same direction as the effect produced in this experiment by [ga]$_1$ and [ga]$_2$ and by the [ba] adaptor in Experiment 1 (mean boundary shift = 3.04 msec, $t(15) = 3.21, p < 0.01$. This effect was somewhat surprising, although by no means implausible, since repetitive listening to an isolated vowel often produces a perceptual illusion of a [b] + vowel syllable (Goldstein & Lackner, 1973, and reports of our own listeners). This illusion may be partly attributable to the relatively abrupt increase in the amplitude of voicing excitation over a broad frequency range at the beginning of the isolated vowel, possibly simulating the broad-band plosive burst found for [b] in real speech (Cooper, Delattre, Liberman, Borst, & Gerstman, 1952). This simulation of a plosive burst for the [a] adaptor might account for the present effect on the [ba]–[wa] test series and at the same time account for the absence of vowel adaptation effects for test series which are comprised of stop consonants (Study 2, Leiter, 1974).

EXPERIMENT 3

In order to determine whether the previously observed effects of adaptation are primarily due to changes in the sensitivity of perceptual analyzers rather than changes in response criterion, it is appropriate to apply a signal detectability analysis. Although the phoneme identification task used in Experiments 1 and 2 was not suitable for such an analysis, a relatively simple modification of the task, used recently by Klatt and Cooper (1975), and suggested for use here by W. F. Ganong, enabled us to study the sensitivity-criterion issue. The modification involves requiring subjects to respond by assigning numbers ranging from 1 through 7 to the test stimuli rather than by merely identifying the stimuli phonemically. This task represents a special case of magnitude estimation known as *absolute identification* (Durlach & Braida, 1972). By analyzing the data for this task in terms of a variant of signal detectability theory, it is possible to determine d' values for adjacent stimuli in the test series to assess whether the listeners' sensitivity changes as a function of selective adaptation.

Method

Subjects. Seventeen M.I.T. undergraduates served as paid volunteers in this experiment. All subjects had the same qualifications as the subjects in Experiments 1 and 2.

Stimuli. The stimuli consisted of the seven [ba]–[wa] stimuli used in Experiment 1.

Procedure. The experiment consisted of two 1-hour sessions conducted on separate days. Each test session began with a warm-up period as in previous work. The subjects were then instructed to practice responding to the [ba]–[wa] stimuli using the integers 1 through 7. The subjects were told to assign 1 to a stimulus that sounded like an exceptionally clear [ba] and to assign 7 to a stimulus that sounded like an exceptionally clear [wa]. The subjects were not told how many different stimuli were contained in the presentations but were told to attempt to use each of the 7 numbers in responding. Subjects practiced assigning numbers to the stimuli until they could do so in a fairly automatic fashion. The practice period generally lasted about 15 min. Following this period, subjects were presented an absolute identification test in which they were instructed to respond with the numbers 1 through 7 to a randomized series of the [ba]–[wa] stimuli, containing 10 presentations of each of the 7 test stimuli. The interstimulus interval was 2.5 sec. Stimuli were played to listeners using the same procedures as in the baseline tests of Experiments 1 and 2.

Following this baseline test for absolute identification, the subjects were presented the same task after periods of repetitive listening to either the [ba] or [wa] end point members of the [ba]–[wa] series. The two adaptation tests were conducted in different sessions. Each adaptation test consisted of 18 trials and was conducted in the format used for the adaptation tests of Experiment 1, with the sole exception that, in the present tests, subjects responded using the integers 1 through 7 rather than the phoneme labels "B" and "W."

All 17 subjects participated in the test session with [ba] adaptation, and 16 of these subjects also participated in the test session with [wa] adaptation. Eight of the subjects took the [ba] adaptation test first, and 8 others took the [wa] adaptation test first.

Results and Discussion

The pooled data for each test condition are presented in the formant of 7 × 7 confusion matrices in Table 2. Although the analysis of absolute identification data is normally performed for individual subjects, we chose to conduct an

Table 2
Confusion Matrices of Pooled Absolute Identification Data for Each Test Condition of Experiment 3

Stimulus	_____ Response _____						
	1	2	3	4	5	6	7
Baseline before [ba] adaptation							
1	94	53	14	2	4	1	2
2	97	48	12	7	5	0	1
3	49	67	28	13	9	1	3
4	6	14	23	37	36	34	20
5	3	8	9	32	50	44	24
6	0	6	4	27	42	51	40
7	1	2	8	19	28	44	68
After [ba] adaptation							
1	89	38	20	16	4	3	0
2	52	49	34	15	12	6	2
3	28	37	27	34	23	16	5
4	7	2	19	29	40	40	33
5	1	3	9	31	42	46	38
6	1	1	8	25	39	55	41
7	0	0	6	21	28	53	62
Baseline before [wa] adaptation							
1	82	46	21	9	1	0	1
2	57	52	31	18	2	0	0
3	27	62	43	10	10	5	3
4	1	11	18	31	54	28	17
5	0	7	15	29	47	41	21
6	3	1	4	29	38	52	33
7	0	2	10	19	28	51	50
After [wa] adaptation							
1	81	42	14	13	7	1	2
2	67	50	19	12	6	2	4
3	63	55	26	7	2	5	2
4	12	44	31	21	28	15	9
5	9	20	24	25	37	28	17
6	6	7	25	32	33	39	18
7	7	5	9	24	34	40	41

analysis of the pooled data here because the individual subjects' data differed only slightly from one another.

The confusion matrix data were analyzed in terms of a model of signal detectability (Durlach & Braida, 1969), in which, given certain assumptions which appear to hold for the present data,[3] it is possible to obtain estimates of listeners' sensitivity that correspond to the estimates of d' obtained in a two-interval discrimination task. The model is applied to the present situation as follows. It is assumed that the duration of formant transitions (D) results in a sensation magnitude (x). When noise and other factors are considered, the distribution of the sensation magnitudes (x) which results from the physical duration (D) is normally distribution with a mean of $\mu(D)$ and a standard deviation of σ. The stimuli $I = 1, 2 \ldots, 7$ have different transition durations (D^I) which produce different average sensation magnitudes, termed $\mu(D^I)$. It is assumed, however, that the standard deviations of the x distributions are not a function of D^I.

The listeners are assumed to compare the sensation magnitude (x) of a given stimulus with six criterion thresholds and to determine a response (R) on the basis of the number of thresholds that are exceeded plus one. The criterion threshold locations as determined by the model are optimized to take into account the response bias of the average subject.

Using the confusion matrix data of Table 2, it is possible to estimate the six criterion thresholds and the six differences between adjacent sensation magnitude means. If the standard deviation is normalized to be 1.0, the difference between the adjacent means is equal to d', the standard measure of stimulus discriminability. A d' value of 1.0 calculated in this fashion would indicate that the adjacent stimuli could be discriminated from one another 75% of the time in a two-interval discrimination test. In the present case, d' values were obtained and then converted into just noticeable differences (JNDs), measured in milliseconds of transition duration, by simply dividing the difference in the duration of the transitions for adjacent stimuli (5 msec in each case) by the d' value for the stimulus pair. The d' and JND values for each pair of adjacent stimuli in the [ba]–[wa] series are presented in Table 3 for each of the four test conditions. In addition, a graph of the d' values appears in Figure 3.

Inspection of Table 3 and Figure 3 reveals the presence of substantial changes in listeners' sensitivity following repetitive listening in both adaptation tests. For many pairs of adjacent stimuli, the JND values obtained before and after adaptation differ by about a factor of 2. These results appear to warrant the conclusion that a primary alteration in listeners' sensitivity accompanies a selective adaptation to speech sounds. Although an independent effect of response

---

[3]The fit between the model and the present data was assessed for each of the four test conditions. The actual confusion matrices were compared with matrices expected on the basis of the model, and chi-square values were then obtained to determine the closeness of the match between the actual and predicted matrices for each column in each confusion matrix. The chi-square values indicated that the fit between the model and the data was adequate for more than 75% of the columns.

Table 3
Values of d' and Just Noticeable Difference (JND) for Each Stimulus Pair (in milliseconds) Calculated for Each Test Condition of Experiment 3

Stimulus pair	[ba]		[wa]	
	d'	JND	d'	JND
Baseline before adaptation				
1–2	.0312	160.26	.2763	18.10
2–3	.5239	9.54	.5412	9.24
3–4	1.4223	3.52	1.3636	3.67
4–5	.3192	15.66	.2125	23.53
5–6	.3276	15.26	.3467	14.42
6–7	.2372	21.08	.1586	31.53
After adaptation				
1–2	.4512	11.08	.1736	28.80
2–3	.5258	9.51	a	a
3–4	1.0397	4.81	.9707	5.15
4–5	.2621	19.08	.4169	11.99
5–6	.1647	30.36	.2213	22.59
6–7	.2684	18.36	.2903	17.22

*The calculated d' for this stimulus pair was −.0929, indicating that the higher-numbered stimulus (3) was assigned slightly lower numbers on the average than the lower-numbered stimulus (2), providing one case in which the fit between the data and the detection model was quite poor.

bias is also induced by the selective adaptation procedure as used in these tests,[4] we will restrict our concern here to accounting for the rather large effects which have been demonstrated for listeners' sensitivity.

First, it is useful to compare the overall sensitivity obtained for the [ba]–

[4]The six criterion values were estimated in terms of the Durlach and Braida (1969) decision model, and it was found that the criterion values decreased systematically after adaptation with either [ba] or [wa], with respect to the criterion values of the baseline conditions. It thus appears that a general response bias effect exists but that this effect is quite different from the effects observed in the phoneme identification task, where shifts in the phoneme boundary occur in opposite directions after adaptation with [ba] versus [wa]. Further work will be required to provide an account of this bias effect.

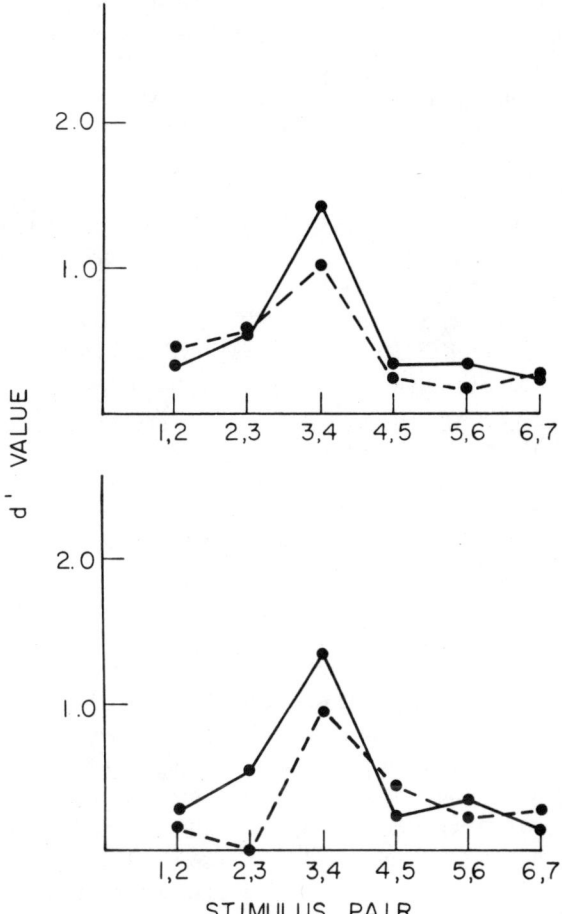

Figure 3. d' values for the six different stimulus pair before and after adaptation. The upper graph shows the d' values before adaptation (solid line) and after adaptation (dotted line) with [ba]. The lower graph shows the d' values before adaptation (solid line) and after adaptation (dotted line) with [wa].

[wa] stimuli, as reflected in the cumulative d' values. In both the [ba] and [wa] adaptation tests, the cumulative d' is less than the cumulative d' obtained in the baseline test for the same session. The decline in cumulative d' is small in the case of [ba] adaptation, going from 2.86 before adaptation to 2.71 after adaptation. The decline is more pronounced in the case of [wa] adaptation, going from 2.90 to 1.98. Both of these results indicate the presence of a general decline in sensitivity following adaptation.

If we now consider the d' values obtained for individual stimulus pairs in the different tests, it is immediately evident that the listeners' sensitivity to different stimulus pairs is not equivalent but that subjects in each test condition are more sensitive to the difference between Stimuli 3 and 4 than for any other adjacent pair of stimuli, by about a net factor of 2. The stimulus pair 3–4 corresponds to the region of the phonetic boundary between [ba] and [wa] as determined in the baseline tests of phoneme identification in Experiment 1 (see Figure 2), and it is thus likely that the heightened d' value obtained for this pair represents an instance of the tendency toward categorical perception (Liberman, Harris, Hoffman, & Griffith, 1957). Recall from Chapter 1 that categorical perception is the term used to describe a situation in which a listener can reliably discriminate two stimuli only to the extent that he can assign these stimuli to different phoneme categories in an identification task. By applying the formula used by Liberman *et al.* (1957) for deriving predicted discrimination functions from obtained identification functions, given the assumption of strictly categorical perception, we noted that the fit between the identification data in the baseline test of Experiment 1 and the JND values of the present baseline test is quite close. In the case of the [ba] and [wa] adaptation tests, however, discriminability between Stimuli 3–4 should not be significantly better than between Stimuli 2–3; nevertheless, it is, so we cannot conclude that the present JND values obtained after adaptation are closely predicted by the identification data of Experiment 1, given the assumption of categorical perception.

3–4 decrease after adaptation with both [ba] and [wa]. The d' value before and after [ba] adaptation decreases from 1.42 to 1.04, whereas the d' value before and after [wa] adaptation decreases from 1.35 to 0.97. These decreases in sensitivity provide another indication that repetitive listening produces a general decline in the sensitivity of a perceptual analyzing system.

Although the most discriminable stimulus pair 3–4 shows a decline in discriminability following adaptation, even after adaptation this stimulus pair was the most discriminable of the [ba]–[wa] series. The absence of a shift in the most discriminable pair after adaptation does not, however, indicate the absence of adaptation effects. Earlier adaptation work of Eimas and Corbit (1973) and in Study 1 showed shifts in discriminability peaks after adaptation for [ba]–[p^{h}a] and [bæ]–[dæ]–[gæ] test stimuli, respectively, but in these cases peak shifts were to be expected on the basis of the differential labeling results of phoneme identification experiments. As a close examination of the formula for deriving predicted discrimination functions (Liberman *et al.*, 1957) will show, such peak shifts would not be expected in this case, given the identification results of Experiment 1. What does appear relevant to the present discussion of adaptation effects is the decline in d' values after selective adaptation.

When the baseline and adaptation values of d' are compared for other individual stimulus pairs, the direction of change in sensitivity differs, depending on the stimulus pair and the particular adaptation condition. For the [ba] adaptation test, repetitive listening produced a sizeable decrease in sensitivity for the stimulus pair 5-6, whereas it produced a sizeable increase in sensitivity for the stimulus pair 1-2. For [wa] adaptation, on the other hand, repetitive listening produced a sizable decrease in sensitivity for the stimulus pairs 1-2, 2-3, and 5-6, whereas it produced a sizable increase in sensitivity for the pairs 4-5 and 6-7.

At present, it is not possible to provide a detailed account of these various directions of change in listeners' sensitivity. One strong possibility is that the increased sensitivity following adaptation for a pair of stimuli including or neighboring the adapting stimulus reflects the listeners' heightened ability to utilize the adapting stimulus as an anchor, or reference stimulus, in assigning members to the stimuli after adaptation (cf. Helson, 1964). Decreased sensitivity, on the other hand, can in many cases be attributed to a decline in differential labeling ability, as evidenced by Experiment 1, coupled with the assumption of categorical perception. This possibility may also account for the increase in sensitivity observed for the stimulus pair 6-7 after [wa] adaptation, since in Experiment 1 it was found that both stimuli were labeled [wa] at least 95% of the time before adaptation but that Stimulus 6 was labeled [ba] 50% of the time (vs. 25% for Stimulus 7) after adaptation with [wa] (see Figure 2). Although much further work is required before the individual instances of sensitivity increase and decrease can be accounted for, it appears from the preliminary analysis given here that work along these lines might eventually lead to a more detailed characterization of both the sensitivity properties of speech analyzers and the nature of adaptation effects.

Postscript to Study 5

Related Studies

Two other studies of the stop-glide distinction were conducted elsewhere about the same time as the present work (Bailey, 1975; Diehl, 1976). Both authors replicated the basic findings of Experiment 1 and conducted additional crossed-adaptation tests. Bailey constructed an unorthodox set of stimuli varying from [bo] to [wa] by varying the duration and extent of the formant transitions. The use of different vowel environments within the series was employed to keep the rate of the formant transitions constant, a control which cannot be achieved using a single vowel. Unfortunately, the listeners' responses to the [bo]-[wa] stimuli were highly variable in the baseline test, and no significant adaptation effects were found.

The failure of this experiment points up a general difficulty faced in current work on the perceptual relevance of various acoustic cues. As we have already noted for the feature voicing, a number of acoustic cues may covary during normal speech to signal a particular feature distinction. For the stop-glide distinction, we find covariation among the rate, duration, acceleration, extent, and rise-time of the formant transitions. A priori, it appears useful to try to isolate and test the separate effects of each of these potential cues, as Bailey had planned (a similar project was undertaken in our laboratory to test the individual effects of acceleration of the formant transitions, but listener responses were highly variable). Yet it is quite possible that this kind of enterprise fails in some cases simply because the acoustic cues are detected jointly *rather than* separately by the perceptual system.

In another study, Diehl (1976) conducted crossed-adaptation tests using nonspeech adaptors with a [ba]-[wa] test series. One nonspeech adaptor contained a fast rise-time to peak amplitude and was perceived as a plucked note; the other contained a slower rise-time and was perceived as a bowed note (see Cutting & Rosner, 1974, for another study of such stimuli). The two adaptors produced oppositely-directed effects on the [ba]-[wa] series. The plucked note produced fewer [b] responses, while the bowed note produced fewer [w]s. The crossed-adaptation results can be attributed directly to adaptation of a detector for rise-time information, since the [ba]-[wa] test stimuli also differed systematically in rise-time from fast to slow. The results do indicate that the use of a speech adapting stimulus is not necessary for producing adaptation effects for a speech test series (see also Tartter & Eimas, 1975).

The Present Study Reconsidered

In a review of speech adaptation work, Ades (1976) expressed the opinion that the present study provides "the best evidence for phonetic level adaptation." He goes on to remark, however, that the demonstration is less than satisfactory because the [ga] adaptor in Experiment 2 may have contained a burst-like onset, rendering it acoustically more similar to the [b] members of the test series. This issue was in fact discussed in our report. Ades fails to consider that, as noted earlier, both the [ga] and [ja] adaptors of Experiment 2 contained identical onset characteristics, yet produced effects in opposite directions. Any similarity between the onset characteristics of the adaptors and test series members cannot in itself provide an account of the adaptation effects. A phonetic interpretation can still be avoided, however, if it is assumed that (1) the small amplitude burst at stimulus onset for both [ga] and [ja] produced a slight adaptation effect on the [b] members of the test series, (2), the duration of the formant transitions for the adaptors exerted another, larger effect of adaptation, with the long transitions of [ja] producing an effect on the [w] members that overrode the effect produced by the burst onset. In view of the small amplitude of the burst onset, it is considered improbable that any adaptation effect for the burst occurred. In any event, the results of Experiment 2 have served to narrow the range of plausible interpretations about the operation of stop-glide detectors.

The results of Experiment 3 on sensory vs. bias effects also deserve further discussion. As noted in Footnotes 3 and 4, the data for this experiment were compared with a decision model of Braida and Durlach (1972). The results for the stimulus pair at the phoneme boundary are adequately modeled, but the fit between data and model was quite poor for stimulus pairs near the endpoint values. For this reason, attention was focused on the d' results for the boundary pair. Recently, Sawusch (1976) has criticized this experiment on the basis of the poor fit for Stimulus Pair 1, which included the [b] endpoint. But, the criticism does not apply to the boundary pair, where the systematic effects for d' were observed, and the results for this pair still appear to provide support for the presence of sensory effects. Alternatively, as suggested by W. F. Ganong (personal communication), it is conceivable that the rating responses obtained near the phoneme boundary are themselves mediated by bias. Ganong and Cooper (1974) tried unsuccessfully to apply a simpler procedure to the problem of measuring sensory vs. bias components of the adaptation effect. A listener's threshold for identifying [ba] vs. [a] or [da] vs. [a] was tested by varying the amplitude of the formant transition portion of a [ba] or [da] syllable. Once a baseline threshold was determined, we hoped to test for a difference in threshold following adaptation with either of these CV syllables. Extensive testing of one listener, however, indicated that a stable baseline threshold could not be maintained. Interestingly, the listener's judgments for identifying a stimulus as [ba] or [da] vs. [a] changed virtually 100% over a change in the amplitude of the formant transitions amounting to no more than 1 dB. Our failure to apply this procedure further was due to the lack of a stable baseline and of a sufficiently wide range of amplitudes for which the listener produced some uncertainty in responding. But other methods of determining thresholds may still provide an appropriate means of testing for sensory and bias effects. It should be noted, however, that studies of *absolute* threshold may not reveal important suprathreshold properties, such as mutual inhibition between opponent detectors (see Chapter 5 model), similar to the case of motion detection in the visual system (Sekuler & Levinson, 1974).

Additional Related Studies

Recently, Ainsworth (1977) and Cole and Cooper (1977) have tested the possibility that selective adaptation represents a *retuning* of the stimulated detector, rather than fatigue. In the form of retuning tested by Ainsworth, adaptation should produce a shift in the stimulus values to which the detector responds, as shown in Figure 4b. Using a tri-valued [di]–[tʰi]–[si] test series varying in the duration of frication from 10 to 160 msec, Ainsworth provided a test of the fatigue vs. retuning hypotheses using adapting stimuli that lay between a phonemic category's modal value and a phoneme boundary. For such adaptors, the fatigue hypothesis predicts an adaptation effect in the same direction as an

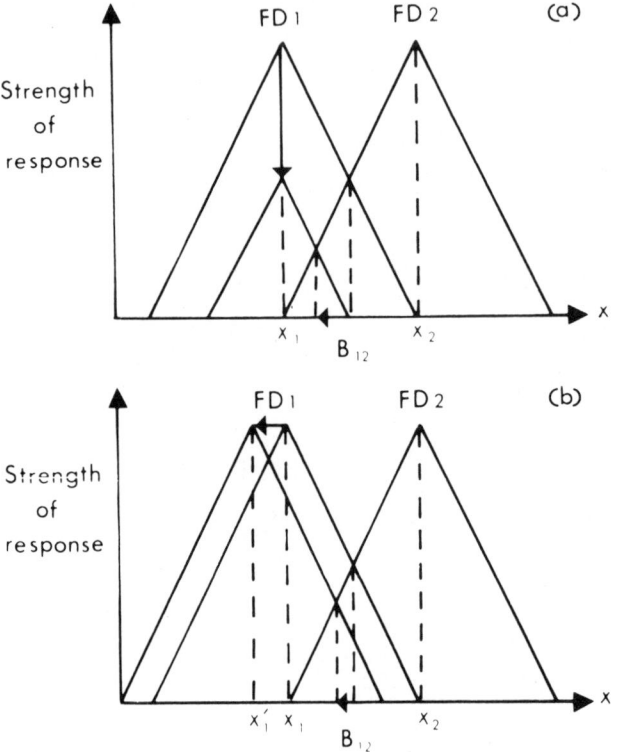

Figure 4. Strength of response of two feature detectors, FD_1 and FD_2, as a function of the signal $S(x)$. (a) Fatigue hypothesis: Adaptation reduces the output of FD_1, causing the perceptual boundary B_{12} to shift. (b) Retuning hypotheses: Adaptation retunes FD_1 so that its strength of response is greater to a signal $S(x_1')$, with a resultant shift in B_{12}. (Reprinted with permission from Ainsworth (1977)).

adaptation effect obtained with a modal adaptor from the same phoneme category, whereas the retuning hypothesis predicts an adaptation effect in the opposite direction. In general, the results provided some support for the fatigue hypothesis, although, as Ainsworth notes, the results may also be accounted for by assuming that both fatigue and retuning occurred.

The retuning hypothesis was also tested by Cole and Cooper (1977).[5] Since the retuning account is based on the notion that adaptation with a given stimulus

---

[5]The retuning hypothesis tested by Cole and Cooper (1977) is slightly different from the one tested by Ainsworth (1977), although both forms of retuning fail to account for the results of the Cole and Cooper experiment. Whereas Ainsworth's retuning includes a shift in the peak sensitivity, Cole and Cooper's retuning includes a restriction of the range of stimulus values to which the detector is sensitive without a peak shift, as shown in Cole and Cooper (1977, Figure 1). The experiment with variable adaptors provides evidence against both retuning accounts.

produces a shift in the detector's modal value to that stimulus (see Figure 4), a shift in the phoneme boundary should not occur if adaptation is attempted using a series of adaptors that include a range of stimulus values within a phoneme category. By testing adaptation on a [d]–[j̑] series with a variety of [j̑] stimuli containing different durations of frication, Cole and Cooper obtained effects equivalent to those obtained with a single adaptor whose duration of frication was approximately the same as the mean frication duration of the variable adaptors. The results suggest that retuning, at least in the plausible form just proposed, does not provide an account of the selective adaptation effects. Rather, the results suggest that adaptation produces a lowered sensitivity of the adapted detector (for further support see Eimas & Miller, 1977; Miller, Eimas, & Root, 1977).

A more elaborate signal detection analysis has recently been carried out using the absolute identification task employed in Experiment 3 (Elman, 1979). In contrast to our experiment, Elman tested only two subjects in each of his experiments but obtained a very large number of responses per subject over a long series of about 20 sessions. By this means, it was possible to obtain a more stable data base appropriate for a signal detection analysis. The results suggested that within-series adaptation effects for three consonantal distinctions ([ápə–ábə], [bæ–dæ], and [bæ–pʰæ]) are attributable to response bias rather than to changes in sensitivity. Elman's study, however, included no tests of crossed-series adaptation, crucial for testing the merits of a *feature* detector account of selective adaptation. Since a response bias account is less likely on a priori grounds in the case of crossed-adaptation than within-series adaptation, it is not yet possible to generalize from Elman's results to the nature of crossed-series effects (for further discussion, see Chapter 7).

Part Two
THE RELATION BETWEEN SPEECH PERCEPTION AND PRODUCTION

In this part of the book, selective adaptation is applied to the problem of whether speech perception and production make use of common processing machinery. At the outset, there was little optimism about the possibility of a perceptuo-motor processor; yet, the adaptation method seemed a good way to put the matter to a test. As data began to come in, it appeared that a perceptuo-motor processor could indeed be tapped.

Unlike the work on perceptual adaptation presented in Part I, the studies reported in these chapters have not yet, to my knowledge, been attempted systematically at other laboratories. The main effects have been replicated in our own laboratory, however, as indicated in the following chapters.

One might charge that we are going too far in setting out to apply the adaptation method to perceptuo-motor processing before all the details of perceptual adaptation have been carefully mapped out. But, on the contrary, the study of the relation between perception and production may help with the former task. In addition, this relation seems worthy of investigation in its own right, especially when one considers the central role that it has been accorded in psychological speculations dating back to at least the 17th century (de Cordemoy, 1668):

Lastly, I am to take notice, that there is so great a Communication and correspondence between the Nerves of the Ear, and those of the Larynx, that whensoever any sound agitates the Brain, there flow immediately spirits towards the Muscles of the Larynx, which duely dispose them to form a sound altogether like that, which was just now striking the Brain. And although I well conceive that there needs some *time* to facilitate those motions of the Muscles of the Throat, so the Sounds, which excite the Brain the first time, cannot be easily expressed by the Throat, yet notwithstanding I do as well conceive, that by virtue of repeating them it will come to pass, that the Brain, which thereby is often shaken in the same places, send such a plenty of spirits through the nerves, that are inserted in the Muscles of the Throat, that at length they easily move all the cartilages, which serve for that action, as 'tis requisite they should be moved to form Sounds like those, that have shaken the Brain.

A belief in a relation between speech perception and production was also expressed by von Humboldt (1836), and as noted in Chapter 1, speculation about the existence of a perceptuo-motor processor has continued in contemporary writings.

chapter five

PERCEPTUO-MOTOR ADAPTATION

Study 6*

The technique of selective adaptation has been employed in previous chapters to study the processing operations that occur during speech perception. Using a variation of this technique, it has been possible in this study to provide a fairly direct test for the existence of a mechanism that mediates one aspect of both speech perception and articulation.

In the present experiments, Ss were required to *listen* to repetitions of an adapting stimulus immediately before *uttering* a selected syllable. The utterances were then analyzed to determine whether a feature of the waveforms systematically varied as a function of perceptual adaptation. Attention was focused on a single phonetic feature, namely, the feature of *voicing* in initial consonants. This feature was chosen for three reasons: (a) it has an acoustic correlate that can be measured from real speech waveforms with a relatively high degree of speed and accuracy; (b) numerous data on perceptual adaptation have already been obtained for this feature; (c) the feature is virtually universal in that it serves to mark phonemic distinctions in most, if not all, natural languages (cf. Lisker & Abramson, 1964).

Method

Subjects. Sixteen M.I.T. students, nine males and seven females, participated in this experiment. All were native speakers of American English. None had prior phonetic training or any known hearing or speech defects.

*Portions of this study are reprinted with permission from *Perception & Psychophysics*, 1974, 16, 229–234.

Stimuli. The adapting stimuli consisted of three synthetically-generated speech syllables, [i], [pʰi], and [bi]. The syllables were five-formant patterns generated on a terminal analog speech synthesizer at the M.I.T. Research Laboratory of Electronics (cf. Klatt, 1973). The acoustic form of the steady-state vowel was identical for the three syllables and simulated the output of a male vocal tract. The two CV syllables, [pʰi] and [bi], differed from each other in VOT and the onset of the formant transitions after voicing onset (cf. Stevens & Klatt, 1974); for [pʰi], the VOT value was +80 msec (voicing onset lagged the release burst of the consonant by 80 msec), whereas for [bi], the VOT value was 0 msec (voicing onset was simultaneous with the release burst of the consonant). The peak amplitudes of the three syllables were matched, and the overall duration of each syllable was 255 msec.

Procedure. The Ss were tested individually in a soundproofed room. Each S was presented 40 adaptation trials during a single, hour-long session. The trials were arranged in blocks of 10, with an approximately 5-min rest period between blocks. Within each block, Ss were presented a single adapting stimulus type ([i], [pʰi], or [bi]). On each individual trial, Ss first listened to 70 repetitions of the adapting stimulus, with an interrepetition interval of 350 msec. The adapting stimulus was played via an Ampex PR-10 tape recorder while the Ss listened binaurally over KLH-Z61 headphones. The Ss were instructed to hold their tongues firmly between their teeth and lips while listening and were told to minimize subvocalization. After 70 repetitions of the adapting stimulus were presented, Ss released their tongues immediately and uttered a single CV syllable (either [pʰi] or [bi] for a given block) in a natural voice as soon as possible. Ss were capable of noticing the cessation of the adapting repetitions on each trial in a virtually automatic manner (mean response latency < 1.5 sec), and for this reason no external signal was employed at the end of the repetitions to prompt a response. Five seconds lapsed between trials, and Ss were told to regard each new trial as a separate task. All utterances were recorded onto tape via a Neumann U87 microphone and a Revox A77 tape recorder.

The four blocks of 10 trials consisted of two major groups; one group of 20 trials required the verbal response [pʰi], the other required the verbal response [bi]. Eight Ss were presented the group of 20 [pʰi]-response trials first; the other eight Ss were presented the two groups of trials in reverse order. Within each group of 20 trials, the first block of 10 trials always involved listening to repetitions of the isolated vowel [i] immediately prior to each utterance (the control condition)[1], while the second block involved listening to repetitions of the syllable belonging to the same CV type as the required utterance. In the second block of trials, Ss thus listened to repetitions of [pʰi] immediately prior to uttering [pʰi] responses and listened to repetitions of [bi] immediately prior to uttering [bi] responses.

[1]Cf. Study 1 for perceptual data showing a close relation between identification of consonants in the unadapted state and after adaptation with an isolated vowel.

Results and Discussion

Each of the 640 utterances was analyzed for VOT oscillographically, aided by the AUDITS computer program written by Huggins (1969). A cursor was manipulated to mark the onset of the consonant release burst and the onset of voicing for each utterance. The time difference between the two markers was displayed on the oscilloscope screen to the nearest 100 microsec. The accuracy of each VOT measurement was estimated to be within ±1 msec, except in the case of those [bi] utterances having VOTs near 0 msec, where the accuracy was reduced to about ±3 msec. Examples of the oscilloscope displays are shown in Figure 1.

The results for each S are shown in Table 1, where the mean VOT value is displayed for each test condition. Figures 2 and 3 show the frequency distribution of the VOT values for the entire group of Ss. For the [p^hi] utterances, a significant decrease in VOT values was obtained after perceptual adaptation to [p^hi], as compared with the VOT values obtained in the control condition (adaptation with the vowel [i]) ($p < 0.05$).[2] Thirteen of the 16 Ss showed this decline in VOT as a function of perceptual adaptation. For the [bi] utterances, no systematic shift in VOT was obtained after perceptual adaptation to [bi]. Some Ss did show marked shifts after [bi] adaptation (cf. Table 1), but these shifts were not systematic in direction across Ss.

The results for the [p^hi] utterances indicate that perceptual adaptation can indeed exert a systematic influence on the speech production values of VOT. The effect was obtained despite a fairly wide range of individual VOT values (cf. Table 1 and Figure 2). In addition, the effect occurred for the male and female Ss to an approximately equal extent, even though the adapting stimuli simulated the output of a male vocal tract.

Since subvocalization was minimized in the experiment, the effect for the [p^hi] utterances is probably central in origin and does not operate at the level of peripheral motor control. A consideration of the direction of the adaptation shift for [p^hi] and the range of individual VOT values adds support to this claim and provides further information about the nature of the effect. From these considerations, it will be argued below that the adaptation effect represents the fatiguing of a single mechanism utilized during both speech perception and speech production. This account of the effect will be contrasted with explanations based on (a) compensation for the effects of perceptual distortion produced during repetitive listening to the [p^hi] adapting stimulus, and (b) voluntary mimicry of the perceived adapting stimulus.

To provide evidence that the effect stems from the fatiguing of a perceptuo-motor component of the speech system, we must, at the very least, establish that the present effect works in the same direction as the shifts obtained during perceptual adaptation for the *voicing* feature. The perceptual adaptation studies of Eimas and Corbit (1973) and Eimas et al. (1973) show that after

---

[2]Two-tailed *t*-test for correlated observations.

(A)

(B)

118

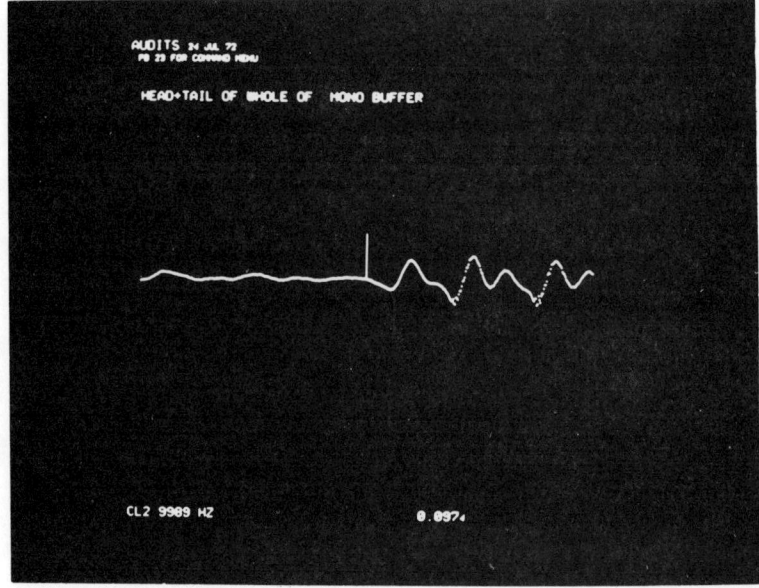

(C)

Figure 1. Sample oscillographic displays of the test utterances, illustrating the method used to analyze VOTs. The top left display shows the initial segment of a [bi] utterance containing a short-lag VOT (voicing onset occurs shortly after release burst of the consonant). The pointer "T" indicates the onset of the release burst, the vertical line to the right of "T" marks the onset of voicing, and the time difference between the "T" pointer and the vertical line is displayed at the bottom right of the oscilloscope screen. For this utterance, the VOT is measured to be 11.6 msec. The bottom left display shows a segment of a prevoiced [bi] syllable (voicing onset precedes the release burst of the consonant). For prevoiced [bi]s, the pointer "T" (not shown in the display segment here) is set at the onset of voicing, while the vertical line cursor is aligned with the onset of the release burst. The time difference between the two markers is taken as the measure of VOT, in this case −86.6 msec (negative VOT values signify prevoicing). The display above shows a segment of aspiration and the onset of voicing for a [p^{hi}] utterance. The "T" pointer is set at the onset of the release burst (not shown in this display segment), and the vertical line cursor is moved to the position of voicing onset as in the case of short-lag VOT [bi] utterances. The actual screen size is 14 × 13 in., and the vertical and horizontal display scales can be magnified to facilitate the marking procedure.

Table 1
Mean VOT Values (in Milliseconds of VOT) for Each Subject in Each Test Condition

S	[pʰi] Utterances Adapt With		[bi] Utterances Adapt With	
	[i]	[pʰi]	[i]	[bi]
B.B.	68.2	50.8	−11.7	5.7
D.B.	66.8	85.0	6.4	−41.4
S.B.	25.9	20.8	−19.7	−9.6
A.C.	94.9	75.9	−23.9	−61.1
J.C.	43.3	37.9	11.3	5.5
L.C.	33.1	29.4	2.3	3.6
L.Ch.	61.0	47.6	8.4	6.3
L.Co.	77.1	71.4	−51.9	−63.8
G.D.	53.3	61.2	14.0	12.2
S.G.	91.0	81.3	6.7	0.5
H.H.	72.5	59.9	5.7	7.5
M.H.	48.4	46.2	7.0	8.5
P.H.	38.8	44.0	−22.8	−41.5
J.I.	88.3	74.4	11.1	16.2
C.L.	93.1	90.1	−10.3	−3.7
H.S.	67.6	58.4	10.7	11.4
Grand Mean	64.0	58.4	−3.5	−9.0

Note. Negative VOT values indicate that voicing onset occurred prior to the release burst of the consonant; positive values indicate that voicing onset occurred after the release burst (see text).

adaptation to a voiceless stop, some VOT stimuli identified as voiceless in the unadapted state where identified as voiced after adaptation. *We can infer from this finding that a given VOT stimulus was perceived as having a shortened VOT after adaptation to a voiceless stop.*[3] If the shifts for speech production represented the same adaptation effect, the articulated VOT values for [pʰi] should have decreased after perceptual adaptation to [pʰi], and our results confirm this prediction.

It should be clear that the present results cannot be accounted for by an effect of perceptuo-motor compensation (cf. Held & Freedman, 1963). According to the compensation hypothesis, the articulated VOT values for [pʰi] should

---

[3] It is important to note that one should consider the perceptual data from the standpoint of the shift in perception for a given VOT stimulus, not from the standpoint of the shift in physical VOT to yield a constant voiceless response. The proper comparison between the perception and production data concerns shifts in perceived and produced VOT, not shifts in the voiced-voiceless response, since the latter is variable in the perceptual studies but is phonetically constant in the production task here.

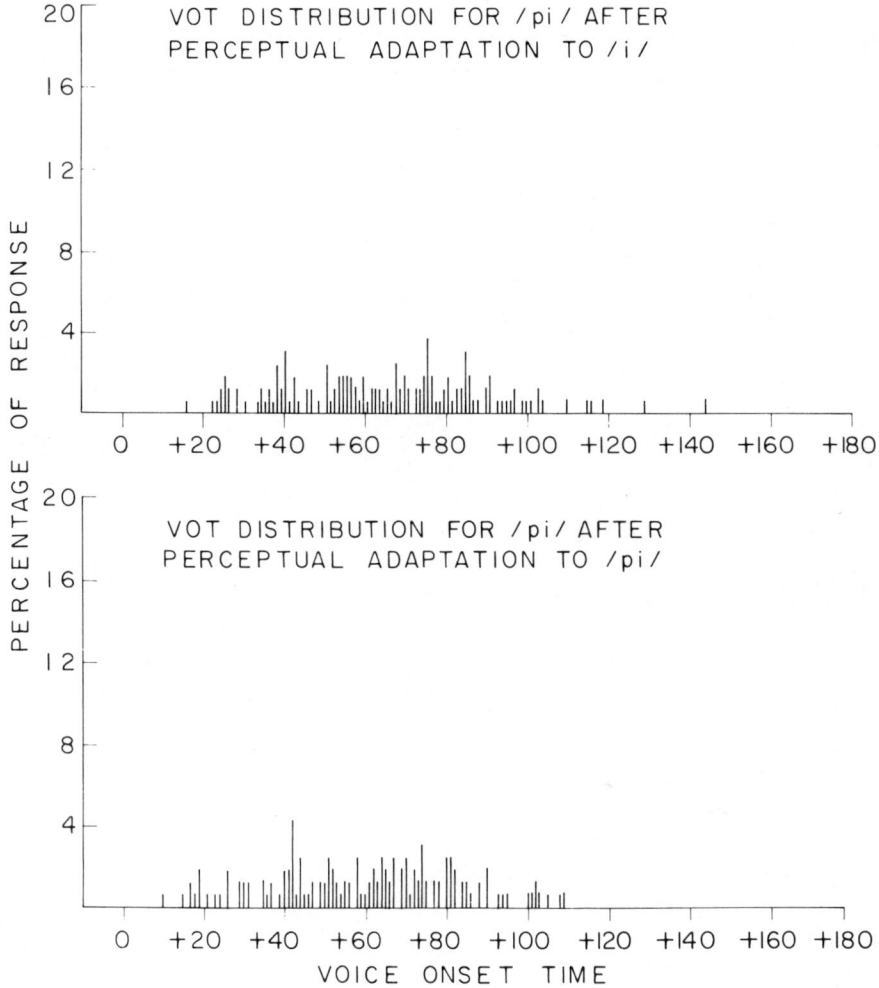

Figure 2. Frequency distribution of the [pʰi] utterances for the group of 16 Ss.

have become *longer* in order to compensate for the perceived shortening of the VOT value of the voiceless adapting stimulus, contrary to fact. Since Ss in this experiment were instructed to make their responses as quickly and automatically as possible on each trial, it is not surprising that compensation (at least in voluntary form) did not govern the results.

Another possibility—that Ss simply mimicked the perceived VOT value of the [pʰi] adapting stimulus—can also be ruled out on the basis of the present

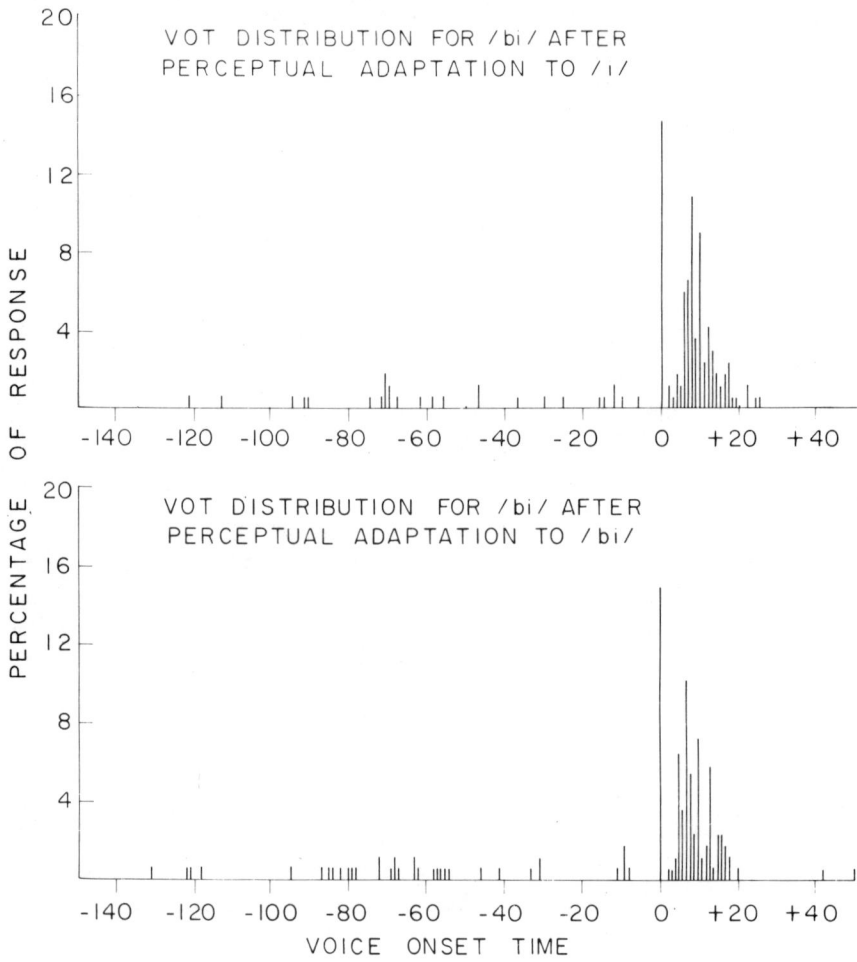

Figure 3. Frequency distribution of the [bi] utterances for the group of 16 Ss.

data. The mimicry interpretation cannot account for the wide range of individual VOT values obtained after adaptation to [pʰi]. Some Ss showing a decline in VOT after adaptation to [pʰi] produced shifts in VOT directed away from the VOT value of the adapting stimulus (+80 msec), whereas other Ss showing the shortening effect produced VOT shifts in the direction toward the adapting stimulus value. In effect, the direction of shift was not systematic in relation to the absolute VOT value of the adapting stimulus; the VOT values for nine Ss shifted away from the +80 value of the adapting stimulus; the VOTs for seven Ss shifted toward it. This finding, plus the generally wide range of VOT values for the [pʰi] utterances, indicates that voluntary mimicry of the perceived adapting stimulus cannot account for the present effect.

Having provided some evidence that the shortening effect for the [pʰi] utterances represents the fatiguing of a perceptuo-motor aspect of the speech system and neither compensation nor mimicry, we now turn to the problematic question, "Why was a systematic effect of adaptation observed for the [pʰi] utterances but not for the [bi] utterances?" Two important differences between the processing of these syllables may lead to an explanation. With regard to speech production, an examination of Figures 2 and 3 shows that the distribution of VOT values for the [pʰi] and [bi] utterances differed greatly in their distributional type. Whereas the VOT values for [pʰi] were distributed in an approximately Gaussian fashion in both test conditions, the VOT values for [bi] provided a poor fit to the Gaussian distribution, and in addition showed a strong clustering of responses within the relatively narrow range between 0 and 20 msec VOT.[4] The basic difference in distributional pattern of the [pʰi] and [bi] VOT values occurred for the individual Ss as well as for the group as a whole. This same distributional difference was also found by Lisker and Abramson (1964) in their original study of VOT production for the syllables [pʰa] and [ba]. The presence of a strong response clustering between 0 and 20 msec VOT indicates that Ss have a well-defined target region of VOT when uttering the syllable [bi], unlike the case for [pʰi] utterances. One might speculate on this basis that [bi] utterances would be less susceptible to the effect of perceptuo-motor adaptation.

Perceptual evidence from the studies of Eimas and Corbit (1973) and Eimas et al. (1973) is in accord with the notion that the voiced stops are less susceptible to adaptation. In these perceptual studies, it was found in a variety of test conditions that the voiceless stops were more affected by selective adaptation than were their voiced counterparts.

Considering the correlated differences in perception and production between the adaptation effects for voiced vs. voiceless stop consonants, it seemed reasonable to ask a further question, namely whether the processing of voiced vs. voiceless stops is carried out independently of each other. This question, of particular importance for evaluating models of the adaptation effects (see below), was taken up in a second perceptuo-motor experiment.

This experiment was designed to test whether perceptual adaptation to [pʰi] would alter the VOT values of [bi] utterances, and vice versa. Eight Ss, six of whom had served in the main experiment, listened to repetitions of the syllables [i], [pʰi], and [bi] as before, only in this case the repetitions of [pʰi]

---

[4]Experiments conducted since the completion of this study indicate that the obtained 16% responses at 0 msec VOT (see Figure 8) is too high a percentage, resulting from the failure to pick up very low-amplitude [b] bursts for some utterances. It should be noted also that Lisker and Abramson (1964) reported 75% [ba] utterances having 0 msec VOT. Lisker and Abramson's measurements were based on an analysis of wide-band spectrograms, and they rounded off each measurement to the nearest 5 msec of VOT. It seems certain that the highly elevated response peak obtained in their study as well as in the present study was due to a failure to notice very low-amplitude onset bursts. As for the present research, it is important to point out that the generally strong clustering of responses between 0 and 20 msec VOT continues to show up consistently in additional work with improved measuring techniques.

immediately preceded [bi] utterances, and vice versa. The 320 utterances were analyzed for VOT in the same manner used in the main experiment.

No systematic effect of adaptation was found for either the [pʰi] or the [bi] utterances (see Table 2).[5] The results of the experiment are of interest because they (a) rule out any remaining explanations of the original adaptation effect for [pʰi] based on notions other than an effect that is dependent on the *voicing* property of the adapting syllable, and (b) suggest that the mechanisms for processing voiced vs. voiceless stop consonants operate independently of each other. The claim for independent processing is supported by the additional fact that the VOT distributions for voiced vs. voiceless consonants show virtually no overlap for individual speakers, contextual factors being equated (cf. Lisker & Abramson, 1964, and present data).

The claim for independent processing of voiced and voiceless stops makes it difficult to account for the perceptual adaptation effects obtained by Eimas and Corbit (1973) as well as for the perceptuo-motor effect observed in the main experiment here. Eimas and Corbit accounted for the perceptual adaptation shifts by proposing the existence of two detector mechanisms, each selectively sensi-

Table 2
Mean VOT Values (in Milliseconds of VOT) for Each Subject in Each Test Condition of Experiment 2

S	[pʰi] Utterances Adapt With		[bi] Utterances Adapt With	
	[i]	[bi]	[i]	[pʰi]
B.B.	61.9	62.5	−34.3	−10.3
D.B.	71.5	70.2	7.8	−7.3
R.B.	32.4	39.5	5.3	5.0
M.C.	61.1	57.8	−0.9	−7.9
L.Ch.	64.4	58.7	10.8	8.6
L.Co.	87.9	90.8	−61.2	−58.3
S.G.	62.6	58.1	4.3	2.5
H.S.	58.0	59.3	14.8	11.9
Grand Mean	62.5	62.1	−6.7	−7.0

Note. Negative VOT values indicate that voicing onset occurred prior to the release burst of the consonant; positive values indicate that voicing onset occurred after the release burst (see text).

[5] Although no systematic shift was obtained for the group data [bi] utterances, there existed a clear trend for the VOT values to decline after perceptual adaptation to [pʰi] for those Ss having a nonnegative mean VOT in the control condition. There was no highly systematic relation in turn, however, between the performance of such Ss after adaptation in this experiment and their earlier performance in the main experiment.

tive to a range of VOT values. They proposed further that the range of VOT values to which each detector is sensitive partially overlaps the range of sensitivity of the other detector. The assumption of overlapping, or alternatively, of inhibition of one detector by the other, forms an essential aspect of the proposed explanation of the adaptation effects, since fatiguing one detector should result in a *directional shift* in VOT perception only if the fatigued detector operates in an opponent-process fashion with the unadapted detector. The effects observed here for speech production appear inconsistent with the notion that the voiced and voiceless stops are processed in such a conjoint manner. In Study 8, however, we propose a model of the perceptuo-motor effects that resolves this apparent dilemma.

Study 7*

Previous studies of perceptual adaptation provided evidence that linguistic *features* may be processed during some stage of speech perception. The present aim was to determine whether these features are extracted at the level of processing which mediates both speech perception and production. We studied this question by examining the case in which both the adapting syllable and the selected utterance shared the relevant voicing property, but differed from each other in place of articulation.

In these experiments, subjects were presented the adapting stimuli [i], [p^{h}i] and [bi] as before. But now, the subjects' task was to utter the syllable [t^{h}i] or [di] after each group of 70 adapting repetitions. For each of the two CV utterance types, perceptual adaptation to [i] was counterbalanced across blocks of ten trials with perceptual adaptation to the CV syllable belonging to the same voicing category as the utterance.

The results of the experiments appear in Figures 4 and 5, where the VOT frequency distribution of the [t^{h}i] and [di] utterances are shown for each test condition. A total of 1280 utterances was examined in these experiments (320 in each of the four experimental conditions). For [t^{h}i] utterances, a systematic decline in VOT was obtained after adaptation to [p^{h}i], compared with the VOT values obtained after adaptation with the isolated vowel (P <0.01). Twenty-three of the 32 subjects showed this effect; the mean magnitude of effect was 3.2 ms. This average magnitude was about 2% larger than that obtained for [p^{h}i] utterances with the same subjects (based on data in Study 6, and additional tests). The obtained effect for the voiceless stops thus seems to be entirely feature-specific. No systematic shift was obtained in the VOT values of the [di] utterances after adaptation to [bi]. The asymmetry observed between the effects for [t^{h}i] and

---

*Portions of this study are reprinted with permission from *Nature*, 1974, *252*, 121–123. Marc R. Lauritsen, coauthor.

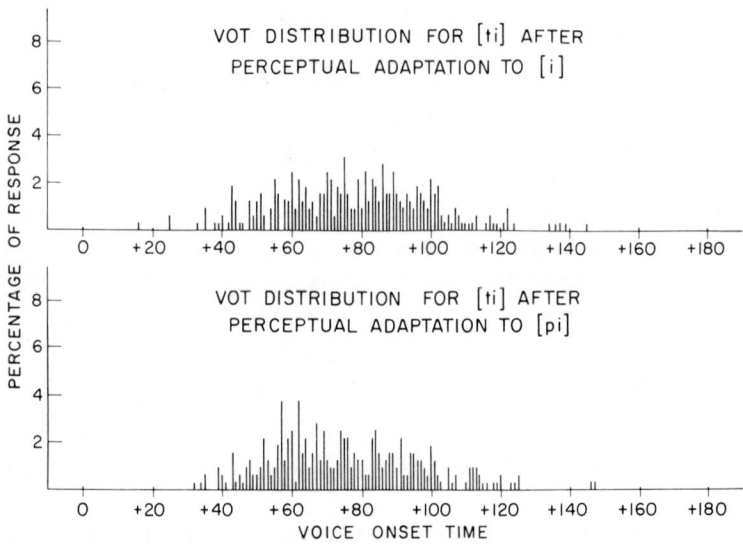

Figure 4. Frequency distribution of the [tʰi] utterances for the group of 32 subjects after perceptual adaptation to [i] (a) or [pʰi] (b). This display provides a good record of the range and distributional pattern of VOT values, although it does not easily reveal the small but significant shift in VOTs between the two test conditions.

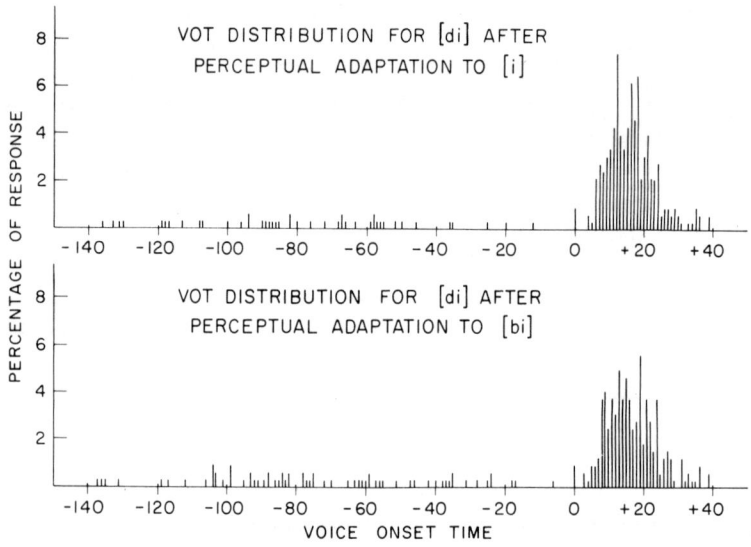

Figure 5. Frequency distribution of the [di] utterances for the group of 32 subjects after perceptual adaptation to [i] (a) and [bi] (b).

[di] utterances corresponded to the asymmetry obtained earlier for [pʰi] and [bi] utterances. In both cases, perceptuo-motor effects were found for the voiceless stop consonants but not for their voiced counterparts. The corresponding difference in the distributional patterns for VOT held as well for the present data (Figures 4 and 5).

The results for the [tʰi] utterances indicate that the stage of processing subserving both the perceptual and motor systems of speech performs at least one highly specialized function—namely, processing information about the voicing property of the consonant. Since the [pʰi] adapting syllable contained a consonant with a different place of articulation from the [tʰi] utterance, the perceptuo-motor effect cannot be attributed to a mechanism that processes consonants as indivisible units.

Study 8*

The current study was aimed at two related problems encountered in the prior perceptuo-motor adaptation experiments—the small magnitude of the effect and the variability of individual speakers' VOT values. In addition to obtaining measurements of VOT, we also decided to measure in this study two other acoustic factors of the utterances produced after repetitive listening, namely, the duration of the closure interval of the voiceless plosive and the duration of the following vowel. Each of these factors has been shown to covary with VOT duration in connected speech (Lisker & Abramson, 1967; Umeda & Coker, 1975), and we wished to test the possibility that one or both of these factors might underlie any observed changes in VOT. The overall aim of these acoustical analyses is to gain a better understanding of the effect so that an explicit model of the relationship between speech perception and speech production mechanisms can be formulated for the particular class of voicing distinctions under consideration.

The present series of experiments was designed in an attempt to both reduce the variability of individual speaker's VOT values and obtain a more sizable perceptuo-motor effect, while providing a valid test of perceptuo-motor processing. In seeking these goals, we chose to use bisyllabic rather than monosyllabic utterances and to embed the voiceless plosive. Although prior studies of VOT provided no explicit basis for the expectation that embedding would reduce the variability of VOT measurements for a given speaker, preliminary data indicated that some reduction could indeed be achieved by this method.

*Portions of this study are reprinted with permission from *Journal of the Acoustical Society of America*, 1975, 58, 256–265, Richard M. Nager, coauthor.

The interest in both reducing variability and gaining a more sizable perceptuo-motor adaptation effect (two goals not necessarily compatible) stems from our interest in carrying out more detailed acoustical analyses of the test utterances and conducting research designed to test specific motor correlates of the perceptuo-motor effect. In the latter research, we hope to study the laryngeal factors commonly associated with variations in VOT, including vocal fold tension and the time course of glottal width (Halle & Stevens, 1971; Kim, 1970; Klatt, 1973). Although such studies present many technical difficulties, it appears that the work can be accomplished using recent innovations with fiberoptic techniques (Sawashima & Hirose, 1968; Sawashima & Ushijima, 1971), transillumination of the larynx (Lisker, Abramson, Cooper, & Schvey, 1969), and electromyography.

EXPERIMENT 1

Method

Subjects. The experiment involved 22 subjects, including both college students and M.I.T. employees. Most of the students were enrolled at M.I.T. or at Harvard Summer School. All subjects were paid volunteers who had little or no phonetic training. The subjects were all native speakers of English with no history of speech or hearing impairments.

Stimuli. The adapting stimuli consisted of two synthetically-generated speech sounds, [i] and [rəp^{h}i]. Both stimuli were five-formant patterns constructed on a terminal analog synthesizer at the M.I.T. Research Laboratory of Electronics (Klatt, 1973). The detailed acoustic specifications of the stimuli appear in Appendix A. The formant frequencies and bandwidths of the [i] portion of [rəp^{h}i] were identical to those of isolated syllable [i]. The duration of the [i] vowel of [rəp^{h}i] was 135 msec; the duration of the isolated [i] syllable was 220 msec. The [rəp^{h}i] stimulus included an unstressed vowel [ə] of 60-msec duration, a silent interval of 35-msec duration (considerably shorter than the silent interval observed in real speech, Suen & Beddoes, 1974), and a voice onset time of 50 msec for the prestressed plosive. The total duration of the [rəp^{h}i] stimulus was 400 msec. The two adapting stimuli were matched in peak amplitude, and 1000 repetitions of each stimulus were recorded onto magnetic tape for playback during the experiment.

Both adapting stimuli were identified unambiguously by listeners at the beginning of the experiment. As in prior work, the isolated vowel stimulus was used as a ''neutral'' or ''dummy'' adapting stimulus to obtain a measure of baseline performance for the utterances that was comparable to the measure obtained after adaptation with a voiceless plosive. The rationale for using the isolated vowel as a neutral adaptor was based on the assumption that such a stimulus would produce no perceptuo-motor effect because the stimulus produces no effect on even the *perception* of a stop consonant series varying in VOT (Leiter, 1974).

Procedure. The subjects were tested individually in a sound-insulated chamber. Each subject was presented 20 adaptation trials during a single 40-min session. Specific procedures were similar to those of earlier perceptuo-motor studies. The trials were arranged in blocks of ten, with a 5-min rest period between blocks. Within each block of trials, the subjects were presented a single adapting stimulus type [i] or [rəp^{h}i]. The order of presentation for these two stimuli was counterbalanced across the 22 subjects. On each trial, subjects first listened to 70 repetitions of the adapting stimulus, with an inter-repetition interval of 350 msec. The adapting stimulus was played via an Ampex PR-10 tape recorder, while the subjects listened binaurally over KLH-Z61 headphones. Subjects were instructed to hold their tongues firmly between their teeth and lips while listening and were told to minimize subvocalization. After 70 repetitions of the adapting stimulus were presented, subjects released their tongues and uttered the bisyllable [rət^{h}i] in a natural voice. The subjects were instructed to place primary stress on the second syllable of the utterance and were given practice beforehand in uttering the bisyllable in a natural, relaxed manner.

As in previous perceptuo-motor work, subjects were capable of noticing the end of the adapting repetitions on each trial in a virtually automatic fashion (mean response latency < 1.5 sec). For this reason, no external signal was used at the end of the repetitions to prompt a response. Five seconds of silence elapsed between consecutive adaptation trials, and the subjects were told to regard each new trial as a separate task. The subjects were instructed not to be overly concerned about how each utterance sounded in comparison with previous utterances and were told to respond on each trial as "reflexively" as possible. All utterances were recorded onto tape via a Neumann U87 microphone and Revox A77 tape recorder.

Results and Discussion. Each of the 440 utterances was analyzed for VOT oscillographically, aided by the AUDITS computer program written by Huggins (1969). A cursor was manipulated to mark the onset of the plosive release burst and the onset of voicing for each utterance. The time difference between the two markers was displayed on the oscilloscope screen to the nearest 100 μsec. The accuracy of most of the VOT measurements was estimated to be within ± 1 msec.[6] Examples of the oscilloscope displays and the marking procedure are shown on pp. 118–119.

[6]The duration of a single glottal cycle for a male speaker is typically about 8 msec. For a few of the utterances, determination of the onset of periodicity on the oscillogram included an error of approximately this magnitude; however, such errors were assumed to be made equally across the two test conditions, nullifying their possible effect on observed VOT shifts.

Table 3
Mean VOT Values (in Milliseconds of VOT) for Each Subject in Each Test Condition of Experiment 1

Subject	[rəth í] utterance after adaptation to [i]	Standard deviation	[rəth í] utterance after adaptation to [rəph í]	Standard deviation
JA	95.6	13.71	84.3	19.79
SB	58.5	11.06	57.3	9.46
NB	80.7	11.23	51.9	23.70
DC	104.1	11.30	93.6	8.25
CC	62.2	9.23	60.2	6.66
CD	72.2	12.59	69.5	19.82
BE	64.4	13.29	63.2	10.76
LG	68.3	7.04	56.2	7.26
FG	64.0	7.25	53.7	7.97
EH	59.1	7.11	57.9	4.50
TK	90.4	5.73	76.9	6.03
DL	71.5	7.71	75.0	6.44
ML	69.5	7.54	59.6	7.90
CM	67.9	8.43	66.1	7.51
RN	87.9	9.48	79.3	6.78
JO	104.1	8.84	104.5	13.55
LQ	80.7	13.41	73.8	9.87
DR	77.9	8.77	81.4	11.76
KR	80.5	8.96	70.7	9.66
CS	88.6	7.60	71.0	13.34
CSt	59.5	10.40	64.2	8.69
LU	73.1	9.22	67.3	4.75
Grand mean	76.40	9.54	69.90	10.20

The results for each subject are shown in Table 3, where the mean VOT value is displayed for each test condition, along with the standard deviation for each condition. Figure 1 shows the frequency distribution of the VOT values for the entire group of 22 subjects.

After perceptual adaptation to [rep^{h}í], a statistically significant shortening in mean VOT duration was obtained, compared with the VOT values obtained after perceptual adaptation with the isolated vowel [i] ($p < 0.001$; two-tailed t-test for correlated observations; $t = 3.88$, df = 21). The average magnitude of shift across all subjects was 6.50 msec of VOT. Eighteen of the 22 subjects showed this net shortening effect.

The effect obtained in the present experiment with [ret^{h}í] utterances was in the same direction as the effect obtained previously for [t^{h}i] utterances after adaptation with [p^{h}i]. The average magnitude of the present effect was about twice as large, however (6.5 msec of VOT compared with 3.2 msec of VOT). In addition, individual speakers' standard deviations for the VOT values of the [ret^{h}í] utterances in the present experiment were slightly smaller than in previous work. The average standard deviation for the VOT values of [ret^{h}í] utterances in the present experiment was 9.54 msec after adaptation with [i] and 10.20 msec after adaptation wiht [rep^{h}í]; in the comparable study using monosyllabic utterances (Study 7), the average standard deviation for VOTs of [t^{h}i] utterances was 10.92 msec after adaptation with

In summary, it appears that the data of the present experiment for bisyllabic [ret^{h}í] utterances indicate that some success has been achieved in both obtaining a larger magnitude of the perceptuo-motor effect and reducing the variability of individual speaker's VOT values, in comparison with previous work using monosyllabic utterances.

A subanalysis was performed on the present data to determine whether the magnitude of the perceptuo-motor effect (as measured in milliseconds of VOT) was correlated with the variability of VOT values for individual speakers. Considering the data for those subjects having relatively low standard deviation scores (less than 11 msec in both test conditions), we found that the average magnitude of the perceptuo-motor effect for this subgroup was 5.57 msec, slightly smaller than the average magnitude of effect for the subjects as a whole. This finding suggests that the magnitude of the perceptuo-motor effect does not covary significantly with the variability of VOT values for individual speakers.

MEASUREMENTS OF VOWEL DURATION AND CLOSURE GAP

Before concluding that the present effect represents a phenomenon that is specific to the voicing property of the voiceless plosive contained in the adapting stimulus, we must consider other acoustic variables which might conceivably underlie the observed changes in VOT. In normal speech, it is known that VOT covaries with the duration of the following vowel (Lisker & Abramson, 1967) as well as with the duration of the plosive closure gap (Umeda & Coker, 1975).

These two measures are normally considered as correlates of stress and speaking rate, and it is conceivable that the effects observed in the present experiment reflect changes in one or both of these underlying variables as opposed to changes in the neural processing of the voicing property of the voiceless plosive. Perhaps, according to one possible alternative, speakers are more likely to place stronger stress on the [i] of [ret^{h}í] utterances after adaptation with the isolated vowel [i] than after adaptation with [rep^{h}í] because of mimicry of the perceptually strong stress associated with the isolated vowel adaptor. The greater stress applied in this baseline test condition would result in relatively shorter VOTs after adaptation with [rep^{h}í], accounting for the present results.

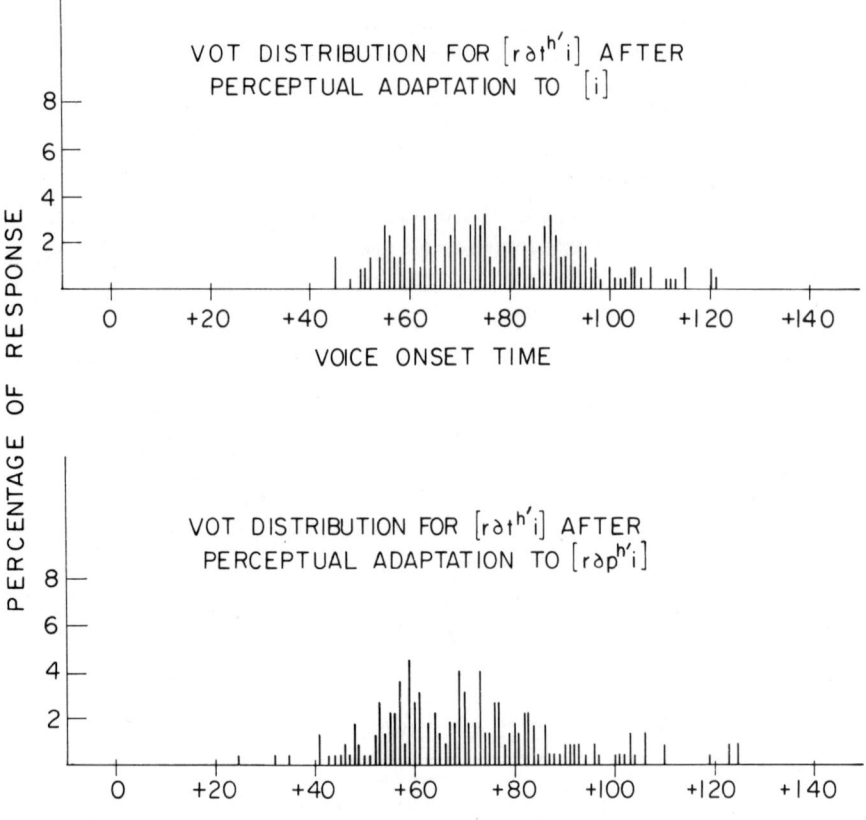

Figure 6. Frequency distribution of the [rəthí] utterances for the group of 22 subjects.

To assess the possible role of both stress and speaking rate in producing the perceptuo-motor effect, we measured the durations of the vowel [i] for the [rethí] utterances as well as the durations of the closure gap of the plosive [t^h]. These measurements were made oscillographically for the utterances of the ten subjects who showed the largest mean shortening in VOT after perceptual adaptation (from 8.6 to 28.8 msec of VOT shift). By using these subjects who show large magnitude VOT shifts, we hoped to provide a strong test of the null hypothesis—that vowel duration and closure gap durations do not covary with VOT shifts in the present experimental context.

The results of the vowel duration analysis appear in Table 4, where the mean vowel duration is shown for each test condition for each of the ten subjects. The results show no consistent differences in vowel duration for the two test conditions ($p > 0.20$, $t = 1.19$, df = 9). Four of the ten subjects showing the

Table 4
Mean Vowel Durations (in Milliseconds) of the Stressed Vowel [i] in [rətʰí]
for Each Subject in Each Test Condition of Experiment 1

Subject	[rətʰí] utterance after adaptation to [i]	[rətʰí] utterance after adaptation to [rəpʰí]
JA	280.7	265.5
NB	249.0	282.4
DC	310.1	294.8
LG	310.7	284.9
FG	224.3	227.2
TK	256.7	257.6
ML	267.6	239.4
RN	224.0	242.4
KR	203.7	180.3
CS	216.4	189.1
Grand mean	254.32	246.36

largest VOT shifts produced average vowel durations that were actually longer after adaptation with [repʰí] than after adaptation with the isolated vowel.

The results of the closure gap analysis appear in Table 5, where the mean duration of closure gap for [tʰ] is shown for each test condition for the ten subjects. The results show no consistent difference in the duration of closure gap for the two test conditions ($p > 0.20$, $t = 0.25$, df = 9). The mean duration of closure gap for five of the ten subjects was longer after adaptation with [repʰí].

The results of the acoustic analyses of both the vowel duration and closure gap duration indicate that the perceptuo-motor effects on VOT are not simply a function of changes in stress or rate of speaking. Rather, the present shifts for VOT appear to represent an effect that is specific to the voicing property of the voiceless plosive contained in the adapting stimulus. Whether this effect is to be identified with VOT *per se* or with still other acoustic cues for voicing the covary with VOT (such as the presence of low-frequency energy at the onset of the rapid spectrum change accompanying voice onset) remains to be determined.

EXPERIMENT 2

Even though the vowel duration and closure gap analyses failed to reveal significant covariation between either of these factors and VOT, we conducted a second experiment to provide a direct test of whether the perceptuo-motor effect is strictly dependent on the voicing property of the voiceless plosive contained in the adapting stimulus. In this experiment, we replaced the adapting stimulus [rəpʰí] with the stimulus [rəbí], changing the plosive from voiceless to voiced while holding all other factors constant.

A secondary purpose of the present experiment was to test the generality of a previous, somewhat unexpected, finding. In the original perceptuo-motor study (Study 6), a crossed-adaptation test was conducted using the adapting stimulus [bi] with [pʰi] utterances, and no systematic effect on VOT values was obtained. That result, while indicating that the perceptuo-motor effect observed after adaptation to [pʰi] was specific to the voicing property of the adapting stimulus, also provided a clue concerning the operation of the mechanism tapped by the perceptuo-motor tests.

As already observed, previous accounts of *perceptual* adaptation effects for stimuli varying in VOT included two detectors, one for voiced plosives and one for voiceless plosives. These detectors contained partially overlapping ranges of response to VOT values and exerted a mutual inhibitory influence on each other. Such a detection scheme could account for the oppositely directed shifts obtained for the perception of stimuli varying in VOT after adaptation with voiced versus voiceless plosives. However, in the perceptuo-motor experiment with [pʰi] utterances, no shift in VOT values was obtained after adaptation with [bi]. This result cast doubt on the applicability of the opponent-process model of voicing analysis at the level of perceptuo-motor processing; such a model would predict that the VOT values for [pʰi] utterances after adaptation with [bi] should shift toward *longer* VOTs, contrary to the results. Because of the importance of the unidirectional character of the perceptuo-motor effect for formulating a workable

Table 5
Mean Closure Gap (in Milliseconds) of the Prestressed Plosive [tʰ] in [rətʰí] for Each Subject in Each Test Condition of Experiment 1

Subject	[rətʰí] utterance after adaptation to [i]	[rətʰí] utterance after adaptation to [rəpʰí]
JA	104.0	109.0
NB	117.4	119.6
DC	107.5	97.3
LG	51.8	58.8
FG	87.4	85.4
TK	78.4	89.0
ML	81.8	65.2
RN	57.6	67.6
KR	100.7	88.2
CS	103.7	102.6
Grand mean	89.0	88.3

model of the processor tapped by the adaptation technique, we considered it advisable to extend the previous cross-adaptation test with monosyllabic utterances to a bisyllabic context to test the generality of this finding.

Method

Subjects. Eighteen subjects participated in this experiment. Six of these had served previously in Experiment 1. One subject served twice in the present experiment. All new subjects had the same qualifications as those who had served previously.

Stimuli. The adapting stimuli consisted of the isolated vowel [i], used in Experiment 1, and the bisyllable [rəbí]. The [rəbí] stimulus contained the same acoustic specifications as the [rəpʰí] stimulus employed in Experiment 1, except that the [rəbí] stimulus contained a VOT value of 0 msec (voicing onset occurred simultaneously with the plosive release). The [rəbí] stimulus was identified unambiguously by all subjects at the beginning of the experiment.

Procedure. The procedure was identical to that of Experiment 1, with the exception that in the present case adaptation with the bisyllable [rəbí] replaced adaptation with [rəpʰí]. The order of test presentation was counterbalanced across subjects.

Results and Discussion

The results appear in Table 6, where the mean VOT value for each subject is displayed for each test condition. No significant effect of perceptuo-motor adaptation was obtained ($p > 0.10, t = 1.48, df = 18$), although the average shift was a shortening effect of 2.33 msec of VOT.

The results of the present experiment extend a previous finding (Study 6) which indicated that adaptation with a voiced plosive does not produce a lengthening of VOT values for voiceless plosive utterances, contrary to the prediction made by an opponent process model of voicing analysis. Indeed, the present results indicate a nonsignificant overall *shortening* of the VOT values. Since this effect is statistically nonsignificant and only about one-third as large as the magnitude of the effect observed in Experiment 1, however, it must be concluded that the major portion of the perceptuo-motor effect observed in the first experiment is attributable to the voicing property of the plosive contained in the adapting stimulus.

As in Experiment 1, a subanalysis was performed on the data for subjects having relatively low standard deviation scores for the VOT values (less than 11 msec in both test conditions). This analysis revealed an average shortening of 2.21 msec of VOT after adaptation with [rəbí], comparable to the magnitude of

Table 6
Mean VOT Values (in Milliseconds of VOT) for Each Subject in Each Test Condition of Experiment 2

Subject	[rətʰí] utterance after adaptation to [i]	Standard deviation	[rətʰí] utterance after adaptation to [rəbí]	Standard deviation
DC	89.4	11.03	90.4	6.53
CH	103.4	6.40	117.3	18.00
EH	81.4	7.33	76.8	7.90
BK	77.3	13.85	69.0	4.82
WK	98.5	16.49	87.3	10.07
ML	64.3	7.18	63.4	8.57
SM	72.0	8.20	67.8	18.30
RN	76.9	4.60	84.9	5.40
DO	100.7	14.00	95.3	8.70
LQ₁	98.3	5.47	88.6	7.20
LQ₂	78.1	7.33	77.2	7.18
JR	81.6	8.55	90.3	8.19
AR	79.4	7.60	83.3	10.60
DR	104.9	4.70	98.2	8.00
DRi	75.0	8.20	71.4	9.46
KR	75.4	5.70	74.6	8.60
MT	82.9	7.72	73.1	8.27
LT	108.2	10.90	101.2	8.30
BT	67.2	9.15	60.5	9.52
Grand mean	84.99	8.65	82.66	9.14

effect observed for the group as a whole. Again, there appears to be no strong correlation between the variability of individual speaker's VOT values and the magnitude of VOT shifts obtained after perceptual adaptation.

EXPERIMENT 3

Since the adapting plosive in Experiment 1 belonged to the class of labial consonants, whereas the plosive of the utterance belonged to the alveolar class, the perceptuo-motor effect observed in that experiment could not be readily attributed to adaptation of a mechanism that detects alveolar consonants as phonemic units. Rather, the effect appeared to be specific to the voicing property of the adapting stimulus and test utterance. The results of Experiment 2 provided additional support for this view. In the present experiment, we wished to determine whether, in addition to the feature-specific effect observed in Experiment 1, a shift in VOT is also produced that is specific to the *phoneme* of the plosive. We thus examined the VOT values for [rəpʰí] utterances after perceptual adaptation with [rəpʰí]. In this experiment, both the adapting stimulus and the test utterance contained a voiceless plosive belonging to the labial class. Thus, if there exists a phonemic component of the perceptuo-motor adaptation effect, as well as a feature-specific component, the magnitude of the VOT shifts in the present experiment should be larger than those observed in Experiment 1.

Method

Subjects. Twenty subjects served in this experiment. Twelve of these had served previously in Experiment 1, and nine had served previously in Experiment 2. The new subjects had the same qualifications as the subjects who had participated in the prior experiments.

Stimuli. The adapting stimuli consisted of the two stimuli used in Experiment 1, [i] and [rəpʰí].

Procedure. The procedure used in this experiment was identical to that used in Experiment 1, with the exception that [rəpʰí] replaced [rətʰí] as the bisyllabic test utterance, to be spoken by the subjects at the end of each period of repetitive listening.

Results and Discussion

The results for each subject are shown in Table 7. A significant shortening was obtained for the VOT values of the [rəpʰí] utterances after perceptual adaptation with [rəpʰí], as compared with the VOT values obtained after adaptation with the isolated vowel ($p < 0.05$, $t = 2.17$, $df = 19$). Twelve of the 20 subjects showed this shortening effect.

In comparison with the results of Experiment 1, the effects observed in the present experiment are relatively small in magnitude and inconsistent across subjects. The present results thus offer no support for the existence of a phonemic component of the adaptation effects, whereby the magnitude of the present effect should have been larger than that observed in Experiment 1.

In previous perceptuo-motor work (Study 6) repetitive listening to [pʰi] produced virtually equivalent VOT shifts for [pʰi] and [tʰi] utterances, the effect for [tʰi] being 2% larger overall. In the present study, the effects for the alveolar plosive in [rətʰí] utterances of Experiment 1 is more than twice as large as that observed for [rəpʰí] utterances after perceptual adaptation with [rəpʰí] (6.50 msec of VOT as compared with 2.73 msec of VOT). We offer no well-motivated explanation for the greater magnitude of effect observed for the alveolar utterances, although one major possibility would be that the alveolar utterances are susceptible to greater VOT shortening than labials because the normal

Table 7
Mean VOT Values (in Milliseconds of VOT) for Each Subject in Each Test Condition of Experiment 3

Subject	[rəphí] utterance after adaptation to [i]	Standard deviation	[rəphí̃] utterance after adaptation to [rəphí̃]	Standard deviation
JB	45.9	9.68	47.0	27.02
DC	71.9	8.47	73.0	10.34
CC	52.7	11.77	46.6	8.63
CD	48.7	7.71	42.1	6.79
BE	49.9	12.41	47.8	8.17
LG	35.9	10.44	31.0	5.50
FG	52.9	8.62	41.1	5.12
EH	54.9	8.87	54.9	14.76
BK	50.7	5.11	50.6	4.16
WK	66.8	20.22	72.7	12.63
SL	69.7	10.01	63.5	6.33
ML	45.1	9.90	38.7	7.69
RN	76.3	14.77	73.8	14.40
LP	52.6	8.27	51.3	13.15
LPo	62.7	11.64	67.1	10.86
LQ	79.9	10.30	64.7	12.54
JR	67.7	13.12	69.5	11.77
DR	81.9	11.65	71.5	10.33
CS	41.7	6.64	45.1	8.75
LU	46.2	10.26	47.5	9.20
Grand mean	57.71	10.49	54.98	10.41

VOT values for alveolars are longer than for labials (Lisker & Abramson, 1964), and there may exist some minimum VOT duration for voiceless plosives which strongly resists the effects of perceptual adaptation, representing, in effect, a compressibility constraint.

GENERAL DISCUSSION

It has been shown in the present series of experiments that perceptuo-motor adaptation effects can be produced for voiceless plosives [p^h] and [t^h] where these plosives are embedded in a CVCV environment. These results, which are particularly consistent in the case of the alveolar plosive [t^h], add weight to the generality and reliability of the perceptuo-motor adaptation effect for voiceless plosives. In addition, the present analyses indicate that this effect is specific to the voicing property of the plosive and is not operating either at a level of the control of stress or speaking rate or at a level of phonemic analysis.

A NEURAL MODEL OF THE PERCEPTUO-MOTOR SYSTEM

To account for the observed effects, we propose that perceptual adaptation produces neural fatigue at a site of processing that mediates both the perception and production of consonant voicing. A model of a neural circuitry believed to be involved is presented in Figure 7. This model is highly speculative, but it is incorporated into the present discussion because it represents a first step toward providing an explicit account of the presently available data obtained from both perceptual and perceptuo-motor adaptation paradigms. The model can be viewed as a more detailed representation of Levels A and B in the model proposed in Chapter 1. In particular, Levels B–D in the present model represent substages of Level B in the general model.

The neural model is comprised of excitatory and inhibitory neural elements with lateral connections only. The neural elements represent either individual cells or cell aggregates.

We will first consider the part of the neural circuit involved in the *perception* of voicing contrasts. This circuitry is designed to account for the effects observed with a strictly perceptual adaptation paradigm, consistent with available evidence from other empirical work on the perception of voicing contrasts as well.

At level A, there exist auditory detectors each of which is narrowly tuned to a particular range of voicing values, represented here as values of VOT solely for purpose of exposition.[7] The existence of level A detectors is needed to account for the fact that listeners are able to discriminate small differences in VOT under appropriate test conditions (Pisoni & Lazarus, 1974). Although prior perceptual adaptation work was not designed to test the presence of adaptation at this particular level of voicing analysis, recent data have indicated that systematic adaptation effects can indeed be produced at this level. Other evidence (e.g., Lisker & Abramson, 1970, Miller *et al.*, 1976; Pisoni, 1977) suggests that the Level A filters exhibit stimulus-response properties that permit especially good discrimination of prevoicing, simultaneity of oral release and voicing onset, and voicing lag.[8] Thus, the specific VOT values assigned to the filters shown in Figure 7 require modification, though this problem is not relevant to the present task of describing the information-flow among stages of the model.

---

[7]A number of recent studies have suggested that VOT *per se* is not the relevant variable (Summerfield & Haggard, 1974). However, the controversy concerning which correlates of VOT are crucial to voicing perception remains unresolved to some extent, and we shall discuss voicing perception in terms of VOT as a coverall term (see also Chapter 3).

[8]Unpublished observations by P. D. Eimas and W. E. Cooper, suggesting that the discriminability of stimuli that differ by 10 msec of VOT can be elevated to about 90% in an AX discrimination test given a period of intensive training.

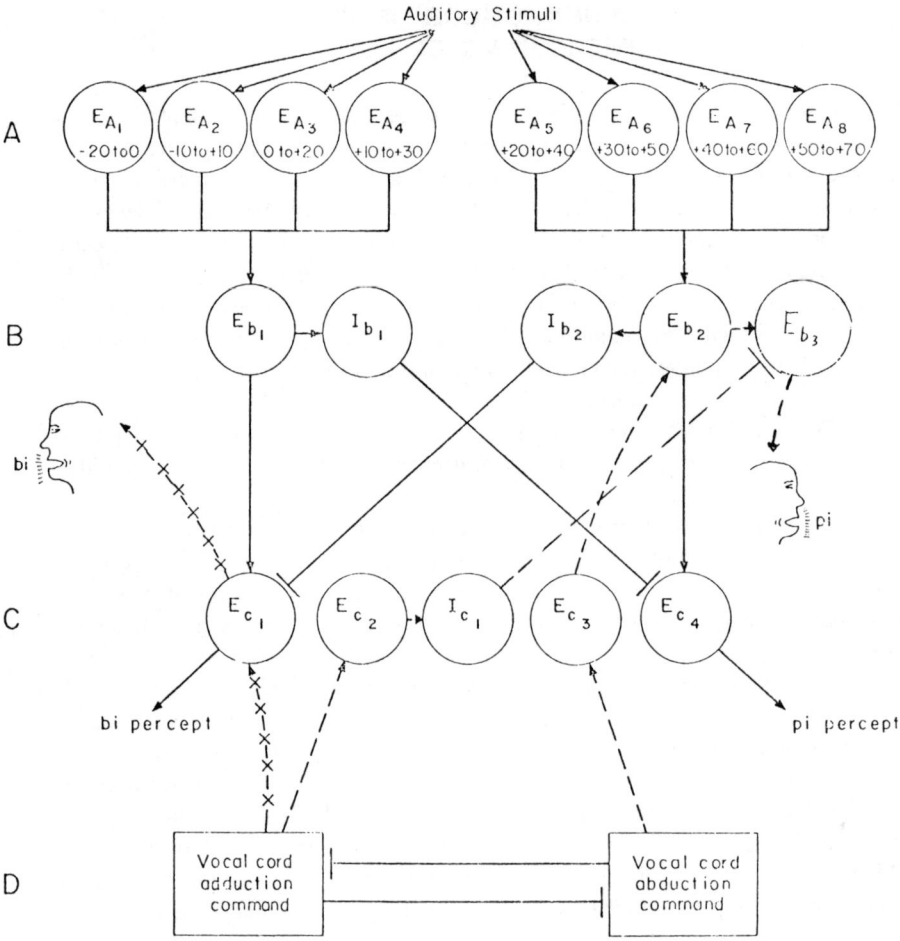

Figure 7. Neural model of the perceptuo-motor system for voiced—voiceless distinctions. Major routes of information-flow are denoted by solid, dotted, and cross-hatched lines. See text for description.

Level B contains two integrators, Eb_1 and Eb_2, each responsive to the output of a separate set of auditory detectors. Eb_1 responds primarily to short-lag and prevoiced VOT values, while Eb_2 responds primarily to longer lags. The existence of these integrators is required within the present framework to account for the nearly categorical nature of the perception of stimuli varying in VOT. Stimuli lying on either side of a VOT value of about +30 msec are discriminated much better than are stimuli lying within the ranges of 0 to +30 msec or +30 to +60 msec of VOT. The peak in VOT discriminability can be accounted for by the notion that stimuli lying on either side of the +30 phonetic boundary excite the two integrators differentially. The degree of overlap in the VOT response ranges of the two integrators is required to account for the degree of inconsistency in listeners' category judgments of stimuli varying in VOT.

The output of these two integrators is transmitted to two different types of neural structure, one excitatory and one inhibitory. The excitatory structure that detects the amount of voicedness is Ec_1, while the complementary structure that detects voicelessness is Ec_4. The output of these level C detectors feeds directly into a decision rule mechanism which correlates the information obtained from level C detectors with other available information from the speech context (e.g., speaker rate, stress pattern, semantics) in order to decide whether a voiced or voiceless signal has been presented. To summarize the excitatory pathway, information regarding short-lag and prevoiced VOTs is transmitted to a structure which determines the extent of voicedness, while information about longer-lag VOTs is transmitted to a structure that determines the extent of voicelessness. The outputs of these structures is then combined with other information relevant to a decision regarding the voiced or voiceless quality of the stimulus.

In contrast to this excitatory pathway, the outputs of Eb_1 and Eb_2 are also transmitted to inhibitory structures. The output of Eb_1 is transmitted to Ib_1, which in turn transmits information to the excitatory structure for voicelessness, Ec_4. A complementary system of cross transmission for inhibitory information exists for Eb_2, whose output is transmitted to Ib_2 and then on to Ec_1. With this system of mutual inhibition, stimulation with a voiced or voiceless plosive actively excites the detector for voicedness or voicelessness, respectively, while at the same time inhibiting the activity of the opponent detector.

This system of perceptual analysis accounts for the perceptual adaptation effects observed as follows. After a certain number of repetitions of a particular plosive are presented, one of the two integrators at level B loses a proportion of its normal response strength, presumably due to a depletion of neural transmitter substance. After adaptation with a voiceless plosive, Eb_2 transmits weaker excitatory signals to the voiceless decision processor. In addition, Eb_2 transmits weaker inhibitory signals to the voiced decision system. Thus, after adaptation with a voiceless plosive, there exists a greater likelihood that a stimulus lying near the phonetic boundary for VOT will be identified as voiced rather than voiceless, *ceteris paribus*. A complementary effect occurs after adaptation with a voiced plosive. In summary, the proposed model accounts for the bidirectional nature of the effects obtained in perceptual adaptation experiments.

Providing an account of the unidirectional effects observed in the perceptuo-motor adaptation experiments is more difficult, but is in fact possible using part of the same neural circuitry postulated for speech perception. In addition to accounting for the general form of the results of the present study, the neural circuitry is designed to account for the results of earlier perceptuo-motor adaptation studies as well. One of the major findings of these previous studies, not dealt with specifically in the present experiments, concerned the fact that adaptation effects were not observed for voiced plosive utterances [bi] and [di]. These results are attributed to the fact that the timing of voicing onset for voiced plosives is a consequence of a straightforward mechanical coupling by airflow (Ohala, 1970), in contrast to the more complicated situation for voiceless plosives. The difference between the degree to which central motor programs must control the timing of voicing onset relative to the release of oral closure in voiced versus voiceless plosives has led us to postulate the existence of a unitary mechanism that mediates speech perception and production for the *voiceless* plosives only. We now turn to the specific neural circuitry.

At level D, commands originate for the production of voiced or voiceless plosives. These commands include the abduction of the arytenoid cartilages for voiceless plosives and the adduction of these cartilages for voicedness. The commands also include tensing of the vocal folds for voiceless plosives and slackening of the vocal folds for voiced plosives. Each of these commands may involve a sophisticated set of instructions to various intrinsic, and, in some cases, extrinsic laryngeal muscles, but for the purpose of explicating the general features of the present neural model we will restrict ourselves to the overall commands for abduction and adduction of the arytenoids.

The neural command to adduct the arytenoids accompanies the production of voiced and voiceless prestressed plosives, since without such adduction the vocal folds are sufficiently spread to prevent the onset of voicing. For the articulation of voiced plosives, the adduction command is the only command necessary for lateral arytenoid movement. In the case of most shortlag VOTs, it is simply necessary that the timing of this command be controlled so that the vocal folds are in adducted position by the time of oral release. For the articulation of voiceless plosives, the situation is more complicated.

Prior to the initiation of the adduction command, an abduction command must be transmitted to the laryngeal control system when producing voiceless plosives. We speculate that this abduction command is transmitted through the neural system via Eb_2, a proposed site of perceptual adaptation (see previous discussion). The strength of this abduction command is weakened to some extent as a function of repetitive listening to a voiceless plosive, resulting in a smaller amount of total abduction of the arytenoids. Assuming that the rate of glottal adduction is constant, the end result of this decrease in total abduction is a shorter delay in the onset of vocal fold vibration relative to the release of oral closure. With this circuitry, we can thus account for the shortening effects on VOT that accompany perceptuo-motor adaptation with voiceless plosives as adapting stimuli and test utterances.[9]

Since the abduction command is involved in the production of voiceless plosives but not voiced plosives, the model accounts for why perceptuo-motor

---

[9]An alternative possibility for obtaining the VOT shortening would be to maintain a constant total amount of abduction but to increase the rate of glottal close-down. However, it appears that the rate of glottal adduction may be constant and not independently controllable by the motor system (cf. R. Kagaya, 1974.)

adaptation is observed for voiceless but not voiced utterances. In addition, since the structures fatigued by repetitive listening to a voiced plosive are not part of the circuitry postulated for abduction, the model also accounts for why perceptual adaptation with a voiced plosive does not alter the VOTs of voiceless plosive utterances. The only perceptuo-motor effect permitted under the present model is a net shortening of VOTs for voiceless plosives uttered after perceptual adaptation with voiceless plosives, the only perceptuo-motor effect observed thus far experimentally.

While the present model has been constructed with the specific intention of providing an account of perceptual and perceptuo-motor adaptation effects, the model makes a number of testable predictions about other speech phenomena as well. For example, since a linkage between the perceptual and motor system is postulated in the case of voiceless but not voiced plosives, the model predicts that voiced plosives are probably mastered first in the speech of young children. Recent research is consistent with this prediction.[10,11]

In addition, the model predicts that, in aphasia, patients are more likely to possess a *concurrent* impairment in the perception and production of voiceless as opposed to voiced plosives (Kewley-Port & Preston, 1974; Yeni-Komshian & Preston, 1967). This prediction can be tested by studying a large aphasic population using the methods described by Blumstein, Cooper, Zurif, and Caramazza (1977). The testing of these and other predictions should further an understanding of the relation between speech perception and speech production for the restricted domain of voicing distinctions dealt with in the present perceptuo-motor experiments. On the basis of additional results, it should be possible eventually to replace the present model with one which describes in greater detail the operation of the perceptuo-motor system.

Appendix A

The adapting stimuli were generated on a digital terminal-analog speech synthesizer, which produces 5-kHz bandwidth speech and contains sources for frication,

[10] The pathway from $EA \rightarrow Eb_1 \rightarrow Ec_1 \rightarrow$ [bi] production and from $Ea \rightarrow Eb_2 \rightarrow$ [p^hi] production represents the route taken during subvocalization of the auditorily presented speech sounds. Similarly, the pathway from the vocal cord adduction command to [bi] percept and from vocal fold abduction command to [p^hi] percept represents an auditory image that accompanies articulation. These auxiliary pathways, which were noted only after the construction of the main circuitry was completed, indicate that the present model, despite its simplicity, can account at a general level for a wide range of likely routes of information transmission during speech perception and production.

[11] One prediction concerning the part of the circuit mediating perception involves the existence of facilitation effects—lowered thresholds for the detection of a voiced or voiceless plosive after adaptation with the opposite plosive type. Such facilitation effects may be expected to occur for difference thresholds but not absolute thresholds (see Sekuler & Levinson, 1974).

Table A-1
Major Acoustic Parameter Values

Parameter	Time	Value
fundamental frequency	0	111 Hz
	100	123
	190	98
	195–280	0
	285	109
	330	115
	395	89
first-formant frequency	0–75	346 Hz
	130–185	391
	190–245	203
	265–395	286
second-formant frequency	0–75	1182 Hz
	130–185	1921
	190–245	1478
	265–395	2241
third-formant frequency	0–75	1495 Hz
	130–185	2522
	190–230	2238
	250–395	2810
fourth-formant frequency	0–395	3500
fifth-formant frequency	0–395	4500
amplitude of voicing	0	41 dB
	20–190	60
	195–275	0
	280–355	60
	375–395	54
amplitude of frication	0–225	0 dB
	230–235	30
	240–395	0
amplitude of aspiration	0–230	0 dB
	235	17
	260	21
	275	16
first-formant bandwidth	0–395	50 Hz
second-formant bandwidth	0–395	70 Hz
third-formant bandwidth	0–395	110 Hz
fourth-formant bandwidth	0–395	170 Hz
fifth-formant bandwidth	0–395	250 Hz

aspiration, and voicing. The parameter values for the fundamental frequency contour, formant frequencies and bandwidths, and source amplitudes were updated in discrete 5-msec steps. In Table A-1 the major acoustic parameter values are presented for the adapting stimuli [rəpʰí] as a function of time. All changes in the value of a parameter over time were linear. The isolated [i] adapting stimulus contained the same frequency and bandwidth parameter values as the [i] portion of the [rəpʰí] stimulus, with the amplitude of voicing increasing linearly during the first 50 msec of the vowel from 41 to 60 dB.

Postscript to Study 8

Follow-up Study

Additional measurements were made of the fundamental frequency (F_0) contours of test utterances for the 10 subjects who showed the largest VOT perceptuo-motor effects. If the adaptation effect produced a fatigue of the motor command which provides tension on the cricothyroid muscle, then the decline in F_0 which normally accompanies the first 40 msec or so of a [pʰi] or [tʰi] syllable (Lea, 1973) might be smaller in magnitude after adaptation. To test this possibility, the difference in F_0 between the first glottal cycle and one occurring 40 msec later was measured, using a hardware pitch detector program provided by Douglas O'Shaughnessy (Gold & Rabiner, 1969).[12] No significant difference in the magnitude of F_0 decline was obtained for the perceptuo-motor test conditions; on the average, the F_0 decline was actually about 5 Hz greater after adaptation with [rəpʰí] vs. [i]. The null result obtained here suggests that fatigue of the motor command for vocal fold tension is not a factor in producing the perceptuo-motor effect. Rather, it appears that the motor command controlling the degree of glottal abduction plays a significant role, as emphasized in the previous discussion.

The focus on glottal abduction naturally leads to experimentation designed to measure the degree of abduction, either directly via fiberoptic methods of viewing the glottal area, or indirectly via electromygraphic measurement of the arytenoid muscles. As indicated in the report, we hoped to conduct such tests as an extension of the perceptuo-motor work, but a shift in research strategy short-circuited this plan.

Interpretation

As noted in this study, the lack of a perceptuo-motor effect for a voiced adaptor on voiceless test utterances is accounted for by the present model. Ades

---

[12]In cases where the estimate obtained for the very first glottal cycle was more than 30 Hz above or below that of the second cycle, the second cycle was taken as the starting point of the F_0 analysis, since the pitch detector makes some errors in detecting the first pulse.

(1976), however, takes this lack of effect to indicate that VOT does not serve as a positive cue for voicing, an assumption proposed by Summerfield and Haggard (1974) and reviewed in Chapter 4. This interpretation is at odds with the present model, and it is not clear which of the two proposals is more plausible.

Ades also mentions that the perceptuo-motor site might be the source of an effect reported by Summerfield (1976), who showed that listeners recalibrate their voicing decisions based on VOT as a function of a speaker's apparent rate of speech. The amount of recalibration, interestingly, is about the same as the amount of acoustical change in the speaker's VOT values produced by the rate change. As Ades observes, the joint findings of perceptuo-motor adaptation and the recalibration effect for VOT are gratifying because the link between production and perception was originally proposed to account for how the perceptual system copes with the context-variation of acoustic cues produced by a speaker.

Finally, the difference observed in this study in the magnitude of perceptuo-motor effects for alveolar vs. labial voiceless stops should be reconsidered. As noted in this report, the greater adaptation effects for alveolars may be attributable to alveolars having longer VOTs in the baseline condition; therefore, they enjoy "more room to move" toward shorter VOTs after adaptation than labials. The labials may in effect be resistant to VOT shortening because of a constraint on voiceless VOT compressibility at a given speaking rate. Summerfield and Haggard (1974) have, in addition, noted that the degree of vocal fold abduction is particularly small for labial voiceless stops in the environment of a high following vowel (such as [i], the vowel used here). If perceptuo-motor adaptation influences the motor command for glottal abduction, as suggested earlier, then the smaller magnitude of effect for labials might be accounted for on this basis.[13]

Study 9*

In this study, we consider perceptual adaptation and perceptuo-motor adaptation for a different type of acoustic feature than the ones tested previously. Here we examine a case in which a silent interval serves to cue the existence of an additional phoneme in the syllable. Bastian (1959, 1960) reported a classic series of experiments showing that the perceived distinction between words such as *sag*

---

*Portions of this study are reprinted with permission from *Journal of Experimental Psychology: Human Perception and Performance*, 1976, 2, 105–112, Robert R. Ebert and Ronald A. Cole, coauthors.

[13]Note that this explanation might undermine the rationale for a conclusion reached in Study 7—that the 100% transfer indicates that the site of perceptuo-motor processing operates solely on feature information, as opposed to information about whole phonemes or syllables.

and *stag* could be signaled by the duration of silence between the [s] and the steady-state vowel. In speech production, this silent interval corresponds to the period during which a complete obstruction of airflow exists at some location in the supralaryngeal tract. In the case of *stag*, the obstruction is produced by moving the tongue tip against the alveolar ridge, which lies just behind the upper teeth. Bastian's experiments showed that silent intervals greater than 20 msec produced a [t] percept in most cases, even though other possible cues normally accompanying [t] in speech production (including the presence of a noise burst at the release of oral closure) were not present in the stimuli.

In this study, we ask whether repetitive listening to [si]-[sti] stimuli alters the speech production of these sounds after adaptation. For voiceless plosives [p] and [t] in syllable-initial position, it has been shown in three separate studies (Studies 6-8) that small but systematic effects could be obtained in speech production following repetitive listening to voiceless plosives.

In speech production, it has been shown that the VOT of [t] in [st] clusters is virtually as short as that accompanying a syllable-initial [d] and that this VOT is much shorter than that accompanying voiceless plosives in syllable-initial position. Davidsen-Nielsen (1974), who studied VOT in [s] + plosive clusters using speakers of both British and American English, measured the average VOT for [t] in [st] clusters to be 26 msec, as compared with 23 msec for syllable-initial [d] and 76 msec for syllable-initial [t]. Klatt (1973), in a study of American English, reported an average VOT of 23 msec for [t] in [st] clusters, as compared with 14 msec for syllable-initial [d] and 64 msec for syllable-initial [t]. The VOT for [t] in clusters is thus more similar to that of a voiced than a voiceless plosive in syllable-initial position. Such VOT data account for earlier perceptual observations of Lotz, Abramson, Gerstman, Ingemann, and Nemser (1960) and Reeds and Wang (1961) who found that by splicing out the [s] in [st] clusters they were able to obtain a [d] percept.

A study of airflow during speech production of [st] clusters (Klatt, Stevens, & Mead, 1968), as well as a photoelectric glottographic study of changes in glottal width (Ohala, 1970), have indicated that the vocal folds themselves are approximated (i.e., nearly touching one another) at the time of the release burst for most [st] utterances, as in the case of initial voiced plosives. It can be inferred from this finding that the observed VOT values for [st] clusters are primarily a result of mechanical coupling, as in the case of initial voiced plosives. On this basis, it is predicted that repetitive listening to [sti] should produce no effect on the VOT duration of [sti] utterances, similar to the prediction for [di] proposed in the model of the previous study. In the second and third experiments of the present study, we tested perceptuo-motor adaptation for [st] clusters to determine whether the VOT would in fact be altered by repetitive listening.

EXPERIMENT 1

Method

Subjects. Eight Massachusetts Institute of Technology (M.I.T.) undergraduates participated as paid volunteers in this experiment. All were native speakers of American English and had no known hearing or speech impairment. The subjects had little or no prior training in phonetics.

Stimuli. The test stimuli consisted of seven synthetic speech syllables, ranging from [si] to [sti] by variations in the silent interval between the [s] and the following vowel. The stimuli were five-formant patterns constructed on a digital terminal-analog speech synthesizer at the M.I.T. Research Laboratory of Electronics (Klatt, 1972).

As noted earlier, this synthesizer produces 5-kHz bandwidth speech and contains sources for frication, aspiration, and voicing. The stimuli were generated using the sources for frication and voicing only. The parameter values of the fundamental frequency contour, formant frequencies and bandwidths, and source amplitudes were updated in discrete 5-msec steps. The acoustic parameter values for the [sti] end-point member of the [si]-[sti] series are presented in Table 8. Other members of the series were generated from this set of parameters by starting the onset of the voicing source at shorter invervals after the silent interval, as well as by starting the formant transitions of the vowel portion of the syllable simultaneously with the onset of voicing. The duration of silent interval ranged from 10 to 40 msec in 5-msec steps. Pilot work conducted by author WEC indicated that the 10–40-msec range was sufficient for listeners to categorize the stimuli into roughly equal categories of [si] and [sti].

Procedure. The experiment consisted of two sessions which were conducted on separate days. Each session involved two tests: a baseline test, in which subjects identified the stimuli of the [si]-[sti] series in the unadapted state, and an adaptation test, in which the subjects identified the same stimuli after repetitive listening to one of the two endpoint members of the [si]-[sti] series (these two members contained silent intervals of 10 and 40 msec, respectively). The order of the two adaptation tests was reversed for half of the subjects.

Each session began with a warm-up period during which the subjects listened to a randomized sequence of the speech sounds. The baseline test was then presented, including 10 presentations of each of the 7 [si]-[sti] stimuli and two extra test items. The stimuli were presented in random order with an interstimulus interval of 2.5 sec. The subjects identified each stimulus as "S" or "ST" by writing their choices on answer sheets. The stimuli were played to the listeners at an intensity of approximately 70 dB re 20 $\mu N/m^2$ via Telex head-

Table 8
Acoustic Parameter Values for the [sti] End-Point Member of the [si]–[sti] Series of Synthetic Speech Sounds

Parameter	Time (in msec)	Value
fundamental frequency	0–250	139 Hz
	395	96 Hz
first-formant frequency	0–170	117 Hz
	190–395	289 Hz
second-formant frequency	0–170	1,959 Hz
	190–395	2,296 Hz
third-formant frequency	0–170	3,382 Hz
	190–395	2,947 Hz
fourth-formant frequency	0–395	3,500 Hz
fifth-formant frequency	0–395	4,500 Hz
amplitude of voicing	0–165	off
	170–210	65 dB.
	380	52 dB.
	385–395	off
amplitude of frication	0–15	off
	20	20 dB.
	30–85	30 dB.
	100	20 dB.
	105–395	off
first-formant bandwidth	0–395	50 Hz
second-formant bandwidth	0–395	70 Hz
third-formant bandwidth	0–395	110 Hz
fourth-formant bandwidth	0–395	170 Hz
fifth-formant bandwidth	0–395	250 Hz

Note. Other members of the series were constructed as described in the text. All changes in the value of a parameter as a function of time were linear.

phones from the output of an Ampex PR-10 tape recorder and an AR amplifier. A rest period was provided after half of the test presentations.

The adaptation test of each session included periods of repetitive listening to either the [si] or [sti] end points, followed by presentation of test sounds taken from the same [si]–[sti] series. These test sounds were to be identified as "S" or "ST," as in the baseline test. Each adaptation test consisted of 18 trials. On each trial, the subjects were first presented 40 repetitions of the adapting stimulus, with an interrepetition interval of 350 msec. Following this period of repetitive listening, 4 stimuli were presented for identification. These stimuli were chosen randomly from the [si]–[sti] test series. The first of the 4 test stimuli was presented 2.5 sec. after the final repetition of the adapting stimulus on the trial, and the remaining 3 test stimuli followed at 2.5-sec. intervals. Five seconds of silence elapsed between the presentation of the last of the 4 test items and the beginning of the next adaptation trial. A 5-min. rest period was provided after 9 of the 18 adaptation trials. With this testing procedure, a total of 10 identification responses was obtained for each of the 7 [si]-[sti] test stimuli after adaptation, as in the baseline test. Two extra stimuli were identified in the adaptation tests in order to make a total of 72 test presentations, 4 on each trial. All timing intervals were specified by computer, and the stimulus presentations for each session were recorded onto magnetic tape.

Results and Discussion

The results are presented in Figure 8, where the pooled identification responses for the listeners are shown for the baseline and adaptation conditions. In addition, phonetic boundaries were computed by a least-mean-squares analysis for each individual listener in each test condition.[14]

The results of the baseline tests indicate that the duration of silent interval adequately distinguishes [si] from [sti] in speech perception, as expected on the basis of Bastian's earlier work (1959). In the present case, the crossover between [si] and [sti] responses occurs at a silent interval between 20 and 30 msec for each of the 8 listeners.

The results of the selective adaptation tests showed the presence of systematic shifts in listeners' identification of the [si]-[sti] stimuli after adaptation with [si] and [sti]. After adaptation with [si], each of the 8 listeners assigned fewer identification responses to the [si] category, in comparison with the baseline performance during the same test session (mean boundary shift = 5.1 msec). Statistical analysis of the phonetic boundary values revealed that this effect was significant, $t(7) = 3.022$, $p < 0.05$; two-tailed t-test for correlated observations. After adaptation with [sti], on the other hand, 7 of the 8 listeners assigned fewer identification responses to the [sti] category, in comparison with baseline performance (mean boundary shift = 4.8 msec). Again, this result was statistically significant in terms of a shift in the locus of the phonetic boundary, $t(7) = -2.723$, $p < 0.05$. The results of the selective adaptation tests thus indicate the presence of bidirectional perceptual adaptation effects for the [si]-[sti] series, similar to the effects observed previously for other speech sounds. In each case, listeners assigned fewer identification responses to the phonetic category of the adapting stimulus, the effect being most pronounced at the region of the phonetic boundary (see Figure 9).

Hirsh (1959) has shown for a variety of acoustic stimuli that a duration of 15–20 msec of silence is required between two successive acoustic events in order for a listener to correctly perceive the temporal order of these events. The

---

[14]Tables of phonetic boundary values for individual subjects are available from the author upon request, as are tables of individual subjects' data for Experiments 2 and 3.

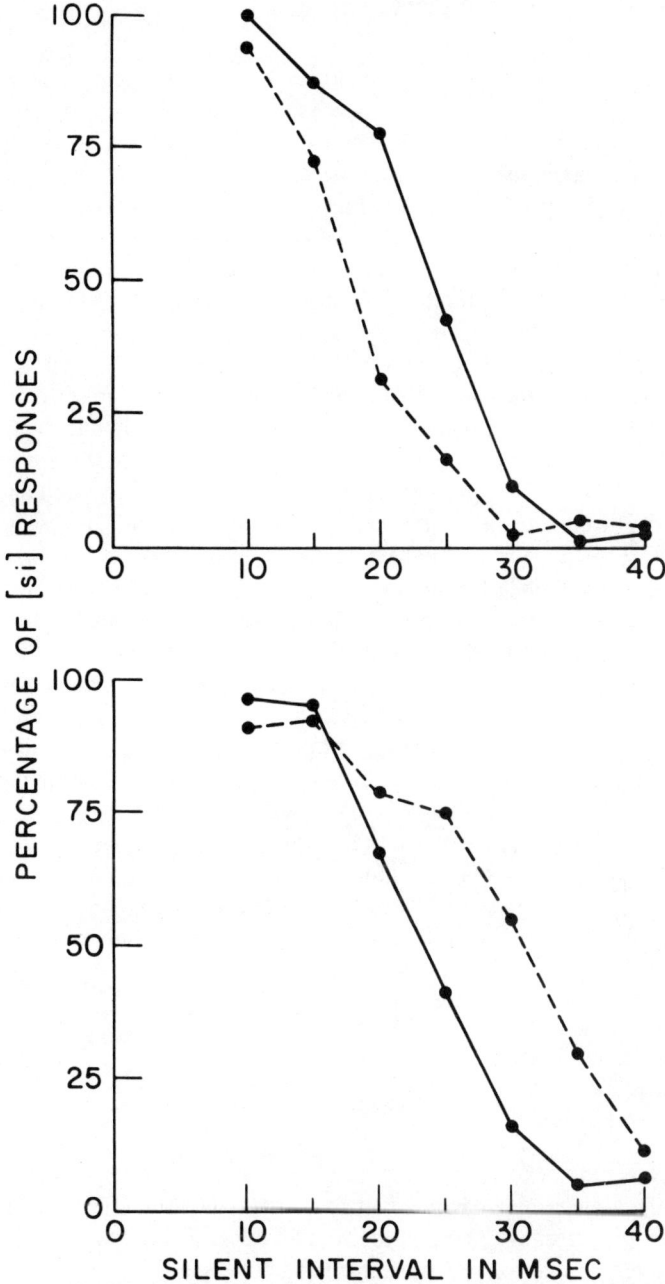

Figure 9. The percentage of [si] responses for the group of 8 subjects before and after adaptation with [si] and [sti]. The solid lines denote identification before adaptation and the dotted lines denote identification after adaptation. The curves in the upper graph represent the identification functions obtained before and after adaptation with [si]; the curves in the lower graph represent the functions obtained before and after adaptation with [sti].

15–20-msec range is close to the 20–30-msec crossover points obtained for the perceived distinction between [si] and [sti] in the present study. It would be difficult, however, to provide an account of the bidirectionality of the present adaptation effects if such effects represented fatigue of a detector which simply computed the duration between two successive temporal events (in this case, the events being the end of [s] and the start of the [i] portion of the waveform) having a lower threshold of between 15 and 20 msec. Whereas postulating fatigue of such a detector might account for the adaptation effect produced after repetitive listening to [sti], it could not account for the effect observed after repetitive listening to [si] because the silent duration of this adapting stimulus was below the detector's threshold and therefore could not produce an effect of fatigue on the detector that was equal to or greater in magnitude than the effect produced in the opposite direction after [sti] adaptation (cf. Figure 9).

It appears that the present results are more adequately accounted for by postulating that the adaptation effects operate at a level of processing slightly beyond that of the detector which computes physical duration between two temporal events with a lower threshold of 15–20 msec. At this high level of processing, two detectors are postulated: one which responds when the output of the duration detector is zero and another which responds when this output is nonzero. It is possible to arrange a system of inhibitory neural elements to represent the operation of the two higher level detectors. Repetitive listening to [si] versus [sti] differentially fatigues one of these two detectors, according to the present view. Assuming that the outputs of these two detectors mutually inhibit one another, a fatigue effect on one detector should shift the listeners' phonetic boundary in the expected direction.

It is quite likely that the aforementioned detectors are sensitive to the duration of silent interval only when such an interval occurs between two speech or speechlike parts of an acoustic signal. Perhaps, according to one viewpoint, the detectors respond not to the silent interval *per se* but to the overall envelope of the wave form in this case.

EXPERIMENT 2

Given the results of the perceptual adaptation tests of Experiment 1, it seemed worthwhile to determine whether perceptuo-motor effects could also be obtained for [t] in [st] clusters. Thus, in the present experiment, [sti] utterances were spoken after periods of repetitive listening to either [si] or [sti]. The [si] adaptor served as a neutral or negative-biasing adaptor in the present test since this adaptor contained no voiceless plosive and in Experiment 1 produced an effect of perceptual adaptation that was opposite in direction to that produced by [sti].

The [sti] utterances were analyzed for both VOT and the duration of silence preceding the plosive release burst. According to the model for perceptuo-motor processing proposed in Study 8, the VOT values for [sti] utterances should remain unchanged after perceptual adaptation, unlike the results obtained for VOT with syllable-initial [t].

Method

Subjects. All eight of the subjects who served in Experiment 1 also participated in this experiment.

Stimuli. Three adapting stimuli were used in this experiment, including one exemplar of [si] containing no silent interval and two exemplars of [sti] containing silent intervals of 40 and 70 msec. All other acoustic parameters were the same as those used in Experiment 1. The two exemplars of [sti] were chosen because extensive pilot work using the [sti] adaptor having a 40-msec silent interval failed to produce perceptuo-motor adaptation effects for 20 subjects. To provide a stronger test of the null hypothesis, we also chose to use a [sti] having a 70-msec silent interval in the present experiment. Of the two [sti] adaptors, the one having a 40-msec silent interval will hereafter be referred to as [sti]$_1$ and the adaptor having a 70-msec silent interval will be referred to as [sti]$_2$. One thousand repetitions of each of the three adapting stimuli (interrepetition interval = 350 msec) were recorded onto magnetic tape for playback during the experiment.

Procedure. The experiment was conducted in the manner used in prior perceptuo-motor adaptation work. The present experiment was conducted in a single, 45-min session consisting of 3 blocks of adaptation trials, separated by a 5-min rest period. Each block of trials consisted of 10 adaptation trials. On each trial, subjects listened to 40 repetitions of a particular adapting stimulus ([si], [sti]$_1$, or [sti]$_2$ in separate blocks) and immediately thereafter uttered the syllable [sti] in a natural voice. During the periods of repetitive listening, the subjects held their tongues between both teeth and lips to prevent movement of the articulators and to maintain a fixed starting position for each [sti] utterance. As in prior perceptuo-motor work, the subjects were trained to respond as automatically as possible as soon as they detected the cessation of the adapting repetitions and to regard each new trial as a separate task instead of trying to maintain the same utterance quality throughout by conscious effort. The adapting repetitions were played to the listeners at an intensity of approximately 70 dB re 20 $\mu N/m^2$ via KLH-Z61 headphones from the output of an Ampex PR-10 tape recorder. The utterances were recorded onto magnetic tape via a Neumann U87 microphone and a Revox A77 tape recorder.

The three blocks of adaptation trials were presented to half of the subjects in the order [si], [sti]$_1$, [sti]$_2$ and to the other half in the reverse order.

Results and Discussion

Each of the 240 utterances was analyzed oscillographically, aided by a computer controlled cursor (Huggins, 1969). The wave-forms were analog-to-digital converted using a sampling rate of 10 kHz at the outset of the computer processing. Measurements of the VOT and the interval of silence preceding the plosive release burst were made for each utterance. The accuracy of each measurement was estimated to be within ±1 msec.

No systematic differences were found between either of the two [sti] adaptation conditions and adaptation with the baseline adaptor [si] ([sti]$_1$ vs. [si]: $t(7) = -1.743$, $p > 0.10$; [sti]$_2$ vs. [si]: $t(7) = -1.127$, $p > 0.20$). Clearly, repetitive listening to either [sti]$_1$ or [sti]$_2$ did not produce any systematic shortening effects on the subjects' VOTs. In actuality, the mean VOT after adaptation with the [sti] stimuli was about 2 msec longer than after adaptation with [si]. In all three test conditions, the mean VOT lies at approximately 20 msec, which is slightly shorter than the mean VOTs for [st] averaged over a number of different words as reported by Davidsen-Nielsen (1974) and Klatt (1973). The average standard deviation for the VOT values in the present experiment was approximately 5 msec, which is less than half as large as the 11-msec standard deviation average found for voiceless plosive in syllable-initial position (Study 8; Klatt, 1973) and comparable to the standard deviations for voiced plosives in syllable-initial position when utterances with voicing lead are excluded (Study 6; Klatt, 1973).

Like the VOT analysis, the results of the silent interval measurements revealed no significant differences between either of the two [sti] adaptation conditions and the [si] adaptation baseline ([sti]$_1$ vs. [si]: $t(7) = -1.262$, $p > 0.10$; [sti]$_2$ vs. [si]: $t(7) = -1.399$, $p > 0.10$). The average silent intervals after adaptation with [si], [sti]$_1$, and [sti]$_2$ were 59.2, 62.1, and 64.4 msec, respectively. On the basis of the significant perceptual adaptation results of Experiment 1, it would have seemed reasonable to predict that if any perceptuo-motor effect were to be observed at all, the effect should be manifest as a shortening of the silent interval following adaptation to [sti]. However, the mean duration of silent interval was longer following [sti] adaptation in the present experiments, averaging 3 msec longer for [sti]$_1$ and 5 msec longer for [sti]$_2$, although neither of these shifts was statistically significant.

The results of the VOT analysis in Experiment 2 support the model of perceptuo-motor adaptation effects observed previously for voiceless plosives in syllable-initial position. In addition, the results of the silent interval analysis provide generality to the prior finding that the silent interval preceding a plosive release is not altered in speech production by repetitive listening. A more detailed account of the present results in terms of the model and other alternatives is provided in the general discussion.

EXPERIMENT 3

Although the results of the preceding VOT analysis provided some support for the model, it could reasonably be argued that the absence of VOT shortening effects in the previous experiment were attributable to the absence of a long VOT in the [sti] adapting stimuli rather than to the nature of motor commands that accompany [sti] utterances. Thus, a third experiment was conducted to determine whether repetitive listening to a [st^{h}i] adaptor containing a long VOT would produce shortening effects. In addition to this [st^{h}i] adaptor, a [t^{h}i] adaptor was also used in the present experiment to provide a further test of perceptuo-motor effects. Finally, the neutral adapting stimulus in the present experiment was an isolated vowel [i] instead of the [si] syllable used in Experiment 2. The vowel adaptor was used in earlier perceptuo-motor work in which VOT shortening effects were observed for voiceless plosives in syllable-initial position.

Method

Subjects. Seven M.I.T. undergraduates, none of whom had served previously, took part as paid volunteers in the present experiment. All of the subjects had the same qualifications as the subjects in Experiment 1.

Stimuli. Three adapting stimuli were used in this experiment—[i], [st^{h}i], and [t^{h}i]—each having an overall duration of 365 msec, the same as previously used synthetic stimuli (cf. Table 8). The [i] adaptor contained formant frequency values identical to those of the vowel portion of the [si]–[sti] stimuli used in Experiment 1. The [st^{h}i] and [t^{h}i] adaptors both contained a noise burst and an interval of aspiration in the [t] portion of the syllable. Both a noise burst and aspiration accompany [t] in syllable-initial position in real speech. A [t] in a cluster such as [st], however, typically contains a noise burst but little, if any, aspiration in real speech (the aspiration interval is usually less than 10 msec).

The present synthetic speech [st^{h}i] adaptor contained an [s] identical to the [s] of previously used [si]–[sti] stimuli (cf. Table 8), followed by a silent interval of 75 msec, a noise burst of 15 msec, an aspiration interval of 30 msec, and finally the steady-state vowel. The VOT for this syllable was 45 msec.

The [t^{h}i] adaptor was constructed by removing the [s] friction noise from the [st^{h}i] adaptor and then lengthening the vowel portion of the syllable to render an overall duration of 365 msec.

Procedure. The experiment was conducted in the manner used in Experiment 2. The only difference between the previous experiment and this one was that the adapting stimuli [i], [st^{h}i], and [t^{h}i] replaced [si], [sti]$_1$, and [sti]$_2$. Four of the subjects listened to the adapting stimuli during the adaptation blocks in the order [i], [stʰi], and [tʰi], whereas the other three subjects listened to these adapting stimuli in the reverse order.

Results and Discussion

Each of the 210 utterances was analyzed for VOT and silent interval oscillographically using a computer controller cursor as in Experiment 2. No significant differences were found between the VOT values of the [sti] utterances produced after repetitive listening to either [sthi] or [thi] in comparison with the [i] adaptation baseline condition ([sthi] vs. [i]: $t(6) = 0.114, p > 0.20$; [thi] vs. [i]: $t(6) = -0.528, p > 0.20$. As in Experiment 2, the VOT values averaged close to 20 msec in all three test conditions. The results provide additional support for the view that repetitive listening to syllables containing voiceless plosives does not alter the VOT values of [sti] utterances, consistent with the model proposed in Study 8.

As in the case of the VOT analysis, no significant differences were found between the closure intervals of the [sti] utterances produced after adaptation to either [sthi] or [thi] in comparison with adaptation to [i] ([sthi] vs. [i]: $t(6) = 0.576, p > 0.20$; [thi] vs. [i]: $t(6) = 0.012, p > 0.20$). Unlike Experiment 2, the present data revealed no tendency for silent intervals to become longer after adaptation with voiceless plosives. The mean silent interval after adaptation with [i], [sthi], and [thi] was 73.4, 70.8, and 73.2 msec, respectively. A consideration of individual differences suggests the possibility that significant effects are present, but that these effects are different in direction for different subjects. An interesting trend emerged from the silent interval data when the baseline condition of each experiment ([si] or [i] adaptation) was compared with the two other adaptation tests ([sti]$_1$ and [sti]$_2$ in Experiment 2 and [sthi] and [thi] in Experiment 3). The shifts in mean silent interval for the latter two test conditions were in the same direction with respect to the baseline for 14 of the 15 subjects. A similar trend was noted for 11 of the 15 subjects for the VOT data. Although it is probably premature to conclude that either of these *post hoc* analyses represents reliable individual perceptuo-motor effects, we should continue to study the possibility of such regularities in future work with the perceptuo-motor paradigm. If significant effects do exist which are opposite in direction for different subjects, then our current review of perceptuo-motor control, as outlined in the general discussion, will require considerable revision.

GENERAL DISCUSSION

The present experiments demonstrate the presence of perceptual adaptation effects for a series of speech syllables ranging from [si] to [sti], as well as the absence of perceptuo-motor adaptation effects for [sti] utterances after repetitive listening to [sti], [sthi], or [thi]. As we have already observed, this marked contrast between the results of the perceptual and perceptuo-motor adaptation tests is in accord with a neural model of perceptual and perceptuo-motor processing proposed earlier on the basis of evidence for voiced and voiceless plosives in syllable-initial position.

The model was constructed to account for the presence of adaptation effects for initial voiced plosives in a strictly perceptual adaptation paradigm as well as for the absence of such effects in a perceptuo-motor paradigm, while at the same time accounting for the presence of adaptation effects for initial voiceless plosives in both testing situations. The model postulated that repetitive listening to a voiceless plosive in syllable-initial position selectively fatigues a neural processor which both (a) transmits information about voice timing relations from the auditory system to a perceptual decision processor for voiced–voiceless distinctions, and (b) transmits information to the motor commands which regulate the amount of abduction of the vocal folds at approximately the time of plosive release (Kagaya, 1974; Kim, 1965, 1970). The motor command to adduct, or close down the opening of the glottis, which accompanies the production of both initial voiced and voiceless plosives, was assumed not to be under perceptuo-motor control. The model accounted for the observed shortening of VOT in speech production of initial voiceless plosives after repetitive listening to a voiceless plosive by postulating a weakening in the abduction command, along with a constant rate of glottal close-down (cf. Kagaya, 1974, for some supporting evidence of the latter postulate). Because laryngeal pulsing is initiated only after the vocal folds move sufficiently close to one another (Halle & Stevens, 1971), this schema accounted for the observed shortening effects of VOT for the initial voiceless plosives.

For initial voiced plosives containing a short lag in voicing onset, the vocal folds are sufficiently close to one another at the release of the consonant to initiate laryngeal pulsing, and the precise time at which such pulsing begins with respect to the release is believed to be determined by the time needed for a sufficient drop in intraoral pressure (cf. Klatt, 1973; Lisker & Abramson, 1971; Ohala, 1970). Thus, the VOT values obtained for such utterances are determined by mechanical factors rather than central neural commands. This situation indicates that the null results obtained for voiced plosives in perceptuo-motor adaptation experiments are quite reasonable. Perhaps the neural commands controlling the adduction of the vocal folds are in fact subject to perceptuo-motor adaptation, as evidenced by variations in the VOT values for voiced plosives when a period of voicing lead is observed (cf. Study 6). However, analysis of the data from both Studies 6 and 7 revealed no systematic effects when utterances containing such voicing lead were analyzed separately from utterances containing short lags in voicing onset with respect to the release burst. Thus, we have put forth the possibility in the model that the timing of glottal adduction is not under perceptuo-motor control with respect to the timing of the release burst, unlike the case for glottal abduction.

Since, as we noted in the introduction, the VOT values for [sti] utterances appear to be primarily a consequence of mechanical coupling as in the case of syllable-initial voiced plosives, it was predicted that no perceptuo-motor adaptation effect for VOT values would be observed, and the data from Experiments 2 and 3 support this prediction. An additional indication that the VOT values were primarily determined by mechanical factors[15] was provided by the small standard deviation values obtained (about 5 msec for each speaker), similar to the standard deviations observed in our previous data for initial voiced plosives that contained short-lag VOTs. In contrast, the standard deviations for voiceless plosives in syllable-initial position averaged about 11 msec in our earlier data, consistent with the view that voice timing relations for such plosives involve relatively complex central control, probably involving more than one motor command. In addition to the command to abduct the vocal folds, there exists, for example, the possibility of commands to increase the tension of certain laryngeal muscles during the production of initial voiceless plosives, including commands to increase tension on the *cricothyroid* and *lateral cricoarytenoid* (Halle & Stevens, 1971; Maeda, 1975).

In summary, it appears that the model of the adaptation effects provides an adequate account of the present results as well as the previous results obtained with the perceptuo-motor paradigm. Although this model provides an account of the available data, we view the present model primarily as a working hypothesis which requires continued critical appraisal and empirical testing.

It must also be recognized that the present null results of perceptuo-motor adaptation, while predicted by our model, are also predicted by models which posit no link between perception and production at any stage of speech processing. Such models cannot, however, account for the positive perceptuo-motor effects observed for voiceless plosives in syllable-initial position found in three previous studies, whereas the model proposed in Study 8 provides a means of accounting for both positive and negative results selectively observed for voiceless plosives contained in different syllable environments.

Postscript to Study 9

The work on perception has been extended to include a comparison between the syllable-initial cluster [st] and a syllable-*final* cluster [ts]. A series of stimuli varying from [is] to [its] was constructed, analogous to the series used in

---

[15]A high-level problem which the present account cannot resolve is how a speaker converts from an internal representation of the stop consonant in [st] to the level of motor commands. It is likely that the internal representation of the stop in [st] is T, yet the motor commands that accompany the production of this stop in [st] clusters are more similar to those for a word-initial [d] than [t]. A process of translation from the internal representation to the motor commands must be postulated, according to this view, and a reverse translation process must be postulated for speech perception. Chomsky and Halle (1968) discuss the nature of internal representations and the problem of translation to and from such representations at some length, although work has yet to uncover any of the details of how the proposed translation process occurs.

Experiment 1, by varying the interval of silence between the formant transitions of the vowel and the fricative [s]. The aim of the study was twofold: to determine (a) the degree to which acoustic differences in silent duration could be used to make phoneme decisions for initial vs. final clusters, and (b) to determine whether crossed-adaptation effects could be obtained using syllable-final clusters as adaptors and syllable-initial clusters as test stimuli. The baseline results showed that listeners could distinguish [si] from [sti] using a much smaller range of silent interval than [is] from [its], by about a factor of two. Crossed-adaptation tests revealed a number of significant effects for a group of 17 listeners, but the direction of these effects was in some cases uninterpretable. For the [si]–[sti] test series, fewer [si] responses were obtained after adaptation with [is], [its] than with the isolated vowel [i] (only 8 listeners participated in this last test, but the effect was statistically significant at p <0.01). These results would appear to rule out the possibility that adaptation for the [si]–[sti] distinction affects a detector for silence which operates irrespective of the location in the syllable where the silence occurs. No single account can be provided for the effects obtained, and the detection system for the consonant cluster remains a topic for future study.

NEW PERCEPTUO-MOTOR STUDIES

Recent work on perceptuo-motor adaptation has focused primarily on studies with Hindi stops in syllable-initial position and with English stops in syllable-final position.

Unlike English, the Hindi language has a phonemic contrast between aspirated and unaspirated voiced stops, as in [b^h] vs. [b]. According to the model presented in Study 8, perceptuo-motor adaptation should be observed for the aspiration interval of stop consonant, so it was decided to test this hypothesis for the Hindi voiced aspirates. Native speakers of Hindi now at M.I.T. served as subjects in an experiment conducted with Steven Lapointe. The data for two speakers have been analyzed. The aspiration interval was measured spectrographically to test whether the interval of aspiration in the syllable [$d^h a$] differed after repeated listening to either the isolated vowel [a] (the control condition) or the voice of aspirate of [$b^h a$]. Perceptuo-motor adaptation effects were observed in the predicted direction for both speakers. The aspiration interval was shortened by an average of about 11 msec for each speaker after adaptation with [$b^h a$] vs. [a].

An additional perceptuo-motor study was conducted to determine whether cross-adaptation effects would be observed for stop consonants in different syllable environments. The adapting stimuli consisted of a vowel control [i] and CV syllables [$t^h i$] and [$k^h i$], with test utterances including the VC syllables [it] and [ik]. Unlike stops in CV syllables, a major cue for voiceless stops in VC syllables consists of the interval of silence following the vowel (Wang, 1959). This interval is typically shorter for a voiceless stop than for a voiced one. Steven Lapointe and I tested to see whether this interval would be lengthened after perceptuo-motor adaptation with the CV adaptors, as might be expected if the site of adaptation is a very high-level phonetic processor (Level D in the model of Chapter 1) for the voiced-voiceless distinction. In fact, a small shortening effect was obtained for a group of 16 subjects, averaging close to 6 msec for [it] and less than 2 msec for [ik] utterances. The effect did not approach statistical significance, however. Thus, it seems likely that the earlier perceptuo-motor effects should be assigned to Level B in the Chapter 1 model.

chapter six
MOTOR–PERCEPTUAL ADAPTATION

In the previous chapter we considered perceptuo-motor tests in which the acoustic properties of utterances were measured after periods of repeated listening. In this chapter, we study a converse situation, in which subjects' perception was tested after repeated articulation. The results obtained with this procedure were less systematic than those obtained in the previous chapter, yet, they were by no means random. For each case where the effect was observed, the effect's direction was the same as that obtained using a strictly perceptual adaptation test. The results thus added a further measure of support to the notion that speech perception and production rely to some extent on the same processing machinery.

Study 10*

According to the model presented in the previous chapter, perceptuo-motor adaptation effects are attributable to the fatiguing of a mechanism that processes consonant feature information jointly for the perception and production of speech. Such a model predicts that, in addition to the effects observed in previous research, there should exist a converse perceptuo-motor effect in which repetitive articulation alters the perception of speech, even in the case where the repetitive articulation is not accompanied by auditory feedback.

*Portions of this study are reprinted with permission from *Journal of Phonetics*, 1975, *3*, 87–98, Sheila E. Blumstein and Georgia Nigro, coauthors.

However, the existence of this complementary effect is by no means certain, since the prior perceptuo-motor effects could conceivably be attributed to a one-way regulation of speech production by mechanisms that normally subserve perception. Although the case in favor of such one-way regulation is rather weak at present, there does exist at least one line of reasoning which lends some plausibility to this view. The starting point for this approach is the recent observation that young infants can perceive distinctions between consonants that belong to different adult phonetic categories long before they can produce such distinctions (Eimas, Siqueland, Jusczyk, & Vigorito, 1971; Eimas, 1974; Butterfield & Cairns, 1974). Given this finding, it is quite reasonable to suppose that the articulation of different consonant sounds is initially established with the help of auditory monitoring, in much the same way that the development of birdsong is accomplished in some species (Konishi, 1965; Marler, 1974).

We might go on from here to suppose that the regulation of speech production by auditory feedback in childhood is retained as a useful feature in the speech system of adults. Experiments by Ringel and Steer (1963), Ladefoged (1967), Scott and Ringel (1971), and Sussman and his co-workers (Sussman, 1971; Sussman, MacNeilage, & Lumbley, 1974) have provided fairly strong support for this proposal, although not in the particular case of consonants. Ringel and Steer (1963) and Ladefoged (1967) found that the elimination of auditory feedback during speech production (by means of white noise masking) affected the length and quality of many vowel sounds, as well as nasalization and pitch.

Sussman and his colleagues have approached the feedback question using a different experimental approach consisting of an auditory motor-tracking task. In this task, subjects are presented a tone of slowly varying frequency and amplitude to one ear, and a cursor tone, whose frequency–amplitude modulation is controlled by movements of the subjects' own tongue, to the opposite ear. Sussman found that subjects track the target tone better when the cursor tone is presented to the right ear than when it is presented to the left. This right ear advantage for tongue tracking, later extended to tracking with the jaw as well, is analogous to the right ear advantage typically obtained in dichotic perception tests (cf. Kimura, 1967). Sussman also demonstrated that parts of the body not involved in speech communication, such as the hand, produced no significant ear advantage in the tracking task. This latter result indicated that the ear advantage obtained for the articulators was not simply a reflection of a general lateralization of somatic sensorimotor control.

On the basis of these results, Sussman proposed the existence of a hemispherically specialized system which provides the articulatory motor commands with auditory feedback. Granting the existence of this regulatory system, and extending it for the sake of argument to the case of consonant sounds, it is possible to account for our prior perceptuo-motor adaptation effects in terms of one-way regulation, provided that one further assumption is made. In our perceptuo-motor adaptation experiments, systematic effects were obtained for utterances after periods of repetitive listening. Thus, we must assume, according to the one-way regulatory account of these effects, that the regulatory system operates not only to provide auditory feedback to the motor commands after an utterance but that the system is also capable of providing input to the motor commands via externally produced speech prior to the initiation of self-produced utterances. This assumption derives some support from constraints on our ability to mimic speech sounds. It has been shown that the ability to mimic different consonants is constrained by the ability to perceive distinctions among such sounds (cf. Harris, Bastian, & Liberman, 1961). Although the Haskins researchers prefer to account for this limitation in terms of a motor constraint on perception, a converse auditory-to-motor regulatory system could account for the finding equally well. Overall, then, we must conclude that the possibility of a one-way regulation of speech production by speech perception cannot be strictly ruled out.

If in fact such a one-way regulatory system is operative, it is of interest to consider why complementary effects of speech production on speech perception might *not* be obtained. This possibility might rely on the notion of *efferent copy* (von Holst & Mittelstaedt, 1950; von Holst, 1954; Mittelstaedt, 1960), known also as *corollary discharge* (Sperry, 1950; Teuber, 1964). According to this concept, motor commands are accompanied by a motor-to-sensory discharge which serves to cancel out the afferent signal that is produced as a consequence of motor activity (reafference). The efferent copy signal prohibits the system from mistaking the reafferent signal for one which is environmentally produced (exafference). Although the efferent copy was originally proposed to account for such phenomena as the stability of visual perception during saccadic eye movements, it has recently been proposed by Lackner (1974) that such a discharge accompanies speech production as well.

In Lackner's study, subjects were asked to repeat a given CV syllable at a very rapid rate (one repetition every 300 ms) for periods of 30 s. During each of these repetition periods, the experimenter observed that the phonetic identity of the syllable uttered by the subject did not change. In addition, the subjects reported that their perception of this syllable was seldom altered during the repetitions. However, when the same subjects later listened to recordings of their own repetitive speech, numerous perceptual alterations were reported.

Lackner argued that the failure to obtain perceptual alterations in the case of self-produced speech indicated the presence of a corollary discharge signal sent in a feed-forward manner from the production system to the perceptual system. However, while it may be true that corollary discharge information accompanies articulation, there exists certain drawbacks with Lackner's experiment which make it difficult to draw any conclusions regarding the role of corollary discharge in perceptual stabilization.[1] In the present research, we wished to study the possibility of an influence of speech production on speech perception which could not be attributed to a one-way regulatory system such as the one presumed to mediate the efferent copy. In order to bypass any possible effects of neural fatigue that may occur in such a system, we employed exafferent, or environmentally produced, stimuli while testing subjects' perception. With exafferent test stimuli, it was possible to obtain a more sensitive measure of perception as well, by using synthetically generated speech signals which differed from one another by small amounts along a specified acoustic dimension.

A proper test of the influence of speech production on perception must involve an open loop testing situation, in which repetitive articulation is not accompanied by auditory feedback to the speaker, since such feedback could induce purely perceptual adaptation effects. In order to eliminate this possibility, we employed an experimental task in which subjects whispered a syllable during the periods of repetitive articulation, while they simultaneously listened to a white noise masking stimulus over headphones. The combination of whispered speech and white noise masking served to prevent auditory feedback in the case of both air- and bone-conducted signals (cf. Ladefoged, 1967, p. 163; Tonndorf, 1970).

Since we employed whispered (i.e., nonvoiced) speech, it was inappropriate in this study to investigate the feature *voicing*, the topic of our prior perceptuo-motor work. Instead, the present testing procedure was more condu-

---

[1] A number of difficulties exist with Lackner's experiment. (1) Concerning his observation that the produced syllable does not change its phonetic identity during the repetitions, it should be noted that this result holds only when subjects are required to repeat a *single* syllable. It has been observed by Jakobson (1941) for normal adult speakers, and by Luria (1970) for aphasics, that speech production is quickly distorted when subjects are required to repeat an alternating sequence of two similar syllables (e.g., [ba] and [pʰa]). Since aphasics appear to be particularly susceptible to this effect, it is unlikely that this effect is entirely attributable to peripheral motor difficulties. Thus, in the case of an alternating sequence, stability of the production system is not maintained. Whether or not the perceptual system remains stable with respect to produced speech in this situation is not yet known. In any event, the claim that produced speech remains stable during repetitive articulation seems limited to the case of single-syllable repetitions, and in this case stability can be attributed to the simplicity of the task and to the fact that little or no phonetic processing is required of the subject. (2) Lackner's measures of both speech production and speech perception are gross measures of phoneme identity. It is quite possible that subtle but systematic acoustic changes occur in the repetitive productions of a single syllable, but that these changes would only be revealed by acoustical analysis of the utterances. An analogous problem arises with his measure of perceptual alterations, a problem which can be avoided by the use of synthetic speech sounds. (3) The extremely fast rate of articulation demanded of his subjects was not conducive to normal auditory monitoring of the self-produced speech. It could thus be argued that suppression of normal auditory monitoring may have played a role in limiting the perceptual alterations reported during the periods of repeated articulation. In summary, there exist sufficient grounds for questioning the validity of Lackner's findings with regard to the normal functioning of the perceptuo-motor system.

cive to a study of *place of articulation*, the focus of perceptual adaptation studies in Chapter 2.

Pilot Work

We began by conducting an experiment in which four subjects were asked to utter repetitions of the syllable [bæ] for 1-min periods while listening to white noise, each repetition period being followed by identification of auditorily presented stimuli from a synthetic series of [bæ]–[dæ]–[gæ] syllables. These syllables varied from one another only in the starting frequency and direction of the second- and third-formant transitions. During repetitive articulation, subjects spoke in a whispered voice at a rate of about one syllable per second.

With this procedure, we obtained systematic effects of perceptuo-motor adaptation for three of the four subjects. The direction of the effects was analogous to that obtained in prior perceptual adaptation work with the [bæ]–[dæ]–[gæ] test series, using [bæ] as the adapting syllable. In both the case of perceptual and perceptuo-motor adaptation, subjects' phonetic boundary between [b] and [d] shifted toward the [b] category, signifying that the subjects assigned fewer identification responses to the [b] category after adaptation, as compared with a baseline measure in which the subjects identified the syllables without adaptation. On the other hand, the subjects' phonetic boundary detween [d] and [g] remained fixed after adaptation with respect to the baseline measure. These results provided additional support for the model of place feature analysis presented in Study 1, in which three separate analyzers are utilized to process labial, alveolar, and velar consonants.

Although encouraging, these initial results were far from conclusive, since the magnitude of the effect was quite small for two of the subjects and since the effect was absent in the case of another (the average phonetic boundary shift for the [b]–[d] boundary across the four subjects was 0.9 stimulus values; see below for details on method of data analysis). In order to try to produce a greater magnitude of effect, while at the same time making the experiment a more valid test of phonetic perceptuo-motor control, we decided to make one major modification in the experimental procedure before resuming the study. In the pilot work, it had been noted that the use of a single articulatory adapting stimulus demanded very little phonetic processing on the part of the subjects. Indeed, subjects could simply put their lips together, mimicking a bilabial closure, without effectively articulating the target syllable [bæ]. We chose to increase the amount of phonetic processing required of the subjects by having them utter a sequence of syllables sharing the same approximate place of articulation. We hoped that, in addition to increasing the phonetic processing load, the use of this sequence would reduce somewhat the tedium encountered in the experimental task, a factor unanimously reported by our subjects.

The sequence of syllables consisted of [bæ], [mæ], and [væ], all containing labial initial segments. In prior perceptual adaptation work, it was shown that each of these three syllables was effective in selectively adapting listeners' [b]–[d] phonetic boundary in the direction toward [b], indicating that the adaptation effects were specific to the *place* feature of the consonant and independent of the particular *manner* class to which the consonants belonged (i.e., plosive, nasal, or fricative, Study 2).

The main experiment reported included six test conditions. Two of the tests were baseline measures; the remaining four tests included open loop (repetitive articulation with no auditory feedback) and closed loop (repetitive articulation with auditory feedback) perceptuo-motor adaptation, a perceptual adaptation test, and a test in which subjects were instructed to simply "think" the [bæ]–[mæ]–[væ] sequence repetitively.

Method

Eight Brown University students participated as paid volunteers in this experiment. All subjects were native speakers of English and had no known speech or hearing impairments.

The test stimuli consisted of 13 synthetic speech CV syllables ranging from [bæ] to [dæ] to [gæ]. These syllables were constructed on a parallel resonance synthesizer by Pisoni (1971). The syllables varied from one another only in the starting frequency and direction of the second- and third-formant transitions. The starting frequencies and steady-state frequencies of these formant transitions are presented in Table 1; other acoustic specifications for these stimuli appear in Pisoni (1971).

The experiment included six tests, (1) unadapted auditory identification of the [bæ]–[dæ]–[gæ] syllables, and the remaining tests, (2) through (6), consisting of auditory identification of these same syllables after 1-min periods of: (2) listening to white noise, (3) repetitive whispered articulation of the [bæ]–[mæ]–[væ] sequence while listening to white noise, (4) repetitive "thinking" of the [bæ]–[mæ]–[væ] sequence, (5) repetitive articulation (nonwhispered) of the [bæ]–[mæ]–[væ] sequence with auditory feedback, and (6) repetitive listening to a [bæ]–[mæ]–[væ] sequence. All eight subjects were presented the first two tests, the baseline conditions, on the first day of the experiment. Half of the subjects were then presented tests (3) through (5), each test on a separate day, while the other half of the subjects were presented these same tests in the reverse order. All eight subjects were presented test (6) on the final day of the experiment. A minimum of 20 h and a maximum of 5 days separated adjacent test sessions. The perceptual adaptation test (condition 6) was administered on the last day of testing so that any effects of perceptuo-motor adaptation could not be attributed to carry-over effects induced during the perceptual adaptation test.

Test condition (1), the unadapted baseline test, was administered in the manner used previously. The 13 test stimuli were presented to subjects 10 times

Table 1
Starting Frequencies of the Second- and Third-Formant Transitions for the Synthetic CV Stimuli

Stimulus number	Starting frequencies (Hz) F_2	F_3
1	1232	2180
2	1312	2348
3	1386	2525
4	1465	2694
5	1541	2862
6	1620	3026
7	1695	3195
8	1772	3026
9	1845	2862
10	1920	2694
11	1996	2525
12	2078	2348
13	2156	2180

Note. The fixed steady state formants were centered at 743 Hz (F_1), 1620 Hz (F_2) and 2862 Hz (F_3) (after Pisoni, 1971).

each in random order over Koss Pro 4AA headphones with circumaural seal, from the output of a Revox A77 tape recorder. The stimuli were played at a comfortable listening level (approximately 70 dB SPL). Adjacent stimuli were separated by 2.5 s of silence.

In test conditions (2) through (6), the test stimuli were presented in groups of 4 as in prior perceptual adaptation work. Ten occurrences of each stimulus were presented during each test in this manner.

Test condition (2) represented a second baseline test in which any possible effects of repeated exposure to white noise were assessed. The white noise, 3 dB down at 50 and 10,000 Hz, was generated by a Grason Stadler 901B noise generator and was played to subjects at an intensity of approximately 70 dB SPL.

Prior to the beginning of test conditions (3) and (5), the tests in which repetitive articulation was required, subjects were trained to articulate the [bæ]-[mæ]-[væ] sequence at a fixed rate of about one syllable per second in time with a flashing light. In the case of condition (3), the subjects were required to whisper this sequence, while in condition (5), they spoke the sequence normally. In both conditions, the subjects were instructed to articulate each syllable fully from a fixed starting position, with mouth closed. Occasional deviations from the fixed rate of articulation were called to the subjects' attention by a tap on the shoulder from the experimenter, who monitored the articulation throughout.

In test condition (3), subjects listened to the white noise masking stimulus during the periods of repetitive articulation. The noise level was set at approximately 70 dB SPL as in the noise baseline test. Subjects reported in pilot work that they received no auditory feedback at this noise intensity. In condition (5), auditory feedback was provided over the headphones, by having subjects articulate into a Sony microphone connected to a Sony TC-630 tape recorder.

In test condition (4), subjects were told to "think" the [bæ]-[mæ]-[væ] sequence at the same fixed rate as in the repetitive articulation conditions. The subjects were instructed to hold their tongues firmly between both teeth and lips to prevent supraglottal movements during this test, and they were told to minimize subvocalization as well.

Test condition (6), the perceptual adaptation test, involved repetitive listening to a sequence of the three syllables [bæ]-[mæ]-[væ], spoken by WEC. These stimuli, each 300 ms in duration, were recorded, dubbed, and then played back to subjects in a repetitive sequence with 350 ms separating adjacent stimuli. In this test condition, as well as in test conditions (2) through (5), 2s of silence intervened between the end of the adapting period and the onset of the first of the four test stimuli on each trial. Adjacent test stimuli were separated by 2.5 s of silence, while 5 s separated the fourth test stimulus from the onset of the next adaptation trial.

Results and Discussion

The results appear in Table 2, where the phonetic boundary values are computed by a least-mean squares analysis for each subject in each test condition. The phonetic boundary value in each case was determined by first assigning to each stimulus a number ranging from 1 to 13 (see Table 1) and then performing a least-mean squares analysis on the transformed percentages of identification responses.

A one-way analysis of variance was applied to the phonetic boundary values. No significant main effect was obtained. A subsequent t-test comparing performance on the unadapted baseline (condition 1) and the baseline in which white noise was administered (condition 2) was also nonsignificant. We chose to employ the noise baseline values for making additional comparisons between baseline and adapted performance. Subsequent t-tests for conditions (2) through (6), including all pair-wise comparisons, showed two significant differences for the [b]-[d] phonetic boundary and no significant differences for the [d]-[g] phonetic boundary. For the [b]-[d] boundary, the values for test condition (2) (noise baseline) and for test condition (4) ("think" [bæ]-[mæ]-[væ]) were both significantly larger than the values for test condition (6) (perceptual adaptation to [bæ]-[mæ]-[væ]) ($P < 0.05$). These results indicate that fewer [b] responses were assigned by subjects in the strictly perceptual adaptation test than in either the noise baseline or the "think" adaptation conditions. The outcome

Table 2
Individual and Mean Phonetic Boundaries for Each Test Condition

(a) [b]–[d] Phonetic boundary
Test conditions

Subjects	(1)	(2)	(3)	(4)	(5)	(6)
M.F.	3.50	4.00	3.93	4.39	3.17	3.83
G.G.	4.16	4.27	3.61	5.59	4.61	4.51
S.G.	3.33	3.28	3.24	4.12	3.12	0.00
M.L.	2.76	3.97	3.93	3.62	4.36	3.34
P.M.	4.64	4.50	4.96	5.06	4.38	3.09
C.M.	3.59	4.03	4.83	4.50	4.03	4.17
C.P.	3.82	3.96	0.00*	0.74	0.00	0.00
J.S.	4.37	4.41	2.53	3.82	0.00	0.00
Mean	3.77	4.05	3.38	3.98	2.96	2.37

*Identification functions which contained no percentage of [b] responses greater than 50% for any of the 13 test stimuli have phonetic boundary estimates of 0.00.

(b) [d]–[g] Phonetic boundary
Test conditions

Subjects	(1)	(2)	(3)	(4)	(5)	(6)
M.F.	10.75	10.44	9.83	10.23	9.43	9.58
G.G.	9.79	9.61	10.55	10.44	9.01	10.50
S.G.	10.61	10.44	9.56	9.35	9.92	10.46
M.L.	9.45	9.69	9.55	9.45	9.07	9.07
P.M.	9.07	9.45	9.50	9.18	9.33	9.50
C.M.	10.50	9.83	9.89	9.61	10.22	10.16
C.P.	9.89	8.89	9.03	8.67	9.91	10.00
J.S.	10.39	10.50	9.92	11.22	9.78	10.89
Mean	10.06	9.86	9.73	9.77	9.58	10.02

Note. The value of each phonetic boundary was determined by first assigning to each stimulus an arbitrary number, ranging from 1 to 13, and then performing a least mean squares analysis.

for the perceptual adaptation test vis à vis the baseline test was as predicted from previous work (Study 2), while the results for the "think" test are discussed below.

A comparison of the boundary values for the open and closed loop perceptuo-motor adaptation (test conditions 3 and 5) with the noise baseline revealed nonsignificant differences in the same direction as the comparison between the baseline and the perceptual adaptation test; namely, after repetitive articulation of the [bæ]-[mæ]-[væ] sequence, subjects assigned somewhat fewer responses to the [b] category (open loop vs. noise baseline, $t = 1.227$, $0.20 < P < 0.30$; closed loop vs. noise baseline, $t = 1.588$, $0.10 < P < 0.20$).

While the overall effects of the open and closed loop perceptuo-motor test failed to reach statistical significance, analysis of the data for individual subjects revealed a clear pattern of results which did offer support for the presence of a systematic perceptuo-motor effect. Of the eight subjects tested, three (namely J.S., C.P. and S.G.) showed relatively large adaptation effects in the perceptual adaptation test. These same subjects also showed effects of perceptuo-motor adaptation in the expected direction in both the open and closed loop test. Two of these subjects, J.S. and C.P., showed quite sizable perceptuo-motor effects, amounting to a shift of about two stimulus values, or a shift of about 150 Hz in the starting frequency of the second-formant transition. The data for one of these subjects, J.S., are shown in Figure 1.

In addition, the data on Table 2 show a fairly good overall correlation between the performance of individual subjects on the perceptual adaptation test and their performance on both the open and closed loop perceptuo-motor tests. To assess this correlation statistically, we performed a Spearman's rank order correlation on the [b]-[d] phonetic boundary for the magnitude of shift in the perceptual adaptation test compared with the magnitude of shift in each of the two perceptuo-motor tests (the amount of shift in each case was determined by subtracting the boundary value obtained in the noise baseline from the boundary value of the adaptation test). The results of this correlational analysis showed a significant rank correlation between the effects of perceptual adaptation and closed loop perceptuo-motor adaptation ($\rho = 0.77$, $P < 0.05$) and a similar though statistically non-significant correlation between the effects of perceptual adaptation and open loop perceptuo-motor adaptation ($\rho = +0.59$, $P > 0.05$).

In summarizing the results of this experiment, it should be mentioned first of all that, as expected on the basis of prior work, perceptual adaptation to a sequence of [bæ]-[mæ]-[væ] syllables produced a systematic effect on the phonetic boundary between [b] and [d], the boundary being displaced toward the [b] category after adaptation. On the other hand, no systematic effect was obtained for the phonetic boundary between [d] and [g]. The results of the open and closed loop perceptuo-motor test indicate the presence of a similar effect restricted to the [b]-[d] phonetic boundary, although only six of the eight subjects showed the effect, and in some cases the magnitude of the effect was negligible. A comparison of performance on the perceptual adaptation test and the two perceptuo-motor tests revealed a strong relationship between the perceptual and perceptuo-motor effects. The overall conclusion drawn from these results is that a perceptuo-motor effect is present, even in the case of open loop testing, but that its appearance depends on a strongly adaptable speech processing system, present in only some of our subjects. According to our view, a large

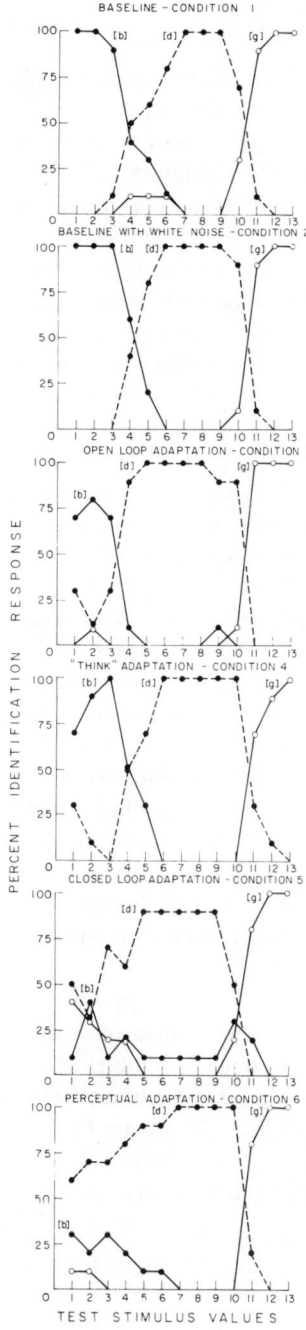

Figure 1. Percentages of identification responses ([b], [d], or [g]) obtained for subject J.S. in each of the six test conditions.

part of the effect produced in the strictly perceptual adaptation test is attributable to fatigue of the same processing site which accounts for the perceptuo-motor effects—a site which jointly processes information about the *place* feature for both speech perception and speech production.[2]

In comparison with the baseline, the results for the "think" condition showed an overall nonsignificant effect in the direction opposite that obtained for the perceptual and perceptuo-motor tests. It thus appears that merely thinking a repetitive sequence of labial consonant + vowel syllables is not a sufficient condition for producing the adaptation effects. This finding indicates that it is unlikely that the adaptation effects reflect the fatiguing of a simple auditory-motor mental image.

Follow-up Experiment

Like the results of our pilot work, the overall results of the main experiment provided less-than-convincing support for the existence of a perceptuo-motor adaptation effect, although the results for some individuals were quite clearly supportive. We made one further attempt to improve the task by trying to reduce the tedium associated with the present experiment. We hoped to accomplish this goal by decreasing the duration of each period of repetitive articulation from 1 min to 40 s. In a follow-up experiment, four new subjects were tested using this modified procedure, and three of these four showed sizable perceptuo-motor adaptation effects (average effect for the three subjects for the open loop test = 2.11 stimulus values, for the closed loop test = 1.62 stimulus values). In addition, the three subjects showing perceptuo-motor effects also showed larger adaptation effects in the perceptual adaptation test than the single subject who failed to show the perceptuo-motor effect.

We then conducted a replication experiment for the open loop test with these same subjects. In the replication experiment, only one of the four subjects showed the expected effect. However, as in our earlier experiments, we again found a correlation between the effect obtained in the perceptuo-motor test and in the perceptual test. The single subject who showed the perceptuo-motor effect in the replication study showed the largest of the effects induced by strictly perceptual adaptation of the four subjects. This latter finding reinforces the view that a perceptuo-motor effect is present but strongly dependent on the presence of a large-magnitude effect of perceptual adaptation.

---

[2]More specifically, we believe that the magnitude of the perceptual adaptation effect is composed of two components, one reflecting the fatigue of acoustic feature detectors which are part of the perceptual system, and another reflecting the fatigue of a centralized perceptuo-motor control mechanism. Because these two effects are combined in a test condition in which subjects' identification is measured, the magnitude of the effect obtained in the perceptual adaptation test should be larger than the magnitude obtained in the perceptuo-motor test, since in the former case the perceptuo-motor and perceptual effects are combined. This expected difference in magnitude generally holds true for the present data.

General Discussion

For the subjects who showed the perceptuo-motor effects, these effects can be accounted for by postulating that repetitive articulation induces neural fatigue within a perceptuo-motor control system, analogous to the one proposed in Study 8 for one aspect of the feature *voicing*. The site of fatigue is believed to be a processor that both initiates motor commands to the articulators and processes phonetic feature information during a late stage of perceptual analysis. However, future research must be conducted before we can decide whether the centralized processor actually operates on units the size of phonetic features or on still smaller units, corresponding to individual acoustic cues and their motor correlates. An example of the latter possibility would be a processor that operates on formant transition information to the exclusion of other information relevant to *place* decisions (in particular, information contained in the initial burst portion of the consonant). In order to test the presence of such a processor, crossed-adaptation tests might be carried out, similar in format to those performed to determine priorities of the perceptually induced adaptation effects.

Postscript to Study 10

In a follow-up study (Cooper, Billings, & Cole, 1976),[3] articulatory effects on perception were tested for three other speech sound distinctions, including [ba]–[wa], [si]–[sti], and [ba]–[pʰa]. Perceptual adaptation had been obtained for each of these distinctions in previous chapters. The perceptual effects were replicated, and some articulatory effects on perception were also obtained. The motor-perceptual effects were less systematic than those obtained with a strictly perceptual adaptation test, and a precise account of the results has not been formulated. It does appear, however, that some systematic motor-perceptual effects have been produced, providing support for the general type of model proposed in Chapter 5.

---

[3]This study utilized the integer rating response described in Chapter 4. As noted in the Postscripts to Chapter 4, the d^1 values obtained by this method provide only rough estimates of sensitivity. Further work with moto-perceptual adaptation should include better d^1 estimates, either by obtaining much more data per individual listener as well as a more rigorous test of the decision model's assumptions (e.g., Elman, 1979) or by using a different response measure.

chapter seven
NEW DIRECTIONS

In preceding chapters, we have seen how the selective adaptation method can be applied to a number of issues about speech processing. A number of general findings have emerged from the studies reviewed thus far. Chief among these are the effects of crossed-adaptation, including effects obtained with the use of different consonants as adaptors and test stimuli, interaural transfer, and perceptuo-motor adaptation. Taken together, these results point to the existence of a centralized processing component that integrates acoustics information over a relatively large domain of frequency, time, and intensity. This component can be identified with Level B in the information-flow diagram presented in Chapter 1. By examining the results of such cross-adaptation studies, we have been able to infer some salient characteristics of this stage of processing. In addition, the adaptation method has been useful in probing a peripheral component of the speech processor at Level A, which processes acoustic information over much narrower domains. That the same method can tap these two distinct stages of processing is best illustrated by the findings of Sawusch (1977a), to be reviewed later in this chapter.

In discussing the many results obtained for consonantal distinctions of place, voicing, and others, we have been able to propose a fairly large number of candidate explanations for the data, and our major contribution has been first to identify these and then whittle this set down to a few alternatives. In most if not all cases, we are nowhere near the enlightened state of arriving at a single valid explanation for a particular set of results. Time and again, we have been struck by the variety of plausible accounts, and this embarrassment of riches will not subside until further crossed-adaptation studies are combined with converging work obtained from other experimental paradigms (see later).

In this chapter, we review recent work that offers some opportunity for imposing further constraints on candidate explanations of selective adaptation. The framework adopted here is also intended to serve as a convenient means of classifying new adaptation studies as they continue to emerge.

Generalization and Higher-Order Processing

We begin with a relatively simple question: How general is the selective adaptation effect? Recent studies have shown that perceptual adaptation effects can be produced for test stimuli distinguishing stops from nasals (Cole, Cooper, Singer, & Allard, 1975; Samuel, 1975; Miller & Eimas, 1977), liquids [r] from [l] (Verbrugge & Liberman, 1975), affricates [č] from [ǰ] (Cole & Cooper, 1975), and vowels [i] from [I] from [ə] (Morse, Kass, & Turkienicz, 1976), among others. It thus appears that the selective adaptation method can be applied to study the properties of the processing system that enables listeners to distinguish members of each of these sound classes.

One should note that the effects for vowels (and perhaps others) may not represent adaptation in the sense of fatigue, however, since vowels are subject to range effects that might produce results similar to those obtained by Morse et al. (see Sawusch, Pisoni, & Cutting, 1975; Sawusch & Nusbaum, 1978). Range effects (Parducci, 1974) have also been reported for consonant distinctions (Brady & Darwin, 1978; Darwin, 1976; Simon & Studdert-Kennedy, 1978; Studdert-Kennedy, 1976), although their direct relation to selective adaptation results has not been established. Although range effects may occur in the same direction as adaptation effects, it is not expected that range effects exhibit a long-time course of recovery similar to adaptation (Eimas & Corbit, 1973) nor exhibit perceptuo-motor transfer of the type reviewed in Chapter 5. In a similar vein, parallels have been noted between effects of selective adaptation and response contrast (e.g., Diehl, Lang, & Parker, 1978; Diehl, Elman, & McCusker, 1978), yet no direct relation has been established.

In light of the numerous differences which have already been observed between the processing of isolated vowels and CV syllables, caution must be exercised in trying to develop a reinterpretation of adaption studies with CV syllables on the basis of new studies with isolated vowels. Recently, Remez (1979a) has suggested that the selective adaptation effects originally obtained for CV syllables do not provide evidence for feature detectors because similar effects are observed for a series of vowel-like stimuli which are perceived as speech or nonspeech as the bandwidths of the formants are increased. Attempting to develop a *reductio* argument, Remez concludes that selective adaptation does not provide evidence for feature detectors, even in CV syllables, because this line of reasoning would suggest the existence of speech vs. nonspeech opponent detectors when applied to his experiment. The argument is unconvincing because the results for isolated vowel-like stimuli ought to reflect different processing characteristics than those involved with CV syllables. Remez attempts to counter this drawback by demonstrating that his stimulus series is perceived categorically, yet this similarity between the processing of his vowel-like stimuli and CV syllables is not sufficient to warrant his general comparison of the two. The case for or against a *feature* detector model for CV syllables must be tested on its own terms, by considering *crossed*-adaptation tests with CV syllables in a signal detection task. Remez fails to meet these requirements in the study just cited as well as in a more recent one in which the same general procedure was applied to a speech vs. non-speech series conveyed by consonantal-like stimuli (Remez, 1979b).

This tendency toward over-generalization also applies to the study of signal detectability reported by Elman (1979), reviewed in Chapter 4. Elman found that within-series adaptation results reflect changes in listeners' response bias rather than sensitivity. These results are not surprising in light of the fact that the same syllables were used as adaptors and test stimuli in these experiments. Yet, on the basis of this limited finding, Elman calls into question the more general interpretations put forth in studies that utilize crossed-adaptation results as a basis for their conclusions. In the absence of a signal detectability analysis of crossed-adaptation data, a generalization from within-series to crossed-series is not warranted, since on logical grounds there is reason to suspect that crossed-adaptation results are more representative of changes in sensitivity.

Aside from this issue, a major test of generality concerns whether the selective adaptation effect is restricted to syllabic adapting and test stimuli or whether the effect can be obtained when the listener is engaged in normal sentence processing, aimed at recovering a semantic interpretation. One aspect of this question has been studied by Rudnicky and Cole (1977), who tested whether perceptual adaptation could be produced using sentences and paragraphs as adapting material. They obtained significant effects for syllabic test series using sentence and paragraph adaptors heavily weighted in a particular consonant feature value, and these effects closely resembled those obtained with syllable adaptors. The results suggest that adaptation is not eliminated when a listener is engaged in relatively normal processing of semantic and syntactic information, as required by their experiment.

It would be useful to conduct an additional study in which sentence materials were used as *test* stimuli. Each test sentence would include a key word whose interpretation depended on a single consonant distinction, such as voicing with the words *bears* and *pears*. A sentence such as *At the gallery we saw a painting of two -ears* could then be used to test whether adaptation would influence a listener's interpretation of the final word for an acoustically ambiguous consonant. By using a variety of different test sentences, an adequate test could be provided of whether the selective adaptation effect applies to the realm of normal speech processing.

The use of sentences as adaptors and test stimuli would pave the way for using the adaptation method for probing the relation between the processing of acoustic and phonetic feature information and other components of the speech processing system. One such component, noted in the model in Chapter 1, concerns normalization for speaking rate. In speech production, the values of voice onset time distinguishing [b] from [p^h] vary considerably with speaking rate. At faster rates, the VOT values for [p^h] become progressively shortened. Summerfield and Haggard (1972) and Summerfield (1976) have shown that listeners adjust the perceptual boundary between [b] and [p^h] as a function of speaking rate. That is, the listeners' phoneme boundary lies at a longer VOT for slow vs. fast rates.

It would be of considerable interest to determine whether the listeners' normalization for speaking rate occurs before or after the site(s) at which perceptual adaptation are produced (see Figure 7, Chapter 1). This question could be answered using sentences as adaptors, spoken at fast vs. slow rates. If the fast-rate sentences are spoken with voiceless [p^h] whose VOT values are shorter than the VOT defining the unadapted phoneme boundary for [b]– [p^h] syllabic test syllables, then the direction of the adaptation effect should depend on whether the adaptation effect is produced at a site of processing before or after rate normalization. Of course, as noted in preceding chapters, it is quite possible that the selective adaptation effect applies at more than a single processing site. If so, the normalization test would be appropriate in conjunction with a testing method (see later) which isolates a single adaptation site.

In summary, generalization of the adaptation effect may help to establish the validity of the technique for testing aspects of processing used in normal sentence perception. In addition, such generalization may permit extension of the technique to questions of information-flow between acoustic-phonetic processing and other components of the system. The case of speech rate normalization just mentioned represents only one such possibility. Another, quite general, possibility involves testing information-flow relations between the acoustic-phonetic processing and syntatic and semantic levels of processing. As recent work on speech recognition by machine (e.g., Reddy, 1975) and psycholinguistics (Fodor, Bever, & Garrett, 1974) shows, this area requires extensive study before we can arrive at an overall theory of speech perception. It had been useful in the beginning stages of adaptation research to confine stimulus materials to single syllables, as in most other areas of controlled experimentation with speech, and the results of this work serve as a useful guide to studies using sentence materials. In future work, however, it is imperative that we keep in mind that, from the listener's standpoint, the goal of speech perception is the recovery of a semantic representation, not the distinguishing of one phoneme from another. The stages of acoustic-phonetic recognition are critical to the ultimate understanding of a sentence, yet these stages need to be studied as aspects of the overall system when the listener is actively engaged in the task of recovering meaning. It is a considerable challenge to design tests in which listeners are so engaged and are yet able to provide the experimenter with information about the early stages of processing. It is expected that the future success of the adaptation method rests largely on its ability to meet this aim.

In order to render adaptation tests more suitable for this purpose, it appears that the use of sentence and paragraph adaptors and sentence test stimuli will be required. The problems of maintaining acoustic control of the stimuli will increase accordingly, although possibilities exist for synthesizing sentence frames or for electronically editing real sentences in precise acoustic steps (Huggins, 1969). In order to engage the listeners' normal processing, however, an additional requirement must be met, involving the use of a large variety of stimuli within an experiment so that listeners cannot predict the approximate identity of upcoming stimuli. In the work on syllable adaptation reviewed earlier, listeners were typically faced with a two-choice perceptual task, clearly unlike the task faced by listeners in normal conversation. It would be interesting to test whether the syllable effects noted in preceding chapters generalize to a situation in which a variety of consonant distinctions are used as test stimuli during the same experimental session. And similarly, future tests with sentence test stimuli might utilize a sufficiently large variety of materials per session so that the listeners cannot predict the approximate identity of the test stimulus on any given trial. Given these requirements, it will become increasingly important to discover means of streamlining the method of obtaining responses from listeners. The selective adaptation procedure is currently quite inefficient, to say the least, and efforts are being directed at minimizing this drawback, much to the delight of both subject and experimenter (e.g., Raz & Wightman, 1978).

Sites of Selective Adaptation

Much of the early and current work on speech adaptation has been designed to test whether adaptation occurs for one or more levels of processing and whether such level(s) of processing occur before or after binaural integration in the auditory system. A test of the latter issue is provided by a measure of interaural transfer. This is a measure of the adaptation effect produced when the adaptor and test series are presented to separate ears, as compared with a same-eared effect. In early work, Eimas, Cooper, and Corbit (1973) obtained a substantial interaural transfer effect of about 95% for a voicing [da]–[tʰa] test series after adaptation with [tʰa]. Niccum and Speaks (1978) have obtained lesser transfer effects (50–60%) for adapting and testing with a series from [ba] to [pʰa]. For a [bæ]–[dæ] place series, Ades (1974) obtained about 55% transfer. In an additional test, Ades used the contingent adaptation method (see Chapter 3) to test the possibility that some part of the adaptation effect operated prior to binaural fusion. He presented the adapting syllable [bæ] to one ear and the adapting syllable [dæ] to the other ear simultaneously. He then tested subjects' identification of a [bæ]–[dæ] test series in each ear separately. Small, but statistically significant, shifts were obtained, indicating the presence of a monaural component of the adaptation effect. After adaptation with [bæ] to the left ear and [dæ] to the right ear, for example, the phonetic boundary location for the test series was shifted toward the [bæ] category when subjects were tested in the left ear; this boundary shifted toward the [dæ] category when the same subjects were tested in the right ear.

In reviewing the studies of Eimas *et al.* (1973) and Ades (1974), Cooper (1975) suggested that both monaural and binaural sites of adaptation exist. In addition, it was speculated that these different sites might be uniquely associated with low-level auditory detectors and higher-level integrative detectors. Based on evidence from studies of dichotic listening (Pisoni, 1975; Studdert-Kennedy & Shankweiler, 1970; Studdert-Kennedy, Shankweiler, & Pisoni, 1972), one would predict that the low-level component is monaurally driven, whereas the more integrative component involves a mechanism which operates subsequent to binaural fusion. If this prediction were confirmed, we would be in a position to isolate the components of the adaptation effect within the same test situation and thereby set the stage for studying the properties of each component in greater detail, as well as their possible interaction.

Sawusch (1977a) has conducted interaural transfer experiments with a [ba]–[da] place series that shows such a dissociation between lower- and higher-level effects. An interaural effect of 100% on the average was obtained for an adaptation test in which the adaptor and test series contained formant frequencies in the vowel that differed by about 1½ critical bands in center frequency. Interaural transfer of only about 50% was obtained, however, using adaptor and test series containing the same format frequencies. It thus appears that both a monaural and binaural component of the adaptation effect exist and that the binaural component integrates information about place over a wider frequency range than the monaural component, consistent with the earlier prediction. If a similar effect of 100% transfer can be demonstrated for other speech distinctions, the interaural transfer technique may become a powerful tool for isolating two components of the adaptation effect. And once the properties of each component are determined, we will be able to study their interplay in a controlled manner.

In light of earlier discussion, it is conceivable that the central component of adaptation reflects a complex form of response bias, whereas the peripheral component most probably represents a change in sensitivity. The difference could be tested by combining a signal detection analysis with transfer studies like those conducted by Sawusch.

Another question concerns whether there is a purely *phonetic* stage of processing tapped by adaptation, a stage distinguishable from a high-level auditory stage. As noted in Cooper (1975), an adequate test of a phonetic site of adaptation must bypass or neutralize the auditory system. In early work, such as that reported in Chapter 2, this stringent requirement was not met. One possible way of providing such a test was presented in Cooper (1975), involving adaptation with visually presented letters in combination with auditory presentation of the test stimuli. Although some adaptation effects were obtained using this procedure, they exhibited directional asymmetries and inconsistencies not mirrored by the typical speech adaptation effects, and testing of this type was abandoned. It may be useful to explore this technique more systematically in the future. In addition, it may be possible to test a phonetic component of speech adaptation by neutralizing rather than bypassing the auditory stages of processing.

Tuning Properties

A number of recent studies (e.g., Cole & Cooper, 1977; Miller, 1975, 1977; Sawusch, 1976a, b) have been aimed at examining some of the tuning characteristics of speech detectors, including their bandwidths and maximum sensitivity values. (See the foregoing references for a detailed discussion.) On the basis of this kind of work, it appears that we will eventually be able to provide a detailed description of the tuning properties of each of the speech detectors tapped by selective adaptation. It is expected that this area of inquiry will represent one of the most useful types of adaptation research.

Although the primary interest of such work is to describe the tuning properties of detectors in their unadapted state, work is also being directed at describing the specific changes in tuning that occur as a result of adaptation based on adaptation effects as exemplified in the work of Sawusch (1977a) on interaural transfer and frequency bands. The results of studies by Miller (1975) and Sawusch (1976b) suggest, for example, that selective adaptation effects occur over the entire detector range as assumed in Chapter 2. Miller (1976) has also shown that the amount of adaptation is dependent on the adaptor's nearness to the value of maximum sensitivity in the unadapted state.

The use of signal detectability measures of the adaptation effect (see Chapter 4; Miller, Eimas, & Root, 1977; Elman, 1979) should permit a more precise account of the adaptation effects on various stimuli within a test series. A number of issues remain unresolved concerning possible changes in sensitivity. It would be interesting, for example, to determine whether a lowering of sensitivity to the adapted value is accompanied by a heightening of sensitivity (facilitation) to the opponent value. At suprathreshold stimulus levels, such facilitation can be demonstrated for visual stimuli varying in movement (Sekuler & Levinson, 1974). The coupled shifts in sensitivity after adaptation would provide important evidence favoring the general view that speech detectors are organized in opponent-process fashion.

Modeling

As descriptions of the adaptation effects become more complete, the possibility opens up for neural and computer modeling as a tool for testing further aspects of adaptation. Such modeling may play a significant role in cases where the predictions of a theory of speech processing are not obvious. The neural modeling in Chapter 5 to account for perceptual and perceptuo-motor adaptation can be extended in a number of specific directions. As shown by modeling of neural inhibition in the visual system (e.g., Barlow & Levick, 1966; Wilson, 1975; Uttal, 1973; MacKay, 1968; Harmon, 1968) a number of candidates exist to account for opponent processing, and it remains a task for future research to test the merits of competing neural models in the domain of speech processing. Computer models of speech adaptation effects, introduced by Sawusch (1976a), may also play an important role.

Verbal Transformations

In each of the perceptual studies discussed so far, we have focused on data obtained by asking listeners to report their perception of test stimuli *following* adaptation. As originally observed by Warren and Gregory (1958), data may also be obtained from listeners *during* adaptation. Typically, listeners report that the adapting syllable is transformed during the course of repetitive stimulation. The transformed percept may be another syllable, a word, or even a sentence. More recently, it has been shown that the transformed percept is closely related to the adapting stimulus in terms of acoustic or phonetic features (Goldstein & Lackner, 1973; Lackner & Goldstein, 1975; Ohde, 1978). In addition, verbal transformations have provided evidence for an analysis-by-synthesis model of stress perception (Lackner & Tuller, 1976).

Cross-language Studies

With one exception, the experiments reviewed thus far involved native speakers of English. The exception, discussed in Chapter 5, involved a perceptuo-motor test with native speakers of Hindi, in order to test for the presence of a perceptuo-motor effect with Hindi's voice aspirated consonant $[d^h]$. More recently, Donald (1976) and Foreit (1977) have conducted independent studies of perceptual adaptation with Thai and English native speakers. The Thai language includes a phonemic distinction between prevoiced stop consonants and stops having a short-lag voice onset time. In English, no such phonemic distinction exists, even though speakers may produce stops having either prevoiced or short-lag VOTs. Donald and Foreit conducted experiments to test whether adaptation to prevoiced and short-lag VOT stimuli would affect identification of the boundary between short-lag and long-lag VOTs, corresponding to the voiced-voiceless distinction which is phonemic in both Thai and English.

The results showed a striking difference between the Thai and English listeners. For the English listeners, the adaptation effects on the voiced-voiceless test simuli were similar for prevoiced and short-lag adaptors. For Thai listeners, however, adaptation on the voice-voiceless test stimuli was obtained for the short-lag adaptor but not the prevoiced adaptor. The results for Thai may be accounted for by postulating a trimodal detector system (including pre-voiced, short-lag, and long-lag detectors), with overlapping response ranges (and/or opponent process connections) existing only between adjacent detectors (that is, between prevoiced and short-lag and between short-lag and long-lag, but not between prevoiced and long-lag). This trimodal system is analogous to the one proposed for place of articulation in Chapter 2.

It appears, then, that functionally distinct perceptual systems must be postulated for English and Thai listeners. It is possible that both sets of listeners possess the same trimodal detection system in infancy but that English listeners lose, in part, the ability to distinguish prevoiced from short-lag VOTs because this distinction is nonphonemic in their language.

As in the preceding cases, further cross-language work might be profitably directed at potential differences between native speakers of English and other languages. This kind of work should be applied systematically to cases in which the outcome may be used to select between alternative theoretical accounts of the selective adaptation effects.

Nonspeech Adaptation

A number of studies have tested for effects of nonspeech adaptors on speech perception (Eimas, Cooper, & Corbit, 1973; Ades, 1973; Bailey, 1975; Pisoni & Tash, 1975; Sawusch, 1976a; Tartter & Eimas, 1975; Verbrugge & Liberman, 1975; Samuel & Newport, 1979). In one study (Verbrugge & Liberman, 1975), the effect of speech adaptors was tested on the perception of nonspeech. Such cross-adaptation tests have generally been aimed at the issue of whether speech adaptation effects tap a level of processing that is specialized for linguistic analysis. Crossing speech with nonspeech in adaptation experiments permits an adequate test of this issue, provided that listeners do not perceive the "nonspeech" stimuli as speech sounds.

It is important to distinguish the cross-adaptation test of a linguistic processor from tests that utilize nonspeech stimuli as both adapting and test stimuli. The latter type of test has been used to study channels of auditory perception (e.g., Kay & Matthews, 1972; Cutting, Rosner, & Foard, 1976), and based on such work, there is no question that selective adaptation as a phenomenon is not restricted to speech stimuli within the realm of auditory stimuli. The selective adaptation procedure, however, can still be used to test the issue of a linguistic-specific processor, with crossed adaptation tests using speech vs. nonspeech as adapting vs. test stimuli.

Other Studies

Aside from the major lines of research outlined in the preceding discussion, there is a need for studies involving certain specific variables. For example, only a few details are known about the effects of stimulus intensity on speech adaptation (see Hillenbrand, 1975; Ganong, 1976; Ohde, 1978), yet work in vision and audition gives every indication that the response properties of detectors change considerably with differences in intensity (see, for example, Kiang, 1975). It appears that detectors exhibit less response-overlap at lower intensities. In addition, little is known about the time course of build-up and recovery from speech adaptation (Bryant, 1977; Sharf & Ohde, 1977; Miller & Morse, 1979). Work in vision has shown that the study of time course can permit isolation of separate components of adaptation effects (see Favreau, 1976), clearly of importance in speech work, as noted earlier. Finally the role of attention has not been studied systematically with reference to speech adaptation. It does appear, however, that listeners need not devote their full attention to the adapting stimulus in order to yield an adaptation effect (e.g., Foreit, 1977).

A Final Note on Features

At the theoretical level, one of the toughest questions concerns whether crossed-adaptation effects, such as those obtained in preceding chapters, indicate the existence of processors that compute information about salient auditory or phonetic features. Ideally, a feature detector should respond whenever the given feature is present in the stimulus, regardless of other acoustic information contained in the signal. If the adaptation method tapped a level of processing exclusively devoted to such feature extraction, then cross-adaptation tests of the type conducted for a [bæ]-[dæ]-[gæ] place series with the adaptors [bæ], [mæ], and [væ], as in Chapter 2, should show an equal magnitude of effect. Yet typically, adaptation with a syllable not contained in the test series (e.g., [mæ]) as in Study 2, results in a somewhat smaller effect, averaging about 80% of the within-series effect. The absence of a 100% transfer in such cases may be accounted for in three very different ways. One possibility, noted in the first study of Chapter 2, is that partial transfer effects reflect the existence of an additional component or components of adaptation other than a feature-specific effect. In particular, it is reasonable to suppose that phoneme- and syllable-level effects of adaptation can be produced. In this way, it is possible to retain the feature-specific account of the existence of crossed-adaptation effects. A second possibility is that feature detectors are context-sensitive to vowel environment (Study 4) and to other feature parameters (see Eimas & Miller, 1977).

Finally, it is possible that the existence of crossed-adaptation effect can be accounted for without assuming the presence of feature extraction. According to this latter possibility, suggested by W. F. Ganong (personal communication) and Bailey (1975), crossed-adaptation effects reflect the degree of holistic similarity between the adapting and test syllables. As noted in Chapter 2, Neisser (1967) pointed out that perceptual confusions in noise (Miller & Nicely, 1955) could also be accounted for in this manner (see Shepard, 1972, also). The gradient of holistic similarity among syllables is in good agreement with predictions of similarity based on a theory of distinctive features, but the holistic vs. feature notions represent very different accounts. At present, it is difficult to distinguish the merits of these competing alternatives, largely because a precise theory of holistic similarity has not been formulated and because a number of possible feature theories abound. There do exist some clear cases where the feature and holistic alternatives make quite distinct predictions, however, and the results of experiments on these cases should permit a selection. But for now, the question of feature extraction remains unresolved, and there is little comfort in knowing that this issue remains controversial in other domains in human information processing, particularly the visual system (see Sachs, Nachmias, & Robson, 1971; Graham & Nachmias, 1971; Henning, Hertz, & Broadbent, 1975; and current issues of *Vision Research*). Whatever the outcome of this question in speech processing, it is fortunate that the results obtained with selective adaptation also provide evidence on a number of orthogonal issues, as evidenced in the previous chapters.

Concluding Remarks

The main point of this book has been to show how experimentation with a relative simple method can be used to explore a variety of issues in some depth. In earlier chapters, studies with syllabic stimuli revealed new information about the workings of the perceptual system, as well as about the way which the perceptual and motor systems share components of processing. In this chapter, the earlier work with syllables has provided a framework for systematic extensions to larger speech domains and new issues. It thus appears that the application of a single-method strategy has provided an entering wedge into a number of problems about speech processing.

Although a single-method strategy is well suited to the goals of an individual research laboratory over a two-to-three year period, it seems equally important that a variety of laboratories utilize quite different methods in studying a given set of issues. Such means give us the opportunity to discover the task-independent aspects of research findings. In the present case, most of the issues dealt with in selective adaptation have not been studied systematically with other procedures, so we have little basis for reporting any significant dovetailing of results using two or more distinct methods. The search for such converging operations (Garner, 1974) provides a focal point for further research designed to ascertain the relevance of particular results to issues in speech processing at large.

Because the 1970s have witnessed such a flurry of activity in selective adaptation, one might easily get the impression that the method's usefulness has by now been exhausted. The discussion in this chapter seems to indicate otherwise. Nonetheless, a period of exaggerated popularity inevitably gives way to disenchantment in some quarters, and this swing of the pendulum has already encroached upon popular methods in speech research, including selective adaptation and dichotic listening. The ultimate value of these paradigms rests largely on how well they provide sources of evidence leading to a better theory of speech processing, and on this score the jury is still out. In the case of selective adaptation, future prospects rest primarily on the extent to which the individual components of the effect can be properly isolated. To date, attempts in this vein have utilized three relatively powerful methods, including crossed-series adaptation, interaural transfer, and measures of signal detectability. However, researchers have so far utilized at most two of these three procedures within the same experimental series, and the inclusion of all three seems to offer the best means of disentangling an otherwise multi-component effect. If such testing is successful, then much valuable work with this paradigm has yet to unfold.

BIBLIOGRAPHY

Abramson, A. S., & Lisker, L. (1973). Voice-timing perception in Spanish word-initial stops. *Journal of Phonetics, 1*, 1–8.
Ades, A. E. (1973). Sone effects of adaptation on speech perception. *Quarterly Progress Report of the M.I.T. Research Laboratory of Electronics, 111*, 121–129.
Ades, A. E. (1974a). How phonetic is selective adaptation? Experiments on syllable position and vowel environment. *Perception & Psychophysics, 16*, 61–66.
Ades, A. E. (1974b). A bilateral component in speech perception. *Journal of the Acoustical Society of America, 56*, 610–616.
Ades, A. E. (1976). Adapting the property detectors for speech perception. In R. Wales and E. Walker (Eds.), *New Approaches to Language Mechanisms*. Amsterdam: North-Holland.
Ades, A. E. (1977). Source assignment and feature extraction in speech. *Journal of Experimental Psychology: Human Perception and Performance, 3*, 673–688.
Ainsworth, W. A. (1977). Mechanisms of selective feature adaptation. *Perception & Psychophysics, 21*, 365–370.
Appley, M. H. (Ed.). (1971). *Adaptation-level theory*. New York: Academic Press.
Bailey, P. J. (1972). Adaptation paradigms in speech perception-a preliminary report. *Speech Perception: Report on research in progress in the Department of Psychology, The Queen's University of Belfast, Northern Ireland, 2.1*, 13–19.
Bailey, P. J. (1973). Perceptual adaptation for acoustical features in speech perception. *Speech Perception: Report of speech research in progress in the Department of Psychology, The Queen's University of Belfast, Northern Ireland, 2.2*, 29–34.
Bailey, P. J. (1974). Procedural variables in speech adaptation. *Speech Perception: Report of speech research in progress in the Department of Psychology, The Queen's University of Belfast, Northern Ireland, 2.2*, 29–34.
Bailey, P. J. (1975). Perceptual adaptation to speech: Some properties of detectors for acoustic cues to phonetic distinctions. Unpublished doctoral dissertation, University of Cambridge.
Bailey, P. J., & Haggard, M. P. (1973). Perception and production: Some correlations on voicing of an initial stop. *Language and Speech, 16*, 189–195.

Barlow, H. B. (1972). Dark and light adaptation: Psychophysics. In D. Jameson & L. M. Hurvich (Eds.), *Handbook of sensory physiology: vol. VII/4 Visual psychophysics*. New York: Springer-Verlag. 1–28.

Barlow, H. B., & Levick, W. R. (1965). The mechanism of directionally selective units in rabbit's retina. *Journal of Physiology, 178*, 477–504.

Bastian, J. (1959). Silent intervals as closure cues in the perception of stop phonemes. Paper presented at the 58th Meeting of the Acoustical Society of America, Cleveland, Ohio, October 1959.

Bastian, J. (1960). Silent intervals as closure cues in the perception of stops. Paper presented at the 75th Meeting of the Modern Language Association of America, Philadelphia, Pennsylvania, December 1960.

Bibikov, N. G. (1974). Encoding of the stimulus envelope in peripheral and central regions of the auditory system of the frog. *Acustica, 31*, 310–314.

Blumstein, S. E., Cooper, W. E., Zurif, E. B., & Caramazza, A. (1977). The perception and production of voice-onset time in aphasia. *Neuropsychologia, 15*, 371–383.

Blumstein, S. E., & Stevens, K. N. (1977). Acoustic invariance for place of articulation in stops and nasals across syllabic contexts: *Journal of the Acoustical Society of America, 62*, S26–S27. (Abstract)

Blumstein, S. E., Stevens, K. N., & Nigro, G. N. (1977). Property detectors for bursts and transitions in speech perception. *Journal of the Acoustical Society of America, 61*, 1301–1313.

Brady, S. A., & Darwin, C. J. (1978). Range effect in the perception of voicing. *Journal of the Acoustical Society of America, 63*, 1556–1558.

Braida, L. D., & Durlach, N. I. (1972). Intensity perception II. Resolution in one-interval paradigms. *Journal of the Acoustical Society of America, 51*, 483–502.

Bryant, J. (1977). The effects of number of presentations and processing time on the selective adaptation of speech. Unpublished master's thesis, University of Wisconsin, Madison.

Butterfield, E. C., & Cairns, G. F. (1974). In R. Schiefelbush & L. L. Lloyd (Eds.), *Language perspectives*. Baltimore, Md.: University Park Press.

Chiba, T., & Kajiyama, M. (1941). *The Vowel—its nature and structure*. Tokyo: Tokyo-Kaiseikan.

Chomsky, N., & Halle, M. (1968). *The sound pattern of English*. New York: Harper and Row.

Cole, R. A., & Cooper, W. E. (1975). Perception of voicing in English affricates and fricatives. *Journal of the Acoustical Society of America, 58*, 1280–1287.

Cole, R. A., & Cooper, W. E. (1977). Properties of frication analyzers for [j]. *Journal of the Acoustical Society of America, 62*, 177–182.

Cole, R. A., Cooper, W. E., Singer, J., & Allard, F. (1975). Selective adaptation of English consonants using real speech. *Perception & Psychophysics, 18*, 227–244.

Cole, R. A., Jakimik, J., & Cooper, W. E. (1979). Segmenting speech into words. *Journal of the Acoustical Society of America* (under editorial review).

Cole, R. A., & Scott, B. (1972). Distinctive feature control of decision time: Same-different judgments of simultaneously heard phonemes. *Perception & Psychophysics, 12*, 91–94.

Cole, R. A., & Scott, B. (1974). Toward a theory of speech perception. *Psychological Review, 81*, 348–374.

Cooper, F. S., Delattre, P. C., Liberman, A. M., Borst, J. M., & Gerstman, L. J. (1952). Some experiments on the perception of synthetic speech sounds. *Journal of the Acoustical Society of America, 24*, 597–606.

Cooper, F. S., Liberman, A. M., & Borst, J. M. (1951). The interconversion of audible and visible patterns as a basis for research in the perception of speech. *Proceedings of the National Academy of Science, 37*, 318–325.

Cooper, W. E. (1975). Selective adaptation to speech. In F. Restle, R. M. Shiffrin, N. J. Castellan, H. Lindman, & D. B. Pisoni (Eds.), *Cognitive theory (Vol. I)*. Hillsdale, N.J.: Lawrence Erlbaum Associates.

Cooper, W. E., Billings, D., & Cole, R. A. (1976). Articulatory effects on speech perception: A second report. *Journal of Phonetics, 4*, 219–232.
Cooper, W. E., & Cooper, J. P. (1979). *Syntax and speech coding*. (Forthcoming).
Cooper, W. E., & Nager, R. M. (1975). Perceptuo-motor adaptation to speech: An analysis of bisyllabic utterances and a neural model. *Journal of the Acoustical Society of America, 58*, 256–265. (See also Chapter 5, Study 8, this volume).
Corbit, T. E., & Engen, T. (1971). Facilitation of olfactory detection. *Perception & Psychophysics, 10*, 433–436.
deCordemoy, G. (1668). *A philosophical discourse concerning speech*. London: J. Martin.
Cutting, J. E., & Rosner, B. S. (1974). Categories and boundaries in speech and music. *Perception & Psychophysics, 16*, 564–570.
Cutting, J. E., Rosner, B. S., & Foard, C. F. (1976). Perceptual categories for musiclike sounds: Implications for theories of speech perception. *Quarterly Journal of Experimental Psychology, 28*, 361–378.
Dallenbach, J. W., & Dallenbach, K. M. (1943). The effects of bitter-adaptation on sensitivity to the other taste qualities. *American Journal of Psychology, 56*, 21–31.
Darwin, C. J. (1976). The perception of speech. In E. C. Carterette & M. P. Friedman (Eds.), *Handbook of perception* (Vol. IV). New York: Academic Press.
Davidsen-Neilsen, N. (1974). Syllabification in English words with medial sp, st, sk. *Journal of Phonetics, 2*, 15–45.
Delattre, P. C., Liberman, A. M., & Cooper, F. S. (1955). Acoustic loci and transitional cues for consonants. *Journal of the Acoustical Society of America, 27*, 769–773.
Denes, P. B. (1963). On the statistics of spoken English. *Journal of the Acoustical Society of America, 35*, 892–904.
Diehl, R. L. (1975). The effect of selective adaptation on the identification of speech sounds. *Perception & Psychophysics, 17*, 48–52.
Diehl, R. L. (1976). Feature analyzers for the phonetic dimension *Stop vs. Continuant*. *Perception & Psychophysics, 19*, 267–272.
Diehl, R. L., Elman, J. L., & McCusker, S. B. (1978). Contrast effects on stop consonant identification. *Journal of Experimental Psychology: Human Perception and Performance, 4*, 000–000.
Diehl, R. L., Lang, M., & Parker, E. M. (1978). A further parallel between selective adaptation and response contrast. *Journal of the Acoustical Society of America, 64*, S19 (Abstract).
Diehl, R. L., & Rosenberg, D. M. (1977). Acoustic feature analysis in the perception of voicing contrasts. *Perception & Psychophysics, 21*, 418–422.
Donald, S. L. (1976). The effects of selective adaptation on voicing in Thai and English. *Haskins Laboratories Status Report of Speech Research, SR-47*, 129–136.
Dorman, M. F., Studdert-Kennedy, M., & Raphael, L. J. (1977). Stop-consonant recognition: Release bursts and formant transitions as functionally equivalent, context-dependent cues. *Perception & Psychophysics, 22*, 109–122.
Durlach, N. I., & Braida, L. D. (1969). Intensity perception. I. Preliminary theory of intensity resolution. *Journal of the Acoustical Society of America, 46*, 372–382.
Eimas, P. D. (1963). The relation between identification and discrimination along speech and nonspeech continua. *Language and Speech, 6*, 26–217.
Eimas, P. D. (1974). Auditory and linguistic processing of cues for place of articulation by infants. *Perception & Psychophysics, 16*, 513–521.
Eimas, P. D., Cooper, W. E., & Corbit, J. D. (1973). Some properties of linguistic feature detectors. *Perception & Psychophysics, 13*, 247–252.
Eimas, P. D., & Corbit, J. D. (1973). Selective adaptation of linguistic feature detectors. *Cognitive Psychology, 4*, 99–109.
Eimas, P. D., & Miller, J. L. (1977). Effects of selective adaptation on the perception of speech and visual patterns: evidence for feature detectors. In H. L. Pick, Jr. & R. D. Walk (Eds.), *Perception and experience*. New York: Plenum, in press.

Eimas, P. D., Siqueland, E. R., Jusczyk, P., & Vigorito, J. (1971). Speech perception in infants. *Science, 171*, 303–306.

Elman, J. L. (1979). Perceptual origins of the phoneme boundary effect and selective adaptation to speech: A signal detection theory analysis. *Journal of the Acoustical Society of America, 65*, 190–207.

Engen, T., & Bosack, T. N. (1969). Facilitation in olfactory detection. *Journal of Comparative and Physiological Psychology, 68*, 320–326.

Fant, G. (1956). On the predictability of formant levels and spectrum envelopes from formant frequencies. In *For Roman Jakobson*. The Hague: Mouton.

Fant, G. (1960). *Acoustic theory of speech production*. The Hague: Mouton.

Fant, G. (1973). *Speech sounds and features*. Cambridge, Mass.: M.I.T. Press.

Favreau, O. E. (1976). Motion aftereffects: Evidence for parallel processing in motion perception. *Visual Research, 16*, 181–186.

Ferguson, G. A. (1959) *Statistical analysis in psychology and education*. New York: McGraw-Hill.

Fidell, L. S. (1970). Orientation specificity in chromatic adaptation of human "edge-detectors". *Perception & Psychophysics, 8*, 235–236.

Flanagan, J. L. (1972). *Speech analysis, synthesis and perception*. Heidelberg: Springer-Verlag.

Fodor, J. A., Bever, T. G., & Garrett, M. F. (1974). *The psychology of language: An introduction to psycholinguistics and generative grammar*. New York: McGraw-Hill.

Foreit, K. G. (1977). Linguistic relativism and selective adaptation for speech: A comparative study of English and Thai. *Perception & Psychophysics, 21*, 347–351.

Forster, K. I. (1975). In search of the mental lexicon. In R. Wales & E. Walker (Eds.), *New approaches to language mechanisms*. Amsterdam: North-Holland.

Fujimura, O. (1961). Some synthesis experiments on stop consonants in the initial position. *Quarterly Progress Report of the M.I.T. Research Laboratory of Electronics*, April, 153–162.

Ganong, W. F., III. (1975). An experiment on phonetic adaptation. *Quarterly Progress Report of the M.I.T. Research Laboratory of Electronics, 116*, 206–210.

Ganong, W. F., III. (1976). Amplitude contingent adaptation to speech. Paper presented at the 91st Meeting of the Acoustical Society of America, Washington, D.C., April.

Ganong, W. F., III. (1977) Selective adaptation and speech perception. Unpublished doctoral dissertation, M.I.T.

Ganong, W. F., III, & Cooper, W. E. (1974). Unpublished data.

Garner, W. R. (1974). *The processing of information and structure*. Hillsdale, N.J.: Lawrence Erlbaum Associates.

Gold, B., & Rabiner, L. (1969). Parallel processing techniques for estimating pitch periods of speech in the time domain. *Journal of the Acoustical Society of America, 46*, 442–448.

Goldstein, L. M., & Lacker, J. R. (1974). Alternations of the phonetic coding on speech sounds during repetition. *Cognition, 2*, 279–297.

Graham, N., & Nachmias, J. (1971). Detection of grating patterns containing two spatial frequencies: A comparison of single-channel and multiple-channel models. *Vision Research, 11*, 251–259.

Green, D. M., & Swets, J. A. (1966). *Signal detection theory*. New York: Wiley.

Haggard, M., Ambler, S., & Callow, M. (1970). Pitch as a voicing cue. *Journal of the Acoustical Society of America, 47*, 613–617.

Halle, M. (1964). On the bases of phonology. In J. A. Fodor & J. J. Katz (Eds.), *The structure of language: Readings in the philosophy of language*. Englewood Cliffs, N.J.: Prentice-Hall.

Halle, M., & Stevens, K. N. (1971). A note on laryngeal features. *Quarterly Progress Report of the M.I.T. Research Laboratory of Electronics, 101*, 198–213.

Hanson, V. L. (1977). Within category discrimination in speech perception. *Perception & Psychophysics 21*, 423–430.

Harmon, L. D. (1968). Modeling studies of neural inhibition. In C. von Euler, S. Skoglund, & U. Soderberg (Eds.), *Structure and function of inhibitory neuronal mechanisms*. New York: Pergamon Press.

Harnett, D. L. (1975). *Introduction to statistical methods*. Reading, Mass.: Addison-Wesley.

Harris, C. S., & Gibson, A. R. (1968). Is orientation-specific color adaptation in human vision due to edge-detectors, after-images, or "dipoles?" *Science, 162*, 1506–1507.
Harris, K. S. (1958). Cues for the discrimination of American English fricatives in spoken syllables. *Language and Speech, 1*, 1–17.
Harris, K. S., Bastian, J., & Liberman, A. M. (1961). Mimicry and the perception of a phonemic contrast induced by silent interval: electromyographic and acoustic measures. *Journal of the Acoustical Society of America, 33*, 842 (Abstract).
Harris, K. S., Hoffman, H. S., Liberman, A. M., Delattre, P. C., & Cooper, F. S. (1958). Effect of third-formant transitions on the perception of the voiced stop consonants. *Journal of the Acoustical Society of America, 30*, 122–126.
Healy, A. F., & Cutting, J. E. (1976). Units of speech perception: phoneme and syllable. *Journal of Verbal Learning and Verbal Behavior, 15*, 73–83.
Heinemann, E. G. (1972). Simultaneous brightness induction. In D. Jameson & J. M. Hurvich (Eds.), *Handbook of sensory physiology: Vol. VII/4. Visual psychophysics*. New York: Springer-Verlag, pp. 146–169.
Held, R., & Freedman, S. (1963). Plasticity in human sensorimotor control. *Science, 142*, 455–562.
Held, R., & Shattuck, S. R. (1971). Color- and edge-sensitive channels in the human visual system: Tuning for orientation. *Science, 174*, 314–316.
Helson, H. (1964). *Adaptation-level theory: An experimental and systematic approach to behavior*. New York: Harper.
Henning, G. B., Hertz, N. G., & Broadbent, D. E. (1975). Some experiments bearing on the hypothesis that the visual system analyses spatial patterns in independent bands of spatial frequency. *Vision Research, 15*, 887–897.
Hillenbrand, J. M. (1975). Intensity and repetition effects on selective adaptation to speech. *Research on Speech Perception*. Progress Report No. 2. Department of Psychology, Indiana University.
Hirose, H., Lisker, L., & Abramson, A. S. (1972). Physiological aspects of certain laryngeal features in stop production. *Haskins Laboratories Status Report on Speech Research SR 31/32*, 183–191.
Hirsh, I. J. (1959). Auditory perception of temporal order. *Journal of the Acoustical Society of America, 31*, 759–767.
Von Holst, E. (1954). Relation between the central nervous system and the peripheral organs. *British Journal of Animal Behavior, 2*, 89–94.
Von Holst, E., & Mittelstaedt, H. (1950). Das Reafferenzprincip. *Naturwissenschaften, 37*, 464–76.
House, A. S., & Fairbanks, S. (1953). Influence of consonant environment upon the secondary accoustical characteristics of vowels. *Journal of the Acoustical Society of America, 25*, 105–121.
Houtgast, T. (1974). Auditory analysis of vowel-like sounds. *Acoustica, 31*, 320–324.
Huggins, A. W. F. (1969). A facility for studying perception of timing in natural speech. *Quarterly Progress Report of the Research Laboratory of Electronics, M.I.T., 95*, 81–83.
Von Humboldt, W. (1960). [*Über die Vershiedenheit des mechlischen Sprachbaus*]. Bonn: Fredinand Dümmlers. (Facsimile of 1st German ed., 1836).
Hurvich, L. M. (1972). Color vision deficiencies. In D. Jameson & L. M. Hurvich (Eds.), *Handbook of sensory physiology: Vol. VII/4. Visual psychophysics*. New York: Springer-Verlag.
Hurvich, L. M., & Jameson, D. (1975). An opponent-process theory of color vision. *Psychological Review, 64*, 384–404.
Jakobson, R. (1941). *Kindersprache, aphasie, und allgemeine lautgesetze* Uppsala: Almqvist & Wiksell.
Jakobson, R., Fant, C. G. M., & Halle, M. (1963). *Preliminaries to speech analysis*. Cambridge, Mass.: M.I.T. Press.
Jameson, D., & Hurvich, L. M. (1955). Some quantitative aspects of opponent-colors theory—I: Chromatic responses and spectral saturation. *Journal of the Optical Society of America, 45*, 546–552.

Jameson, D., & Hurvich, L. M. (1968). Opponent-response functions related to measured cone photopigments. *Journal of the Optical Society of America, 58*, 429–430.

Jameson, D., & Hurvich, L. M. (1972). Color adaptation: Sensitivity, contrast, and after-images. In D. Jameson & L. M. Hurvich (Eds.), *Handbook of sensory physiology, Vol. VII/4*, Berlin: Springer-Verlag.

Just, M. A., Suslick, R. L., Michaels, S., & Shockey, L. (1978). Acoustic cues and psychological processes in the perception of natural stop consonants. *Perception & Psychophysics, 24*, 327–336.

Kagaya, R. A. (1974). A fiberscopic and acoustic study of the Korean stops, affricates, and fricatives. *Journal of Phonetics, 2*, 161–180.

Kavanagh, J. F., & Mattingly, I. G. (Eds.). (1972). *Language by ear and by eye.* Cambridge, Mass.: M.I.T. Press.

Kay, R. H., & Matthews, D. R. (1972). On the existence in human auditory pathways of channels selectively tuned to the modulation present in frequency-modulated tones. *Journal of Physiology, 25*, 657–677.

Keating, P., & Blumstein, S. E. (1978). Effects of transition length on the perception of stop consonants. *Journal of the Acoustical Society of America, 64*, 57–64.

Kent, R. D., & Moll, K. (1969). Vocal-tract characteristics of the stop cognates. *Journal of the Acoustical Society of America, 46*, 1549–1555.

Kewley-Port, D., & Preston, M. S. (1974). Early apical stop production: A voice onset time analysis. *Journal of Phonetics, 2*, 195–210.

Kiang, N. Y. S. (1975). Stimulus representation in the discharge patterns of auditory neurons. In F. B. Tower (Ed.), *The nervous system. Vol. 3: Human communication and its disorders.* New York: Raven Press.

Kiang, N. Y. S., & Moxon, E. C. (1974). Tails of tuning curves of auditory-nerve fibers. *Journal of the Acoustical Society of America, 55*, 620–630.

Kiang, N. Y. S., Watanabe, T., Thomas, E. C., & Clark, L. F. (1965). *Discharge patterns of single fibers in the cat's auditory nerve.* Cambridge, Mass.: M.I.T. Press.

Kim, C. W. (1965). On the autonomy of the tensity feature in stop classification (with special reference to Korean stops). *Word, 21*, 339–359.

Kim, C. W. (1970). A theory of aspiration," *Phonetica, 21*, 107–112.

Kimura, D. (1961). Cerebral dominance and the perception of verbal stimuli. *Canadian Journal of Psychology, 15*, 166–171.

Kimura, D. (1967). Functional asymmetry of the brain in dichotic listening. *Cortex, 3*, 163–178.

Klatt, D. H. (1972). An acoustical theory of terminal analog speech synthesis. In *Proceedings of the 1972 International Conference on Speech Communication and Processing*, Boston, Mass., IEEE No. 72 CHO 596-7 AE, 131–135.

Klatt, D. H. (1973). Voice onset time, frication, and aspiration in word-initial consonant clusters. *Journal of Speech and Hearing Research, 18*, 686–706.

Klatt, D. H., & Cooper, W. E. (1975). Perception of segment duration in sentence contexts. In A. Cohen & S. G. Nooteboom (Eds.), *Structure and process in speech perception.* Heidelberg: Springer-Verlag.

Klatt, D. H., Stevens, K. N., & Mead, J. (1968). Studies of articulatory activity and airflow during speech. *Annals of the New York Academy of Sciences, 155*, 42–55.

Koenig, W., Dunn, H. K., & Lacey, L. Y. (1946). The sound spectrograph. *Journal of the Acoustical Society of America, 17*, 19–49.

Konishi, M. (1965). The role of auditory feedback in the control of vocalization in the white-crowned sparrow. *Zeitschrift für Tierpsychologie, 22*, 770–783.

Lackner, J. R. (1974). Speech production: evidence for corollary discharge stabilization of perceptual mechanisms. *Perceptual and Motor Skills, 39*, 899–902.

Lackner, J. R., & Goldstein, L. M. (1975). The psychological representation of speech sounds. *Quarterly Journal of Experimental Psychology, 27*, 173–185.

Lackner, J. R., & Tuller, B. (1976). The influence of syntactic segmentation on perceived stress. *Cognition, 4*, 303–307.

Ladefoged, P. (1967). *Three areas of experimental phonetics.* London: Oxford University Press.

Ladefoged, P. (1971). *Preliminaries to linguistic phonetics.* Chicago: University of Chicago Press.

Larimer, J., Krantz, D. H., & Cicerone, C. M. (1974). Opponent-process additivity—I: Red/green equilibria. *Vision Research, 14*, 1127–1140.

Lashley, K. S. (1951). The problem of serial order in behavior. In L. A. Jeffress (Ed.), *Cerebral mechanisms in behavior.* New York: Wiley.

Lass, N. J. (Ed.) (1976). *Contemporary issues in experimental phonetics.* New York: Academic Press.

Lea, W. A. (1973). An approach to syntactic recognition without phonemics. *IEEE Transactions on Audio and Electroacoustics*, AU-21, 249–258.

Lea, W. A. (1973). Segmental and suprasegmental influences on fundamental frequency contours. In L. Hyman (Ed.), *Consonant types and tone. Southern California Occasional Papers in Linguistics.* No. 1.

Leiter, E. (1974). On the abstractness of the feature detectors for voicing in speech perception. Unpublished honors' thesis, Brown University.

Liberman, A. M. (1957). Some results of research on speech perception. *Journal of the Acoustical Society of America, 29*, 117–123.

Liberman, A. M. (1970). The grammars of speech and language. *Cognitive Psychology, 1*, 301–323.

Liberman, A. M., Cooper, F. S., Shankweiler, D. P., & Studdert-Kennedy, M (1967). Perception of the speech code. *Psychological Review, 74*, 431–461.

Liberman, A. M., Delattre, P. C., & Cooper, F. S. (1952). The role of selected stimulus variables in the perception of unvoiced stop consonants. *Psychology, 65*, 497–516.

Liberman, A. M., Delattre, P. C., Cooper, F. S., & Gerstman, L. J. (1954). The role of consonant-vowel transitions in the perception of the stop and nasal consonants. *Psychological Monographs, 68*, 1–13.

Liberman, A. M., Delattre, P. C., Cooper, F. S., & Gerstman, L. J. (1956). Tempo of frequency change as a cue for distinguishing classes of speech sounds. *Journal of Experimental Psychology, 52*, 127–137.

Liberman, A. M., Delattre, P. C., & Cooper, F. S. (1958). Some cues for the distinctions between voiced and voiceless stops in initial position. *Language and Speech, 1*. 153–167.

Liberman, A. M., Harris, K. S., Hoffman, H. S., & Griffith, B. C. (1957). The discrimination of speech sounds within and across phoneme boundaries. *Journal of Experimental Psychology, 54*, 358–368.

Liberman, A. M., Harris, K. S., Kinney, J. A., & Lane, H. (1961). The discrimination of relative onset-time of the components of certain speech and non-speech patterns. *Journal of Experimental Psychology, 61*, 379–388.

Lieberman, P. H. (1975). *On the origins of language: An introduction to the evolution of human speech.* New York: MacMillan & Co.

Lisker, L. (1975). Is it VOT or a first-formant transition detector? *Journal of the Acoustical Society of America, 57*, 1547–1551.

Lisker, L., & Abramson, A. S. (1964). Across-language study of voicing in initial stops: acoustical measurements. *Word, 20*, 384–422.

Lisker, L., & Abramson, A. S. (1967). Some effects of context on voice onset time in English stops. *Language and Speech, 10,* 1–28.
Lisker, L., & Abramson, A. S. (1970). The voicing dimension: some experiments in comparative phonetics. In *Proceedings of the Sixth International Congress of Phonetic Sciences,* Prague. Prague: Academia.
Lisker, L., & Abramson, A. S. (1971). Distinctive features in laryngeal control. *Language, 47,* 767–785.
Lisker, L., Abramson, A. S., Cooper, F. S., & Schvey, M. H. (1969). Transillumination of the larynx in running speech. *Journal of the Acoustical Society of America, 45,* 1544–1546.
Lisker, L., Liberman, A. M., Dechowitz, D., & Erickson, D. M. (1975). On pushing the voice-onset-time boundary about: *Journal of the Acoustical Society of America, 57,* S50, (Abstract).
Lotz, J., Abramson, A. S., Gerstman, L. J., Ingemann, F., & Nemser, W. J. (1960). The perception of English stops by speakers of English, Spanish, Hungarian, and Thai: A tape-cutting experiment. *Language and Speech, 3,* 71–77.
Luria, A. R. (1970). *Traumatic aphasia.* The Hague: Mouton.
MacKay, D. M. (1968). Possible information-processing functions of inhibitory mechanisms. In C. von Euler, S. Skoglund, & U. Soderberg (Eds.), *Structure and function of inhibitory neuronal mechanisms.* New York: Pergamon Press.
Maeda, S. (1975). Electromyographic study on intonational attributes. *Quarterly Progress Report of the M.I.T. Research Laboratory of Electronics, 115,* 261–269.
Malécot, A. (1956). Acoustic cues for nasal consonants. *Language, 32,* 274–284.
Marler, P. (1974). On the origin of speech from animal sounds. In J. F. Kavanagh & J. E. Cutting (Eds.), *The role of speech in language.* Cambridge, Mass.: M.I.T. Press.
Marslen-Wilson, W. (1975). Sentence perception as an interactive parallel process. *Science, 189,* 226–228.
Marslen-Wilson, W., & Tyler, L. K. (1975). Processing structure of sentence perception. *Nature, 257,* 784–786.
Mayer, B. (1927). Messende Untersuchungen über die Umstimmung des Geschmackswerzeugs. *Zeitschrift für Physiologie und Psychologie des Sinnesorgane, 58,* 133–152.
Mayhew, J. E. W., & Anstis, S. M. (1972). Movement aftereffects contingent on color, intensity, and pattern. *Perception & Psychophysics, 12,* 77–85.
McCarter, A., & Silver, A. I. (1977). The McCollough effect: A classical conditioning phenomenon? *Vision Research, 17,* 317–319.
McCollough, C. (1965). Color adaptation of edge-detectors in the human visual system, *Science, 149,* 1115–1116.
Meiselman, H. L. (1968). Adaptation and cross-adaptation of the four gustatory qualities. *Perception & Psychophysics, 4,* 368–372.
Miller, C. L., & Morse, P. A. (1979). Selective adaptation effects in infant speech perception paradigms. *Journal of the Acoustical Society of America, 65,* 789–798.
Miller, G. A., & Nicely, P. E. (1955). An analysis of perceptual confusions among some English consonants. *Journal of the Acoustical Society of America, 27,* 338–352.
Miller, J. D., Wier, C. C., Pastore, R., Kelly, W. J., & Dooling, R. J. (1976). Discrimination and labeling of noise-buss sequences with varying noise-lead times: An example of categorical perception. *Journal of the Acoustical Society of America, 60,* 410–417.
Miller, J. L. (1975). Properties of feature detectors for speech: Evidence from the effects of selective adaptation on dichotic listening. *Perception & Psychophysics, 18,* 389–397.
Miller, J. L. (1977). Properties of feature detectors for VOT: The voiceless channel of analysis. *Journal of the Acoustical Society of America, 62,* 641–648.
Miller, J. L. (1976). Studies on the selective tuning of feature detectors for speech. *Journal of Phonetics, 4,* 119–127.

Miller, J. L. (1977). Studies on the perception of place and manner of articulation: A comparison of the labial-alveolar and nasal-stop distinctions. *Journal of the Acoustical Society of America, 61*, 835–845.

Miller, J. L., & Eimas, P. D. (1976). Studies on the selective tuning of feature detectors for speech. *Journal of Phonetics, 4,* 119–127.

Miller, J. L., & Eimas, P. D. (1977). Studies on the perception of place and manner of articulation: A comparison of the labial-alveolar and nasal-stop distinctions. *Journal of the Acoustical Society of America, 61,* 835–845.

Miller, J. L., Eimas, P. D., & Root, J. (1977). Properties of feature detectors for place of articulation. *Journal of the Acoustical Society of America, 61,* S48 (Abstract).

Monin, L. M., & Huntington, D. A. (1974). Relationship of articulatory defects to speech-sound identification. *Journal of Speech and Hearing Research, 17,* 352–366.

Morse, P. A., Kass, J. E., & Turkienicz, R. (1976). Selective adaptation of vowels. *Perception & Psychophysics, 19,* 137–143.

Murch, G. M. (1976). Classical conditioning of the McCollough effect: Temporal parameters. *Vision Research, 16,* 615–619.

Murch, G. M. (1977). A reply to McCarter and Silver. *Vision Research, 17,* 321–322.

Neisser, U. (1967). *Cognitive psychology:* New York: Appleton-Century Crofts.

Niccum, N., & Speaks, C. (1978). Locus of adaptation effects for the voicing feature: *Journal of the Acoustical Society of America, 63,* S19 (Abstract).

Norman, D. A. (1979). In R. A. Cole (Ed.), *Perception and production of fluent speech.* Hillsdale, N.J.: Lawrence Erlbam Associates, in press.

Ohala, J. J. (1970). Aspects of the control and production of speech. *UCLA Working Papers in Phonetics, 15.*

Ohde, R. N. (1978). Relationship between selective adaptation and verbal transformation of stop consonant voicing: Effects of intensity and number of repetitions of adaptors varying in voice-onset time. Unpublished doctoral dissertation, University of Michigan.

Parducci, A. (1974). Contextual effects: A range-frequency analysis. In E. C. Carterette & M. P. Friedman (Eds.) *Handbook of perception* Vol. II. *Psychophysical judgment and measurement.* New York: Academic Press.

Pisoni, D. B. (1971). On the nature of categorical perception of speech sounds. Unpublished doctoral dissertation, University of Michigan. (Also in *Supplement to Status Report on Speech Research,* Haskins Laboratories, New Haven, Conn., November 1971.)

Pisoni, D. B., & Lazarus, J. H. (1974). Categorical and noncategorical modes of speech perception along the voicing continuum. *Journal of the Acoustical Society of America, 55,* 328–333.

Pisoni, D. B., & Sawusch, J. R. (1975). Some stages of processing in speech perception. In A. Cohen & S. G. Nooteboom (Eds.), *Structure and Process in Speech Perception.* Heidelberg: Springer-Verlag.

Pisoni, D. B., Sawusch, J. R., & Adams, F. T. (1975). Simple and contingent adaptation effects perception. *Research on Speech Perception. Progress Report* No. 2. Department of Psychology, Indiana University.

Pisoni, D. B., & Tash, J. (1975). Auditory property detectors and processing place features in stop consonants. *Perception & Psychophysics, 18,* 401–408.

Preston, M. S. (1971). Some comments on the developmental aspects of voicing in stop consonants. In D. L. Norton & J. J. Jenkins (Eds.), *Perception of language.* Columbus, Ohio: Charles Merrill.

Raz, I., & Wightman, F. L. (1978). An adaptive procedure for estimating phoneme-boundaries: Application to selective adaptation for speech. *Journal of the Acoustical Society of America, 64,* S19 (Abstract).

Reddy, D. R. (Ed.), (1975). *Speech recognition.* New York: Academic Press.

Reddy, D. R., Erman, L. D., & Neely, R. B. (1973). A model and a system for machine recognition of speech. *IEEE Transactions on Audio and Electroacoustics,* AU-21, 229–238.

Reeds, J. A., & Wang, W. S-Y. (1961). The perception of stops after [s]. *Phonetica, 6,* 78.

Remez, R. E. (1979a). Adaptation of the category boundary between speech and non-speech: A case against feature detectors. *Cognitive Psychology, 11,* 38–57.

Remez, R. E. (1979b). Adaptation of the category boundary between speech and non-speech: A consonantal case against feature detectors. In J. J. Wolf & D. H. Klatt (Eds.), *Papers presented at the 97th meeting of the Acoustical Society of America.* New York; Acoustical Society of America.

Ringel, R. L., & Steer, M. C. (1963). Some effects of tactile and auditory alterations on speech output. *Journal of Speech and Hearing Research, 6,* 369–378.

Rovner, R., Nash-Webber, B., & Woods, W. A. (1975). Control concepts in a speech understanding system. *IEEE Transactions on Acoustics, Speech, and Signal Processing,* ASSP-23, 133–140.

Rudnicky, A. I., & Cole, R. A. (1977). Adaptation produced by connected speech. *Journal of Experimental Psychology: Human Perception and Performance, 3,* 51–61.

Sachs, M. B., Nachmias, J., & Robson, J. G. (1971). Spatial-frequency channels in human vision. *Journal of the Optical Society of America, 61,* 1176–1178.

Samuel, A. G. (1975). Nasality: a selective adaptation study. Unpublished honors thesis. Cornell University.

Samuel, A., & Newport, E. (1979). Adaptation of speech by non-speech: Evidence for complex acoustic cue detectors. *Journal of Experimental Psychology: Human Perception and Performance,* in press.

Sawashima, M., & Hirose, H. (1968). New laryngoscopic technique by use of fiberoptics, *Journal of the Acoustical Society of America, 43,* 168–169.

Sawusch, J. R. (1976a). The structure and flow of information in speech perception: Evidence from selective adaptation of stop consonants. Unpublished doctoral dissertation, Indiana University.

Sawusch, J. R. (1976b). Selective adaptation effects on end-point stimuli in a speech series. *Perception & Psychophysics, 20,* 61–65.

Sawusch, J. R. (1977a). Peripheral and central processes in selective adaptation of place of articulation in stop consonants. *Journal of the Acoustical Society of America, 62,* 738–750.

Sawusch, J. R. (1977b). Processing of place information in stop consonants. *Perception & Psychophysics, 22,* 417–426.

Sawusch, J. R., & Nusbaum, H. C. (1978). A perceptual locus for anchoring effects in vowels. *Journal of the Acoustical Society of America, 63,* S3 (Abstract).

Sawusch, J. R., & Pisoni, D. B. (1973). Category boundaries for speech and nonspeech sounds. Paper presented at the 86th Meeting of the Acoustical Society of America, Los Angeles, November 1.

Sawusch, J. R., Pisoni, D. B., & Cutting, J. E. (1974). Category boundaries for linguistic and nonlinguistic dimensions of the same stimuli. Paper presented at the 87th Meeting of the Acoustical Society of America, New York City, April 25.

Scott, C. M., & Ringel, R. L. (1971). The effects of motor and sensory disruptions on speech: a description of articulation. *Journal of Speech and Hearing Research, 14,* 819–828.

Searle, C. (1979). Speech as patterns in space. In R. A. Cole (Ed.), *Perception and production of fluent speech.* Hillsdale, N.J.: Lawrence Erlbaum Associates, in press.

Searle, C. L., Jacobson, J. Z., & Rayment, S. G. (1979). Stop consonant discrimination based on human audition. *Journal of the Acoustical Society of America, 65,* 799–809.

Sekuler, R., & Levinson, E. (1974). Mechanisms of motion perception. *Psychologia* (Kyoto), *17,* 38–49.

Sharf, D. J., & Hemeyer, T. (1972). Identification of place of consonant articulation from vowel formant transitions. *Journal of the Acoustical Society of America, 51,* 652–568.

Sharf, D. J., & Ohde, R. (1977). Recovery from selective adaptation to a voiceless VOT stimulus. *Journal of the Acoustical Society of America, 62*, S77 (Abstract).
Shepard, R. N. (1972). Psychological representation of speech sounds. In E. E. David & P. B. Denes (Eds.), *Human communication: A unified view*. New York: McGraw-Hill.
Simon, H. J., & Studdert-Kennedy, M. (1978). Selective anchoring and adaptation of phonetic and nonphonetic continua. *Journal of the Acoustical Society of America, 64*, 1338–1357.
Smith, P. T. (1973). Feature-testing models and their application to perception and memory for speech. *Quarterly Journal of Experimental Psychology, 25*, 511–534.
Sperry, R. W. (1950). Neural basis of the spontaneous optokinetic response produced by visual inversion. *Journal of Comparative and Physiological Psychology, 43*, 482–489.
Stevens, K. N. (1960). Toward a model of speech recognition. *Journal of the Acoustical Society of America, 32*, 47–55.
Stevens, K. N. (1971). The quantal nature of speech. In E. E. David, Jr. & P. B. Denes (Eds.), *Human communication: A unified view*. New York: McGraw-Hill,
Stevens, K. N. (1972). Segments, features, and analysis by synthesis. In J. F. Kavanagh & I. G. Mattingly (Eds.), *Language by ear and by eye: The relationships between speech and reading*. Cambridge, Mass.: M.I.T. Press.
Stevens, K. N. (1975). The potential role of property detectors in the perception of consonants. In G. Fant & M. A. A. Tatham (Eds.), *Auditory analysis and perception of speech*. New York: Academic Press.
Stevens, K. N. (1975). Quantal aspects of consonant production and perception: A study of retroflex consonants. *Journal of Phonetics, 3*, 215–234.
Stevens, K. N., & Halle, M. (1967). Remarks on analysis by synthesis and distinctive features. In W. Wathen-Dunn (Ed.), *Models for the perception of speech and visual form*. Cambridge, Mass.: M.I.T. Press.
Stevens, K. N. (1977). Physics of laryngeal behavior and larynx modes. *Phonetica, 34*, 264–279.
Stevens, K. N., & House, A. S. (1972). Speech perception. In J. Tobias (Ed.), *Foundations of modern auditory theory (Vol. II)*. New York: Academic Press.
Stevens, K. N., & Klatt, D. H. (1971). The role of formant transitions in the voiced-voiceless distinction for stops. *M.I.T. Research Laboratory of Electronics Quarterly Progress Report, 101*, 188–196.
Stevens, K. N., & Klatt, D. H. (1974). Role of formant transitions in the voice-voiceless distinction for stops. *Journal of the Acoustical Society of America, 55*, 653–659.
Stevens, S. S. (Ed.). (1951). *Handbook of experimental psychology*. New York: Wiley.
Studdert-Kennedy, M. The perception of speech. In T. A. Sebeok (Ed.), *Current Trends in Linguistics, XII*, in press.
Studdert-Kennedy, M. (1976). Speech perception. In N. J. Lass (Ed.), *Contemporary issues in experimental phonetics*. New York: Academic Press.
Studdert-Kennedy, M. (1976). Stimulus range as a determinant of phoneme boundaries along synthetic consonant continua. *Journal of the Acoustical Society of America*, 60, S92 (Abstract).
Studdert-Kennedy, M., & Shankweiler, D. (1970). Hemispheric specialization for speech perception. *Journal of the Acoustical Society of America, 48*, 579–594.
Studdert-Kennedy, M., Shankweiler, D., & Pisoni, D. B. (1972). Auditory and phonetic processes in speech perception: Evidence from a dichotic study. *Cognitive Psychology, 3*, 455–466.
Suen, C. Y., & Beddoes, M. P. (1974) The silent interval of stop consonants, *Language and Speech, 17*, 126–134.
Summerfield, Q. (1974). Toward a detailed model for the perception of voicing contrasts. *Speech Perception: report of research in progress at the Department of Psychology, The Queen's University of Belfast, Northern Ireland, 2.3*, 1–26.
Summerfield, A. Q., & Haggard, M. P. (1972). Articulatory rate versus acoustical invariants in speech perception. Paper presented at the 83rd Meeting of the Acoustical Society of America, Buffalo, New York, April 18.

Summerfield, A. Q., & Haggard, M. P. (1974). Perceptual processing of multiple cues and contexts: Effects of following vowel upon stop consonant voicing. *Journal of Phonetics, 2*, 279-295.

Summerfield, Q. (1976). Speech rate influences on the perception of stop voicing. *Journal of the Acoustical Society of America, 59*, S41 (Abstract).

Summerfield, Q., & Haggard, M. (1976). First formant onset frequency as a cue to the voicing distinction in pre-stressed, syllable-initial stop-consonants. *Speech Perception: Report of Speech Research in Progress. Department of Psychology, The Queen's University of Belfast, Northern Ireland, 2.5*, 25-33.

Summerfield, Q., & Haggard, M. (1977). On the dissociation of spectral and temporal cues to the voicing distinction in initial stop consonants. *Journal of the Acoustical Society of America, 62*, 435-448.

Sussman, H. M. (1971). The laterality effect in lingual-auditory tracking. *Journal of the Acoustical Society of America, 49*, 1874-1880.

Sussman, H. M., MacNeilage, P. F., & Lumbley, J. (1974). Sensorimotor dominance and the right-ear advantage in mandibular-auditory tracking. *Journal of the Acoustical Society of America, 56*, 214-216.

Suzuki, H. (1970). Mutually complementary effect of rate and amount of formant transitions in distinguishing vowel, semivowel, and stop consonant. *Quarterly Progress Report of the M.I.T. Research Laboratory of Electronics, 96*, 164-172.

Tartter, V. C., & Eimas, P. D. (1975). The role of auditory feature detectors in the perception of speech. *Perception & Psychophysics, 18*, 293-298.

Teuber, H-L. (1966). Perception. In J. C. Eccles (Ed.), *The brain and conscious experience*. New York: Springer Verlag.

Tonndorf, J. (1970). Bone conduction. In J. Tobias (Ed.), *Foundations of modern auditory theory* (Vol. II). New York: Academic Press.

Umeda, N., & Coker, C. H. (1974). Subphonemic details in American English. *Speech Communication Seminar*, Stockholm, Sweden, 1-3 Aug.

Uttal, W. R. (1973). *The psychobiology of sensory coding*. New York: Harper & Row.

Verbrugge, R. R., & Liberman, A. M. (1975). Context-conditioned adaptation of liquids and their third formant components. Paper presented at the 89th Meeting of the Acoustical Society of America, Austin, Texas.

Wang, W. S-Y. (1959). Transition and release and perceptual cues for final plosives. *Journal of Speech and Hearing Research, 2*, 66-73.

Warren, R., & Gregory, R. (1958). An auditory analogue of the visual reversible figure. *American Journal of Psychology, 71*, 612-613.

Wickelgren, W. A. (1969). Auditory or articulatory coding in verbal short-term memory. *Psychological Review, 76*, 232-235.

Wilson, H. R. (1975). A synaptic model for spatial frequency adaptation. *Journal of Theoretical Biology, 50*, 327-352.

Wolf, C. G. (1978). Perceptual invariance for stop consonants in different positions. *Perception & Psychophysics, 24*, 315-326.

Wood, C. C. (1975). Auditory and phonetic levels of processing in speech perception: Neurophysiological and information-processing analyses. *Journal of Experimental Psychology: Human Perception and Performance, 1*, 3-20.

Yeni-Komshian, G., & Preston, M. S. (1967). *Annual Report, Neurocommunications Laboratory, The Johns Hopkins University School of Medicine*, 291-306.

AUTHOR INDEX

Page numbers in *italics* indicate where complete references are listed.

Abramson, A.S., 4, 27, 69, 74, 78, 79, 80, 115, 124, 127, 128, 131, 138, 139, 147, 157, *187, 191, 193, 194*
Adams, F.T., 83, 84, 85, 183, *195*
Ades, A.E., 48, 50, 77, 83, 85, 108, 146, 179, 180, *187*
Ainsworth, W.A., 109, 110n, *187*
Allard, F., 176, *188*
Ambler, S., 68, 74, *190*
Anstis, S.M., 82, 86, *194*
Appley, M.H., 68, *187*

Bailey, P.J., 14, 20, 47, 64, 74, 107, 183, 184, *187*
Barlow, H.B., 17, 182, *188*
Bastian, J., 146, 150, 163, *188, 191*
Beddoes, M.P., 128, *197*
Bever, T.G., 178, *190*
Bibikov, N.G., 15, *188*
Billings, D., 173, *189*
Blumstein, S.E., 10, 14, 48, 50n, 143, 161n, *188, 192*
Borst, J.M., 11, 29, 52, 61, 89, 100, *188*
Bosack, T.N., 63, *189*
Brady, S.A., 176, *188*

Braida, L.D., 100, 103, 104n, 109, *188, 189*
Broadbent, D.E., 185, *191*
Bryant, J., 184, *188*
Butterfield, E.C., 162, *188*

Cairns, G.F., 162, *188*
Callow, M., 68, 74, *190*
Caramazza, A., 143, *188*
Chiba, T., 9, *188*
Chomsky, N., 158n, *188*
Cicerone, C.M., 19, *193*
Clark, L.F., 15, *192*
Coker, C.H., 127, 131, *198*
Cole, R.A., 18, 22, 100, 110, 110n, 173, 176, 177, 181, *189, 196*
Cooper, F.S., 9, 11, 13, 29, 46, 52, 61, 68, 89, 91, 95, 100, 128, *188, 189, 191, 193, 194*
Cooper, J.P., 18, *189*
Cooper, W.E., 15, 18, 31, 33, 69, 71, 90, 96, 100, 109, 110, 110n, 117, 123, 143, 173, 176, 179, 180, 181, 183, *188, 189, 190, 192*

199

AUTHOR INDEX

Corbit, J.D., 20, 27, 31, 33, 54, 68, 69, 71, 77, 96, 106, 117, 123, 176, 179, 180, 183, *189*
Corbit, T.E., 63, *189*
Cutting, J.E., 12, 17, 108, 176, 183, *189, 191, 196*

Dallenbach, J.W., 63, *189*
Dallenbach, K.M., 63, *189*
Darwin, C.J., 176, *188, 189*
Davidson-Neilson, N., 147, 154, *189*
Dechowitz, D., *194*
deCordemoy, G., 113, *189*
Delattre, P.C., 13, 29, 52, 61, 68, 89, 91, 95, 100, *188, 189, 191, 193*
Denes, P.B., 5, 89, *189*
Diehl, R.L., 48, 49, 66, 77, 95n, 107, 108, 176, *189*
Donald, S.L., 182, *189*
Dooling, R.J., 139, *194*
Dorman, M.F., 9, *189*
Dunn, H.K., 7, *192*
Durlach, N.I., 100, 103, 104n, 109, *188, 189*

Eimas, P.D., 20, 27, 29, 31, 33, 46, 48, 50, 54, 65, 68, 69, 71, 77, 83, 84, 85, 86n, 96, 106, 108, 111, 117, 123, 162, 176, 179, 180, 181, 183, 184, *189, 190, 195, 198*
Elman, J.L., 111, 173n, 176, 177, 181, *190*
Engen, T., 63, *190*
Erickson, D.M., *194*
Erman, L.D., 15, *196*

Fant, C.G.M., 46, 51, *191*
Fant, G., 9, 10, 52, 78, 91, 91n, 97, *190, 191*
Favreau, O.E., 184, *190*
Ferguson, G.A., 23, 32, 57, 168, *190*
Fidell, L.S., 82, 87, *190*
Flanagan, J.L., 3, 10, 16, *190*
Foard, C.F., 12, 183, *189*
Fodor, J.A., 178, *190*
Foreit, K.G., 182, 184, *190*
Forster, K.I., 18, *190*
Freedman, S., 120, *191*
Fujimura, O., 68, *190*

Ganong, W.F., III, 48, 49, 66, 86, 109, 184, *190*
Garner, W.R., 185, *190*

Garrett, M.F., 178, *190*
Gerstman, L.J., 29, 52, 61, 89, 91, 95, 100, 147, *188, 193, 194*
Gibson, A.R., 82, *191*
Gold, B., 145, *190*
Goldstein, L.M., 100, 182, *190, 193*
Graham, N., 185, *190*
Green, D.M., 90, *190*
Gregory, R., 20, 182, *198*
Griffith, B.C., 11, 28, 29, 106, *193*

Haggard, M.P., 14, 68, 74, 77, 84, 84n, 139n, 146, 178, *187, 190, 197, 198*
Halle, M., 46, 51, 52, 128, 157, 158, 158n, *188, 190, 191, 197*
Hanson, V.L., 11, *190*
Harmon, L.D., 182, *190*
Harnett, D.L., 23, *190*
Harris, C.S., 82, *191*
Harris, K.S., 11, 28, 29, 52, 67, 106, 163, *191, 193*
Healy, A., F., 17, *191*
Heineman, E.G., *191*
Held, R., 82, 87, 120, *191*
Helson, H., 68, 90, 107, *191*
Hemeyer, T., 52, *196*
Henning, G.B., 185, *191*
Hertz, N.G., 185, *191*
Hillenbrand, J.M., 184, *191*
Hirose, H., 128, *191, 196*
Hirsh, I.J., 150, *191*
Hoffman, H.S., 11, 28, 29, 106, *191, 193*
House, A.S., *191, 197*
Houtgast, T., 15, *191*
Huggins, A.W.F., 117, 154, 179, *191*
Huntington, D.A., 14, *195*
Hurvich, L.M., 19, 20, *191, 192*

Ingeman, F., 147, *194*

Jacobson, I.Z., 15, *196*
Jakimik, J., 18, *188*
Jakobson, R., 46, 51, 52, 164n, *191*
Jameson, D., 19, 20, *191, 192*
Jusczyk, P., 27, 162, *190*
Just, M.A., 9, *192*

Kagaya, R.A., 142n, 157, *192*
Kajiyama, M., 9, *188*
Kass, J.E., 176, *195*
Kavanagh, J.F., *192*
Kay, R.H., 183, *192*

Keating, P., 48, *192*
Kelly, W.J., 139, *194*
Kent, R.D., 69, 70, *192*
Kewley-Port, D., 143, *192*
Kiang, N.Y.S., 15, 183, *192*
Kim, C.W., 128, 157, *192*
Kimura, D., 162, *192*
Kinney, J.A., 67, *193*
Klatt, D.H., 18, 68, 69, 70, 74, 75, 91, 100, 116, 128, 147, 154, *192, 197*
Koenig, W., 7, *192*
Konishi, M., 162, *192*
Krantz, D.H., 19, *193*

Lacey, L.Y., 7, *192*
Lackner, J.R., 100, 163, 182, *190, 193*
Ladefoged, P., 44, 162, 164, *193*
Lane, H., 67, *193*
Lang, M., 176, *189*
Larimer, J., 19, *193*
Lashley, K.S., *193*
Lass, N.J., 14, *193*
Lazarus, J.H., 11, 139, *195*
Lea, W.A., 18, 145, *193*
Leiter, E., 100, 129, *193*
Levick, W.R., 17, 182, *188*
Levinson, E., 109, 143n, 181, *196*
Liberman, A.M., 9, 11, 13, 15, 28, 29, 52, 61, 67, 68, 89, 91, 95, 100, 106, 163, 176, 183, *188, 189, 191, 193, 194, 198*
Lieberman, P.H., 14, *193*
Lisker, L., 4, 27, 69, 74, 77, 78, 79, 80, 115, 124, 127, 128, 131, 138, 139, 157, *187, 191, 193, 194*
Lotz, J., 147, *194*
Lumbley, J., 162, *198*
Luria, A.R., 164n, *194*

MacKay, D.M., 182, *194*
MacNeilage, P.F., 162, *198*
Maeda, S., 158, *194*
Malecot, A., 52, *194*
Marler, P., 162, *194*
Marslem-Wilson, W., 18, *194*
Matthews, D.R., 183, *192*
Mattingly, I.G., *192*
Mayer, B., 63, *194*
Mayhew, J.E.W., 82, 86, *194*
McCarter, A., 21, *194*
McCollough, C., 21, 82, *194*
McCusker, S.B., 176, *189*

Mead, J., 147, *192*
Meiselman, H.L., 63, *194*
Michaels, S., 9, *192*
Miller, C.L., 184, *194*
Miller, G.A., 65, 184, *194*
Miller, J.D., 139, *194*
Miller, J.L., 65, 83, 84, 85, 86n, 111, 176, 181, 184, *189, 194, 195*
Mittelstaedt, H., 163, *191*
Moll, K., 69, 70, *192*
Monin, L.M., 14, *195*
Morse, P.A., 176, 184, *194, 195*
Moxon, E.C., 15, *192*
Murch, G.M., 21, 86, *195*

Nachmias, J., 185, *190, 196*
Nager, R.M., 15, *189*
Nash-Webber, B., 15, *196*
Neely, R.B., 15, *196*
Neisser, U., 65, 66, 184, *195*
Nemser, W.J., 147, *194*
Newport, E., 183, *196*
Niccum, N., 179, *195*
Nicely, P.E., 65, 184, *194*
Nigro, G.N., 48, 161n, *188*
Norman, D.A., 18, *195*
Nusbaum, H.C., 176, *196*

Ohala, J.J., 141, 147, 157, *195*
Ohde, R.M., 182, 184, *195, 197*

Parker, E.M., 176, *189*
Parducci, A., 176, *195*
Pastore, R., 139, *194*
Pisoni, D.B., 11, 12, 15, 29, 30, 31, 48, 50, 57, 68, 83, 84, 85, 139, 166, 167, 176, 180, 183, *195, 196, 197*
Preston, M.S., 143, *192, 195, 198*

Rabiner, L., 145, *190*
Raphael, L.J., 9, *189*
Rayment, S.G., 15, *196*
Raz, I., 179, *195*
Reddy, D.R., 15, 178, *195, 196*
Reeds, J.A., 147, *196*
Remez, R.E., 176, 177, *196*
Ringel, R.L., 162, *196*
Robson, J.G., 185, *196*
Root, J., 111, 181, *195*
Rosenberg, D.M., 77, *189*
Rosner, B.J., 12, 108, 183, *189*
Rovner, R., 15, *196*
Rudnicky, A.I., 22, 177, *196*

Sachs, M.B., 185, *196*
Samuel, A.G., 176, 183, *196*
Sawashima, M., 128, *196*
Sawusch, J.R., 15, 48, 50, 66, 68, 83, 84, 85, 109, 175, 176, 180, 181, 182, 183, *195, 196*
Schvey, M.H., 128, *194*
Scott, B., 100, *188*
Scott, C.M., 162, *196*
Searle, C.L., 15, *196*
Sekuler, R., 109, 143n, 181, *196*
Shankweiler, D., 9, 13, 23, 46, 180, *193, 197*
Sharf, D.J., 52, 184, *196, 197*
Shattuck, S.R., 82, 87, *191*
Shepard, R.N., 184, *197*
Shockey, L., 9, *192*
Silver, A.I., 21, *194*
Simon, H.J., 176, *197*
Singer, J., 176, *188*
Siqueland, E.R., 27, 162, *190*
Smith, P.T., *197*
Speaks, C., 179, *195*
Sperry, R.W., 163, *197*
Steer, M.C., 162, *196*
Stevens, K.N., 2, 9, 10, 14, 46, 48, 49, 68, 69, 70, 71, 74, 75, 98, 116, 128, 147, 157, 158, *188, 190, 192, 197*
Stevens, S.S., *198*
Studdert-Kennedy, M., 9, 13, 15, 23, 46, 176, 180, *189, 193, 197*
Suen, C.Y., 128, *197*
Summerfield, A.Q., 77, 84, 84n, 139n, 146, 178, *197, 198*
Summerfield, Q., 15, 17, 77, 146, 178, *197, 198*
Suslick, R.L., 9, *192*

Sussman, H.M., 162, *198*
Suzuki, H., 89, *198*
Swets, J.A., 90, *190*

Tartter, V.C., 48, 50, 108, 183, *198*
Tash, J., 48, 50, 84, 85, 183, *195*
Teuber, H-L., 163, *198*
Thomas, E.C., 15, *192*
Tonndorf, J., 164, *198*
Tuller, B., 182, *193*
Turkienicz, R., 176, *195*
Tyler, L.K., 18, *194*

Umeda, N., 127, 131, *198*
Uttal, W.R., 182, *198*

Verbrugge, R.R., 176, 183, *198*
Vigorito, J., 27, 162, *190*
VonHolst, E., 163, *191*
VonHumbolt, W., 114, *191*

Wang, W.S-Y., 147, 160, *196, 198*
Warren, R., 20, 182, *198*
Watanabe, T, 15, *192*
Wickelgren, W.A., 46, *198*
Wier, C.C., 139, *194*
Wightman, F.L., 179, *195*
Wilson, H.R., 182, *198*
Wolf, C.G., 48, *198*
Wood, C.C., *198*
Woods, W.A., 15, *196*

Yeni-Komshian, G., 143, *198*

Zurif, E.B., 143, *188*

SUBJECT INDEX

A

Abduction, of arytenoids, 142–143, 145–146, 157–158
Absolute identification task, 100
Acoustic invariance, 13
Acoustic pattern detection, 46, 63
Adduction, of arytenoids, 142, 157
Affricates, 5
Alveolar, 136
Alveolar-labial distinction, 146
Alveolar ridge, 4, 147
Amplitude, 6, 10, 15–16, 86, 91, 99, 175
Analysis-by-synthesis, 14, 16, 46, 98, 182
Anchor effects, 68, 107
Aphasia, 143, 164
Arytenoid cartilages, 142, 145
Aspiration, 75, 144, 147–148, 155, 159
Associative learning, 86
Attention, 184
Auditory feedback, 22, 161–164, 166, 168

B

Bias, response, 22, 103–104, 111, 177
Bilabial, 51–52, 63
Binaural integration, 179

C

Categorical perception, 11–12, 106
Cepstral analysis, 16
Choice reaction time, 14
Closed-loop testing, 166
Color vision, 19–20 (*see also* Vision)
Consonants
   affricates, 5
   alveolar, 136
   alveolar-labial distinction, 146
   bilabial, 51–52, 63
   fricatives, 5, 49, 51
   grave-compact distinction, 46, 51
   labial, 63, 90, 136
   labial-velar distinction, 96–99
   labio-dental, 51
   nasal, 5, 51
   plosives, 5
   stop-glide distinction, 89, 111
   stop-nasal distinction, 176
   stops, 5, 51, 89–111
   velars, 90
Contingent-adaptation, 21, 83–87, 179
Contrast, 39, 67–68
Corollary discharge, 163–164
Cricothyroid muscle, 145, 158
Crossed-adaptation, 20–22, 47–49, 65, 68, 111, 175, 177, 183–184, 186

D

Dichotic listening, 14, 23, 180, 186
Discriminability, peak of, 36, 39, 106
Discrimination, of consonants, 35–39

E

Efferent copy, 163–164
Electromyography, 128, 145
Exafference, 163–164
Excitatory elements, 139, 141

F

Fatigue, 67, 74
  neural, 139, 152, 157, 164, 172–173, 176
  sensory, 68, 96
  vs. returning, 109–111
Features, 4, 125
  adaptation, 29–30, 39
  detectors, 28–29, 66, 67, 176–177, 184
  extraction of, 184–185
  processing of, 65
  relative mode, 35
  stable mode, 35
Formant, 7, 27
  frequency of, 6, 10, 15–17, 87, 144, 148, 175
  second format (F_2), 12
  steady-state, 28, 31, 40
  steady-state and transition portions, 8
Formant transitions, 8, 29, 31, 41, 44, 48–49, 53, 65, 68–70, 74–75, 84–85, 95–96, 148, 173
  duration of (D), 103
  first formant (F_1), 77, 85, 91
  second formant (F_2), 12, 13, 29, 30, 33, 40, 45, 46, 47, 49, 52, 63, 64, 89, 165, 170
  third formant (F_3), 29–30, 33, 40, 45–47, 49, 52, 63–64, 89, 165
Frication, 51, 111, 148
Fricatives, 5, 49, 51
Fundamental frequency (F_0), 7, 17, 144–145
  contour of, 18, 71, 78, 148

G

Glides, 5, 89–111
Glottis, 2, 145
Grave-compact distinction, 46, 51

H

Hindi, 159, 182

I

Identification
  of consonants, 28, 30–35
  absolute, 60, 100–101
  probabilistic, 60
Inhibitory elements, 139, 141, 152 (*see also* Neural inhibition)
Integrative voicing analyzers, 68, 74, 75–76, 180
Interaural transfer, 20, 175, 179, 180, 184, 186

L

Labial, 63, 90, 136
Labio-dental, 51
Labial-velar distinciton, 96–99
Larynx, 1–2, 4, 7, 113, 128
Lateral cricoarytenoid muscle, 158
Linear prediction, 16
Lips, 2, 4, 6
Liquids, 5, 176
Lungs, 2

M

Mandible, 2
Manner of articulation, 5, 17, 51, 64, 66, 166
Memory
  long-term, 17–18
  short-term, 12
Mimicry, of adapting stimulus, 117, 121–123, 131
Model of speech perception, 15–19
  level A, 15, 18, 139, 175

Model of speech perception *(cont.)*
  level B, 15–18, 39, 47, 99, 139, 141, 160, 175
  level C, 17
  level D, 17, 40, 47
  level E, 17
  level F, 17
  level G, 17
  level H, 17
  level I, 18
Morphemes, 17

N

Nasal, 5, 51
Nasality, 4, 162
Nasal passage, 4
Negative afterimage, 19 *(see also* Vision)
Neural inhibition, 84, 152, 182 *(see also* Inhibitory elements)
Neural model of the perceptuo-motor system, 139–143, 157, 182
  excitatory elements, 139, 141
  inhibitory elements, 139, 141, 152
  integrators (Eb_1, Eb_2), 139–142
  level A, 139–140
  level B, 139–142
  level C, 139–142
  level D, 139–140, 142
Noise burst, 147, 155
Noninvariance, 12, 14
Nonspeech, 12, 50, 68, 108, 176–177
Nonspeech adaptation, 183

O

Open-loop testing, 164, 166
Open vs. closed-loop adaptation, 169–170
Opponent-processing, 19–20, 125, 135, 181–183
Oral release, 139
Oscillographic display, 6–7, 16–17, 118–119

P

Perceptual adaptation, 134, 137
Perceptual masking, 14

Perceptuo-motor compensation, 120–121, 123
Pharynx, 2
Phoneme recognition device, 17
Pitch, 68, 74, 162
Place of articulation, 4, 8–10, 13, 17, 27–66, 78, 83, 85–86, 89, 96–97, 125, 127, 165–166, 172–173, 183
  analyzer modes, 45, 64
Plateau regions, 9
Plosives, 5
Prevoicing, 139

R

Range effects, 176
Reafference, 163
Release burst, 8, 27, 48–49, 70, 100, 108, 117, 119, 129, 147, 153–154
Retuning, 109–111
Rhythm, 17
Rise-time, 99–100, 108

S

Semiconsonants, 52, 64
  glides, 5, 89–111
  liquids, 5, 176
Sensation magnitude, 103
Short-time amplitude-frequency spectrum, 6, 8
Signal detectability, 100, 103, 111, 177, 180–181, 186
Silent interval, 146–156, 159–160
Smell, 63
Speaking rate, 17, 131–133, 138, 141, 146, 178
Spectrogram, 6–7, 11
Speech motor system, 13
Stop-glide distinction, 89–111
Stop-nasal distinction, 176
Stops, 5, 51, 89–111
Stress, 131–133, 138, 141, 182
Supraglottal articulators, 69
Supralaryngeal tract, 2, 4–5, 89, 147
Syllable-recognition device, 17

T

Taste, 63
Thai, 182–183
Throat, 114
Tongue, 1–2, 6, 9, 116, 147, 162
Trachea, 2
Tuning properties, 181

V

Velars, 90
Velum, 2
Vision, 78, 83, 87
  color detectors in, 19–20
  conditioning, 19, 21
  feature extraction in, 185
  intensity and detection, 184

Vision (cont.)
  motion detection in, 109
  negative afterimage, 19
  neural inhibition in, 182
  perception, 163
Vocal cords, 2, 4, 6–7, 142, 145–147, 157
Voice Onset Time (VOT), 27–29, 33, 44, 67–70, 74–78, 80–81, 84–85, 117–147, 178
Voiced-voiceless distinction, 123–124, 133–134, 160, 182–183
Voicing, 4, 27, 29, 31, 45–46, 66–87, 89, 107, 115, 117, 119, 124, 127, 139, 144, 146, 148, 164, 173

X

X-ray motion pictures, 4, 6

LIBRARY OF DAVIDSON COLLEGE